FEDERAL CIVIL JURISDICTION
IN A NUTSHELL®

LUMEN N. MULLIGAN
Earl B. Shurtz Research Professor
University of Kansas School of Law

WEST
ACADEMIC
PUBLISHING

Nutshell Series, In a Nutshell and the Nutshell Logo are trademarks registered in the U.S. Patent and Trademark Office.

444 Cedar Street, Suite 700
St. Paul, MN 55101
1-877-888-1330

West, West Academic Publishing, and West Academic are trademarks of West Publishing Corporation, used under license.

Printed in the United States of America

ISBN: 978-0-314-28772-4

Fult

OUTLINE

TABLE OF CASES

References are to Pages

FEDERAL CIVIL JURISDICTION

JURISDICTION

IN A NUTSHELL®

CHAPTER 1

SUBJECT MATTER JURISDICTION

"Subject-matter jurisdiction . . . refers to a tribunal's power to hear a case."

> —*Morrison v. Nat'l Australia Bank Ltd.*, 561 U.S. 247, 254 (2010)

This entire volume is dedicated to an overview discussion of "subject matter jurisdiction." In particular, the subject matter jurisdiction of the federal courts—as contrasted with the subject matter jurisdiction of the state court systems or to the subject matter jurisdiction of administrative tribunals. Before we jump into that discourse, in this chapter we start with a general discussion of what subject matter jurisdiction is as a concept, why litigants might fight about it, and a brief overview of the mechanics of challenging subject matter jurisdiction in federal court.

A. THE NOTION OF FEDERAL SUBJECT MATTER JURISDICTION

An American court, be it state or federal, must be in possession of four essential conceptual building blocks before it is empowered to address any matters before it. First, the court must have personal jurisdiction over the parties. Second, the defendant must have received constitutionally adequate notice of the pending proceeding. Third, the court must have adequate statutory venue. And fourth, the court must have subject matter jurisdiction over the matter at bar.

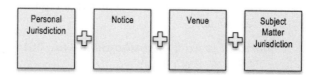

Personal jurisdiction speaks to the power of the court over the litigants themselves. (Or in the case of an in rem dispute, power over the object forming the basis of the case). Personal jurisdiction doctrine derives from the Constitution's due process provisions. The doctrine aims to prevent a faraway court from involuntarily haling parties before it, when litigants have no other connections to the locale.

Notice doctrine addresses the need of defendants to be fairly informed of pending litigation so that they may offer a defense. Akin to personal jurisdiction doctrine, fundamental notice standards flow from the due process clauses and attach as personal rights of the litigants.

Venue is a statutory regime aimed at limiting the number of locations in which a suit may be filed. This is essential because personal jurisdiction is analyzed on a state-by-state basis. Thus, for example, one might conclude that California has personal jurisdiction in the case of *Smith v. Jones*. But California has 58 separate trial courts within the state organized, as is the norm, by county. If a defendant from San Diego was forced to litigate in Del Norte County (one of the northernmost in the state) many of the same fairness concerns that personal jurisdiction doctrine addresses would be implicated. Hence venue doctrine, per statutory directives, whittles these 58 possible trial courts down to a handful of courts, typically focusing upon the residency of the parties or location of the incidents that caused the dispute, in an effort to achieve a fair forum for the litigation.

1.   SUBJECT MATTER JURISDICTION DEFINED

Subject matter jurisdiction, by contrast, is the power of the court to adjudicate cases of the general category to which the current proceeding belongs. Thus while personal jurisdiction speaks to the court's power over the litigants themselves, subject matter jurisdiction addresses the type of dispute at issue. For example, municipal courts are often limited in subject matter jurisdiction to disputes arising out of city-ordinance violations. Hearing a contract suit, to continue the example, would be beyond the subject matter jurisdiction of this hypothetical municipal court.

Of these four essential building blocks of judicial authority, the concept of subject matter jurisdiction is unique. While the first three concepts aim at protecting important fairness interests attaching to the litigants themselves, subject matter jurisdiction aims to protect broad societal resource and expertise allocations.

Many consequences flow from the fact that subject matter jurisdiction doctrine aims to protect these societal decisions, as opposed to protecting due process interests of individual litigants. First, subject matter jurisdictional concerns may not be waived. Whereas a party, should it further his strategic interests, might decide to proceed in a court that otherwise lacks personal jurisdiction over him, this may not be done in the case of subject matter jurisdiction. Following this non-waiver doctrine, the parties themselves are not free to ignore the societal resource and expertise allocations reflected in subject matter jurisdictional rules precisely because these allocations are not meant to protect individual litigants per se. Rather, subject matter jurisdictional rules protect societal (or constitutional) interests.

Second, in a related point, courts themselves are under an obligation to raise objections to subject matter jurisdiction sua sponte (i.e., on their own motion). This constitutes a rare exception to the general adversarial approach in the American judicial system, in which it is decidedly not the function of the court to raise legal issues on behalf of one party or the other.

And third, subject matter jurisdiction may be raised for the first time on appeal. That is to say, even if subject matter jurisdiction was not contested at trial, the issue may be raised anew on appeal. This approach runs contrary to the general rule prohibiting new arguments on appeal.

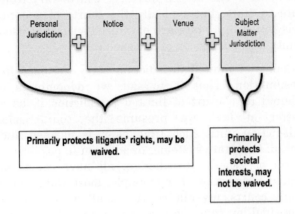

2. COURTS OF GENERAL OR LIMITED JURISDICTION

In regard to subject matter jurisdiction, trial courts may be divided into two broad divisions: courts of general jurisdiction and courts of limited jurisdiction. We denominate a tribunal as a court of general jurisdiction if, as a matter of law, we presume that court to have subject matter jurisdiction over every possible category of claim. What this presumption means is that a court of general jurisdiction possesses subject matter jurisdiction to hear any claim—from violations of state law to federal civil liability to breaches of international law—unless a constitutional or statutory provision specifically excises that basis of authority. Every state in union—as well as D.C., the commonwealths, and territories—has a system of courts of general jurisdiction. The names for these courts vary from state to state, but typically the courts of general jurisdiction in a state are organized such that each county is in possession of one such court.

Courts of limited jurisdiction carry the opposite presumption. That is to say, we denominate a tribunal as a court of limited jurisdiction if, as a matter of law, we presume the court lacks jurisdiction until such time as it is pleaded and proved. Our state systems, in addition to possessing courts of general jurisdiction, all have courts of limited jurisdiction. For example, most states have family courts, juvenile courts, small-claims courts, municipal-law courts, and probate courts. All of these adjudicatory bodies constitute courts of limited jurisdiction because we presume these courts lack jurisdiction; a presumption that may only be overcome within certain defined parameters vis-à-vis each court. Thus, in the case of the typical family court, it is only empowered to hear disputes involving divorce, custody, alimony, and the like. All other controversies must go to the court of general jurisdiction.

3.   ORIGINAL JURISDICTION AND APPELLATE JURISDICTION

Subject matter jurisdiction, in addition to being thought of as either general or limited, may also be categorized as original or appellate. Original jurisdiction, also thought of as trial jurisdiction, is the power of a court over actions in the first instance. This is the type of subject matter jurisdiction that may attach when no other court has adjudicated the case previously. Appellate jurisdiction, as the name implies, speaks to the power of a court to hear appeals regarding alleged errors that occurred in a prior, hierarchically inferior, tribunal.

4.   FEDERAL COURTS AS COURTS OF LIMITED JURISDICTION

Of particular import to our study, the "[f]ederal courts are courts of limited jurisdiction," possessing "only that power authorized by Constitution and statute."[1] Numerous important consequences flow from this axiom:

First, we presume that federal courts lack subject matter jurisdiction until such time as the existence of jurisdiction is pleaded and proved.[2]

Second, parties may not consent to federal subject matter jurisdiction when authority creating such jurisdiction is lacking.[3]

Third, federal judges remain under a duty to consider subject matter jurisdictional challenges *sua sponte*.[4]

---

[1]   *Kokkonen v. Guardian Life Ins. Co. of America*, 511 U.S. 375, 377 (1994).

[2]   See Federal Rule of Civil Procedure 8(a)(1) (requiring plaintiffs to plead subject matter jurisdiction).

[3]   See, e.g., *Wisconsin Dept. of Corr. v. Schacht*, 524 U.S. 381, 389 (1998).

[4]   Id.

Fourth, federal jurisdiction may be challenged for the first time on appeal or even for the first time while on certiorari to the Supreme Court.[5]

And fifth, while federal courts possess only limited jurisdiction, the state courts retain general jurisdiction. This means that in most instances, even if a federal court has subject matter jurisdiction over a matter, its jurisdiction is held "concurrently," as we say, with the state courts. That is, most matters that may be heard in federal court also may be heard in state court as well. If a matter is to be heard "exclusively" in federal court, Congress must state so in clear terms.[6]

The jurisdiction of the federal courts is limited by two bodies of law. First, the Constitution places the outer boundaries for federal jurisdiction. Thus, the courts cannot hear a claim if it would not fall within the scope of one of the constitutional grants of subject matter jurisdiction listed in Article III, clause 2 of the Constitution.

But this full scope of potential federal subject matter jurisdiction under the Constitution, with the exception of the original jurisdiction of the Supreme Court,[7] is not self-enacting. Pursuant to the Madisonian Compromise, which takes its name from events at the Constitutional Convention of 1787,

---

[5]   See, e.g., *Elk Grove Unified Sch. Dist. v. Newdow*, 542 U.S. 1 (2004); *Louisville & Nashville R.R. v. Mottley*, 211 U.S. 149 (1908).

[6]   *Tafflin v. Levitt*, 493 U.S. 455, 459 (1990).

[7]   See *Marbury v. Madison*, 5 U.S. (1 Cranch) 137 (1803).

Congress must also act to vest the lower federal courts with subject matter jurisdiction. Many members of the Constitutional Convention found the creation of a federal judiciary highly controversial. James Madison, in a pitch to save the convention, offered his now-famous compromise, which achieved unanimous support from the delegates. He proposed that the Constitution mandate only the creation of the Supreme Court, leaving the creation of lower federal courts entirely to the discretion of Congress. In line with this history, the majority of commentators and jurists find that the existence of, and by extension the subject matter jurisdiction of, the lower federal courts remains under the near-complete control of Congress.[8] As such, in order to take subject matter jurisdiction in a case, a federal court must have both a statutory basis and a constitutional basis for jurisdiction.

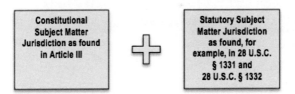

As we will see, Congress seldom enacts jurisdictional statutes that take the full scope of constitutional authority. Typically Congress will

---

[8]   See *Sheldon v. Sill*, 49 U.S. (8 How.) 441 (1850).

deploy but a subset of the potential Article III jurisdictional power.

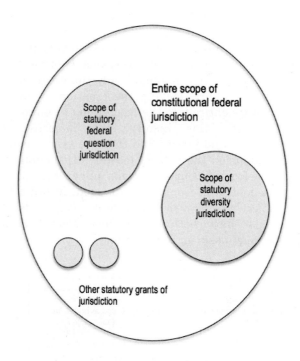

B. STRATEGIC VALUE OF FEDERAL JURISDICTION

Federal subject matter jurisdiction, then, is the power of the federal courts to hear a denominated set of disputes as delimited by the Constitution and federal statutes. Federal jurisdiction, as a result, reflects a series of first-order political decisions about federalism, separation of powers, judicial independence, individual rights, the scope of governmental power, and more. But as often as not, litigants will fight tooth and nail to find, or block, federal subject matter jurisdiction without giving a second thought to any of these grand notions.

While the practicing lawyer will find the following points so obvious as to not be worth mentioning, a new student of the law should bear in mind that disputes about federal jurisdiction often serve as a proxy for strategic or pragmatic advantages that attach to the federal forum. A student is well advised, then, when reading jurisdictional case law, to identify the strategic and pragmatic goals that counsel seek as a means of fully understanding the stakes of the opinion. Similarly, in applying jurisdictional doctrine in their developing practice, students should recall that taking federal jurisdiction is seldom an end in itself, but rather a means of achieving some pre-identified strategic advantage in relation to their particular suits. Without any pretention of presenting an exhaustive list, we next address some common benefits for which federal subject matter jurisdiction often serves as a proxy.

A jurisdictional fight often reflects nothing deeper than convenience to parties. As compared to state courts, which near universally sit in the local county seat, the applicable federal court (especially in the western states) may sit hundreds of miles away from the parties. Such distances not only increase litigation costs, but also in many instances severely hamper the ability of litigants to attend their own court dates and the like.

Similarly, a jurisdictional contest can act as a surrogate for a dispute among attorneys in relation to their comfort with the federal versus state systems. Many litigators focus their practice in the state courts nearly exclusively, while others work most often in the federal system. Dragging an attorney to a different court system, via a subject matter jurisdictional battle, may serve strategic ends by placing the opposing lawyer outside of his or her comfort zone. If opposing counsel has spent the past two decades learning not only the formal rules of the local state court system but also mastering the informal folkways of that system, throwing opposing counsel into the relatively unfamiliar confines of federal court may pay dividends.

A jurisdictional dispute can serve as a stand-in for a fight over jury pools. State courts typically pull jurors only from the county in which they sit. With the exception of geographically small federal districts such as the Southern District of New York, federal courts tend to serve much larger districts, pulling jurors from multiple counties or the entire state. These differences in jury pools, depending upon the district, can have dramatic demographic effects upon composition of the jury pool, which in turn can radically effect the likelihood of victory for one party or the other. In addition to this demographic effect, state and federal juries often vary in size, which can alter the deliberation dynamic.

In a related consideration, the larger federal jury pool and (often) distant location can help thwart one side from getting "home towned." For example, if a defendant is the largest employer in the county, bringing suit in the state court of that county may be unwise. The jury pool likely will have ties to the defendant and the judge may well have a relationship, even if attenuated, with the defendant. In such a situation, the plaintiff may believe that the defendant has a "home field advantage," meaning, that the plaintiff fears that close calls will favor the defendant both when made from the bench and in the jury box. To avoid getting "home towned" in this manner, the plaintiff may seek a more distant federal court forum where these influences seem less likely to affect the trial.

Litigating over federal subject matter jurisdiction may be a proxy for a dispute about varying degrees of judicial independence. The majority of state court systems employ some scheme of electoral appointment or retention for judges. Federal judges enjoy life tenure, following presidential appointment and Senate confirmation. In certain politically charged suits—a school-prayer case or the like—the parties may see this distance from the local electorate afforded by the federal bench as strategically significant.

Federal jurisdiction can serve as a proxy for expertise and resources. For example, the Delaware state chancery courts have great facility with matters of corporate law, likely exceeding the expertise of their federal-court colleagues. Barring federal jurisdiction over a corporate matter in Delaware, then, could be of tactical import. In other matters, such as in an ERISA dispute, the federal court may be seen as having greater expertise. Similarly, the federal courts almost always have more resources and staff than their state-court colleagues, which again might affect the outcome in a particular case.

Resources and expertise also correspond with speed of recovery. If the average time to civil trial in the applicable federal court is substantially faster than the time to recovery in the applicable state court, federal jurisdiction, again, may be of tactical significance.

Finally, but by no means least important, the choice of federal or state forum often affects procedural choice of law. That is to say, despite the prominence of the *Erie* doctrine,[9] which attempts to mitigate this phenomenon as to substantive law, trying a case in state versus federal court can lead to substantial differences in predicted trial outcomes. A few examples will suffice to prove the point. First, the federal courts admit expert testimony under the relatively rigorous *Daubert* standard,[10] whereas several state systems continue to rely on the looser *Frye* approach.[11] In many instances, this change in evidentiary standard entirely controls whether a plaintiff can survive summary judgment. Second,

---

[9]   *Erie Railroad Co. v. Tompkins*, 304 U.S. 64 (1938); discussed in Chapter 4.

[10]   *Daubert v. Merrell Dow Pharmaceuticals, Inc.*, 509 U.S. 579 (1993).

[11]   *Frye v. United States*, 293 F. 1013 (D.C. Cir 1923).

many states now require the awarding of punitive damages to be done by judges, whereas the federal courts tend to find such rules a violation of the right to trial by jury. Third, any number of procedural norm differences—such as the distinction between pleading under the federal *Twombly* standard[12] or the *Conley* standard,[13] which remains the rule in many states—can predictably change trial results in certain cases. As such, the fight over the federal forum will at times be, in reality, a fight over procedural choice of law.

There are more tactical considerations that one might mention, of course, but this would belabor the point. The essential lesson is, while this text will discuss various federal jurisdictional doctrine in the language deployed by the courts—one steeped in broad social-policy goals—the reader must bear in mind that in any particular case these tactical trial advantages are more likely to motivate counsel to seek, or not, federal jurisdiction. That is, one should seek federal jurisdiction only if it furthers the client's interests—broader federalism or separation of powers policy concerns should be deployed only instrumentally insofar as they foster client needs.

---

[12]   *Bell Atlantic Corp. v. Twombly*, 550 U.S. 544 (2007).

[13]   *Conley v. Gibson*, 355 U.S. 41 (1957).

C. OBJECTING TO LACK OF SUBJECT MATTER JURISDICTION

Having gained a general concept of what subject matter jurisdiction is and the strategic values it can play, in this last section, we turn to a brief discussion of the filing of, the timing of, and consequences of motions for lack of subject matter jurisdiction in the federal courts.

The party seeking subject matter jurisdiction bears the burden to plead and prove jurisdiction in the federal courts. Excepting cases of removal from state court (see Chapter 7), this burden will fall upon plaintiffs by virtue of filing the complaint in federal court. Federal Rule of Civil Procedure 8(a)(1) mandates that plaintiffs, as part of their complaints, make "a short plain statement of the grounds for the court's jurisdiction." Federal Rules of Civil Procedure Form 7 illustrates the brevity called for in satisfying Rule 8(a)(1). In the case of a Title VII action, say, pursuant to Form 7, a plaintiff need only allege as follows: "This action arises under a federal statute, 42 U.S.C. § 2000e–5(f)." Absent a challenge from opposing counsel or a sua sponte challenge to jurisdiction from the court, this barebones allegation should be sufficient to ground subject matter jurisdiction in this hypothetical federal civil-rights action.

Further, subject matter jurisdiction attaches claim-by-claim. Thus in the common scenario in which a plaintiff brings multiple claims—or the defendant answers with counterclaim(s)—each claim must have its own basis for subject matter jurisdiction. As such, in challenging subject matter jurisdiction, a party could argue that claims 2, 3, and 6 lack federal jurisdiction, while conceding that claims 1, 4, and 5 do lie in federal jurisdiction.

1.   THE RULE 12(b)(1) MOTION

After the filing of the complaint in federal court, the defendant may contest the court's subject matter jurisdiction. The defendant must contest jurisdiction by motion. The appropriate motion is one to dismiss for lack of subject matter jurisdiction under Federal Rule of Civil Procedure 12(b)(1).

A Rule 12(b)(1) motion, like any other, must contain the appropriate caption for the case following Federal Rule of Civil Procedure 10. The body of the motion should follow, to a large extent, the format of Federal Rule of Civil Procedure Form 40 and any local rules that apply. In most federal courts, the motion itself is a brief one-or two-page document. The motion in turn is supported by a separate document entitled "Memorandum in Support of Defendant's Motion to Dismiss for Lack of Subject Matter Jurisdiction," which is the longer document containing the defendant's argument. The two documents are signed under the dictates of Federal Rule of Civil Procedure 11 and filed with the court and served on all parties. The plaintiff will draft and serve an argument in opposition to the motion. The court may allow the defendant a short reply brief. The court, at its discretion, may schedule a hearing to receive arguments on the matter or set a discovery schedule and/or an evidentiary hearing should it need to resolve contested factual matters relating to jurisdiction. After the conclusion of such a hearing, the court will in due course enter a ruling on the motion. This ruling should include conclusions of law and findings of fact.

In drafting arguments for a Rule 12(b)(1) motion, the defendant may present two basic arguments, which in turn affect the standard of review the court deploys in ruling on the motion. First, a defendant my present a "facial" attack upon the plaintiff's subject matter jurisdictional allegations. A defendant makes a facial attack by accepting plaintiff's assertion of jurisdictional facts as true and contesting only the legal foundation for federal jurisdiction. When adjudicating a facial attack upon its subject matter jurisdiction, the district court assesses only the legal sufficiency of the allegations contained in the plaintiff's complaint. Thus, the court presumes all of plaintiff's factual allegations to be true. The district court will resolve legal disputes, however, without granting deference to the plaintiff's assertion of jurisdiction. In the event of an appeal of such a motion, the appellate court will, like the district court, presume factual allegations to be true, and it will resolve legal questions de novo.

Second, a defendant may present a "factual" challenge to the district court's federal subject matter jurisdiction. For example, a plaintiff may assert that the defendant is a resident of California, thus providing the basis for federal diversity jurisdiction because plaintiff is a resident of Oregon. But defendant could counter that, in fact, she is also a resident of Oregon not California, thus destroying any basis for diversity jurisdiction. When such a factual jurisdictional attack is made by a defendant, the plaintiff must submit evidence in support of the court's jurisdiction, and the plaintiff bears the burden of proving by a preponderance of the evidence that the court, in fact, has subject matter jurisdiction. When considering a factual challenge to jurisdiction no presumption of truthfulness attaches to a plaintiff's allegations. The parties may attempt to prove factual propositions by providing affidavits, live testimony, depositions, documentary and other evidentiary materials challenging the court's jurisdiction. The district court may order discovery, limited in scope to the jurisdictional issue, to aid in collecting needed information to resolve the matter. In ruling on the motion, the district court is free to weigh the evidence for credibility and make any factual findings needed to prove or disprove the existence of federal jurisdiction. On appeal, if the district court determined disputed factual issues, the clearly erroneous standard of review applies to the district court's findings of fact. Remaining questions of law will be reviewed by the court of appeals de novo.

2.   TIMING OF THE RULE 12(b)(1) MOTION

As noted above, a party, or the court itself, may challenge federal subject matter jurisdiction at any time during litigation. Even for the first time on appeal. Federal Rule of Civil Procedure 12(h)(3) codifies this norm.

But this challenge-at-any-time regime is far from best practice. In almost all cases, challenging subject matter jurisdiction at the earliest point in a suit presents the wisest course of conduct. To that end, if done in conformity with the timelines established in Federal Rule of Civil Procedure 12(a), a defendant may challenge the subject matter jurisdiction of the court before serving an answer.

If defendant chooses to file a Rule 12(b)(1) motion prior to the answer, counsel must recall that the joinder and waiver regimes of Rule 12(g)–(h) will apply. Hence filing a Rule 12(b)(1) motion must only be done after counsel has given full consideration to the strategic implications appertaining to the entire suit. Under Rule 12(g)'s joinder provision, the defendant may only file one pre-answer Rule 12(b) motion. Thus, defendant may not challenge subject matter jurisdiction pre-answer in one motion, await disposition of that matter, and then file a separate Rule 12(b)(6) motion pre-answer. Which is to say, if a pre-answer motion is to be filed at all, including a challenge to subject matter jurisdiction, all other Rule 12(b) motions that will be served pre-answer must be joined to that original motion.

Moreover, the serving of a Rule 12(b)(1) motion pre-answer will also waive any Rule 12(b)(2)–(4) motions not joined with the original motion. Hence if a defendant files a subject matter jurisdictional challenge pre-answer and fails to join an objection to, say, venue under Rule 12(b)(3) to that motion, the defendant's venue objection will be waived pursuant to Rule 12(h)(1). Rule 12(b)(6)–(7), however, are not amenable to this waiver regime as established in Rule 12(h)(2).

3.   EFFECT OF JURISDICTIONAL DISMISSAL

Dismissing a case for lack of subject matter jurisdiction does not mean the prevailing party of the motion wins the entire lawsuit. Quite the contrary is the case. Ruling that federal jurisdiction does not attach in a particular controversy means little more than that plaintiff filed the suit in the wrong court. The plaintiff remains free to file the suit in the correct court. Or put more formally, a jurisdictional dismissal is not a decision "on the merits," and as a result res judicata preclusion does not attach to the dismissal.

The granting of a Rule 12(b)(1) motion is immediately appealable in most instances. Granting such a motion constitutes a final judgment within the meaning of 28 U.S.C. § 1291. As such, when coupled with timely notice of appeal, the losing party to a granted Rule 12(b)(1) motion may appeal. If the Rule 12(b)(1) motion, however, is denied, the losing party may not immediately appeal. This so because the proceedings in the federal district court are not completed. That is, as the case was not dismissed, there remain active disputes for the district court to resolve, rendering the ruling not a final one for § 1291 purposes. A denied 12(b)(1) motion, then, may only be appealed after the resolution of all further trial court proceedings.

Finally, the statute of limitations will seldom serve to bar a suit from being filed again, if a case was dismissed from federal court for lack of subject matter jurisdiction. Assume, for instance, that a plaintiff filed her claim in federal court just one day before the statute of limitations ran. Also assume that three months later (i.e., after the statute of limitations has run), her case is dismissed from federal court for lack of subject matter jurisdiction. Plaintiff, by virtue of a body of laws called "saving statutes," will be able to file her suit again in the state court system. Every state has passed a version of a saving statute, which provides plaintiffs a specified grace period to re-file a case in state court after a jurisdictional dismissal from another court system assuming the suit was timely filed originally.

Subject matter jurisdictional dismissals, then, may be of great strategic import as outlined above. But this strategic importance must not be confused with a definitive victory. Indeed, the party losing a Rule 12(b)(1) motion almost always lives to fight another day in the state court system.

* * *

In sum, federal jurisdiction controls the types of questions that the federal courts may hear. If a federal court lacks subject matter jurisdiction, it must dismiss the suit immediately. Federal courts are courts of limited jurisdiction, which are so limited by both the Constitution and federal statute. In the main, federal jurisdiction is held concurrently with the state courts, meaning that the existence of federal jurisdiction, in most instances, does not strip the state courts of jurisdiction over the same matter. While we address many matters of social policy and constitutional interpretation in the remainder of this volume, one should never forget that counsel's motivation for obtaining federal jurisdiction derives from collecting strategic benefits afforded by that forum, not high-minded thoughts about federalism or the like. A party may challenge the existence of federal jurisdiction by serving a Federal Rule of Civil Procedure Rule 12(b)(1) motion. Filing such a motion triggers the joinder and waiver regimes of Rule 12(g)–(h). Finally, one does well to recall that a dismissal for lack of subject matter jurisdiction does not constitute a judgment on the merits, but only the determination that the suit was filed in the wrong court. With these fundamental concepts at hand, we turn in the next chapter to the heart of federal subject matter jurisdiction: Federal Question Jurisdiction.

CHAPTER 2

FEDERAL QUESTION JURISDICTION

"The judicial Power shall extend to all Cases, in Law and Equity, arising under this Constitution, the Laws of the United States, and Treaties made, or which shall be made, under their Authority . . ."

—United States Constitution, Art. III, cl. 2

"The district courts shall have original jurisdiction of all civil actions arising under the Constitution, laws, or treaties of the United States."

—28 U.S.C. § 1331

The vast majority of civil matters heard in federal court obtain subject matter jurisdiction because the suit raises a "federal question." A case presents a federal question if, in the words of the Constitution, it arises "under this Constitution, the Laws of the United States, and Treaties made." While applying this constitutional text, and concomitant statutory language, may appear straightforward at first blush, federal question jurisdiction "masks a welter of issues regarding the interrelation of federal and state authority and the proper management of the federal judicial system."[1] Surveying this broad swath of constitutional and statutory interpretation will occupy our discussion throughout this chapter.

---

[1]   *Franchise Tax Bd. of Cal. v. Constr. Laborers Vacation Trust*, 463 U.S. 1, 8 (1983) (footnote omitted).

In what will become a familiar pattern with most fonts of federal jurisdiction, in the federal question context we find that the Constitution provides broad outer limits of federal question jurisdiction for the federal courts. Despite this broad constitutional scope, following the Madisonian compromise, the Constitution is not self-executing in this regard. Thus, in order for a litigant to make use of federal question jurisdiction as a means of proceeding in federal court, not only must the particular case fall within the constitutional boundaries of Article III jurisdiction but the case must satisfy congressionally set statutory requirements for the exercise of federal question jurisdiction as well. The Supreme Court consistently interprets the primary federal question jurisdictional statute, 28 U.S.C. § 1331, as granting a much narrower scope of federal question jurisdiction than the Constitution permits.

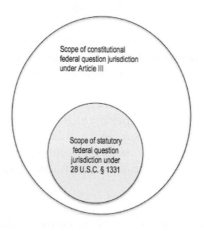

Scope of constitutional federal question jurisdiction under Article III

Scope of statutory federal question jurisdiction under 28 U.S.C. § 1331

As we discussed in Chapter 1, any exercise of federal jurisdiction, including federal question jurisdiction, must satisfy both constitutional and statutory requirements. This chapter, then, proceeds in two parts. First, we discuss the outer boundaries of constitutional federal question jurisdiction as these are established by the *Osborn* "ingredient" test. Second, we consider the narrower parameters set by Congress for statutory federal question jurisdiction under § 1331.

A. CONSTITUTIONAL FEDERAL QUESTION JURISDICTION

As a matter of constitutional law, the scope of federal question jurisdiction—jurisdiction arising under the Constitution, laws, or treaties of the United States as embodied in Article III—is quite broad. Famously, Chief Justice Marshall wrote for the Court in *Osborn v. Bank of the United States* that the existence of any "federal ingredient" in a case is sufficient to satisfy Article III federal question jurisdiction.[2] Under the conventional reading of the ingredient test, Article III jurisdiction lies so long as it is possible, even if not probable, that a question of federal law could arise at some point during the suit.[3] Our discussion of this expansive constitutional definition of federal question jurisdiction proceeds in three parts. First, we consider the early, post-ratification understanding of the provision. We turn

---

[2]   22 U.S. (9 Wheat.) 738, 822–23 (1824).

[3]   *Verlinden B.V. v. Cent. Bank of Nigeria*, 461 U.S. 480, 492–93 (1983).

second to a discussion of the seminal *Osborn* case. Third, we explore whether Article III jurisdiction expands beyond this traditional scope set by the *Osborn* opinion.

1.   RATIFICATION ERA

The notion of federal question jurisdiction made its first appearance at the Constitutional Convention in the Virginia Plan, which would have allowed federal courts to hear "questions which may involve the national peace and harmony." Ultimately, the delegates did not much discuss the concept, but rather approved phraseology revisions that extended federal judicial power to cases arising under the Constitution and treaties in addition to the cases arising under federal laws.

The great scope of the provision stoked criticism by Anti-Federalists during the ratification debates with rebuttals from the Federalists. Alexander Hamilton, for one, argued that supremacy and enforceability of federal law required federal judicial adjudicatory power.[4] This remains the predominant view of federal question jurisdiction's purpose today. As Professor Herbert Wechsler put it, the business of the federal courts "is the vindication of the rights conferred by federal law."[5]

Of course, mapping the general purposes of the provision does not answer the more pressing legal

---

[4]   The Federalist No. 22, at 143 (Alexander Hamilton) (Jacob E. Cooke ed., 1961).

[5]   Herbert Wechsler, Federal Jurisdiction and the Revision of the Judicial Code, 13 Law & Contemp. Probs. 216, 225 (1948).

question of just where the boundaries are of constitutional federal question jurisdiction. The early federal courts, however, did not meet Article III's "arising under" language in a vacuum. English jurisdictional law deployed the term "arising" from time to time, typically meaning that the action must rely upon the source of law from which it arises or the action must arise from a bounded physical territory. Moreover, the English courts had well-developed law regarding how parties could proceed in courts of limited jurisdiction.

The early nineteenth-century federal courts borrowed from this tradition to determine the meaning of Article III federal question jurisdiction. Thus, in *Owings v. Norwood's Lessee*[6] the Court held that it lacked federal question jurisdiction to hear a property claim under the Treaty of Paris ending the Revolutionary War because the treaty merely promised to recognize state-law property rights. If the treaty had created the property rights, then the suit would arise under the treaty, but since it was merely acknowledging pre-existing state-law rights federal jurisdiction did not lie. On the other hand, in *Cohens v. Virginia*, the Court held that the assertion of a federal defense to a state criminal action arose under Article III federal question jurisdiction because a "case in law or equity consists of the right of the one party, as well as of the other, and may truly be said to arise under the constitution or a law of the United States, whenever its correct decision depends

---

6   9 U.S. (5 Cranch) 344, 347–48 (1809).

on the construction of either."[7] As these examples illustrate, the ratification-era Court often found Article III arising under jurisdiction "to mean that a federal court may exercise jurisdiction over cases in which an actual federal law was determinative of a right or title asserted in the proceeding before it."[8]

2. *OSBORN* AND THE INGREDIENT TEST

Leaving the early days of the Republic behind, we turn to what remains the controlling interpretation of Article III federal question jurisdiction. Chief Justice John Marshall delivered the authoritative opinion in *Osborn v. Bank of the United States*.[9] The events leading up to *Osborn* arose during the Banking Crisis of 1819. At that time many banks, including the Second Bank of the United States, demanded repayment for loans which they had issued on credit that they did not have. These practices, in turn, led to an economic downturn and a shortage of money. In response, the state of Ohio placed a tax on the Bank of the United States, hoping that with these funds the state could distribute scarce currency as an economic stimulus. The Supreme Court previously declared such state taxes upon federal entities illegal in *McCulluch v. Maryland*.[10] Nevertheless, Ohio levied a $50,000 tax on the Bank. The Bank sought, and received, a

---

[7]   19 U.S. (6 Wheat.) 264, 379 (1821).

[8]   Anthony J. Bellia Jr., The Origins of Article III "Arising Under" Jurisdiction, 57 Duke L.J. 263, 269 (2007).

[9]   22 U.S. (9 Wheat) 738 (1824).

[10]   17 U.S. (4 Wheat.) 316 (1819).

federal injunction against the collection of the state tax. Ohio then gave its auditor, Ralph Osborn, permission to seize cash from an Ohio branch of the Bank of the United States—by force of arms if necessary. Osborn and his agents promptly confiscated $120,000. Federal agents, again by armed raid, took much of the cash back from the state treasury. The Bank, then, sued Osborn for the return of the remainder.

The suit, filed in federal court, sought equitable relief as provided by state law. Importantly for our discussion, the parties not being diverse, subject matter jurisdiction could arise only as a federal question. So the precise matter before the Court was: Did federal question subject matter jurisdiction exist for the Bank to seek state-law equitable relief? The first issue for the Court was whether statutory jurisdiction existed for the Bank's claim. The Court easily held that the statute creating the Bank also conferred subject matter jurisdiction " 'to sue and be used . . . in any circuit court of the United States.' "[11] Having determined that Congress intended to confer federal question jurisdiction upon the Bank's state-law equity claim by statute, the constitutional issue arose: Did this act of Congress comport with Article III, clause 2 of the Constitution?

Answering this question affirmatively, Chief Justice Marshall gave the constitutional provision a very broad construction. First, Marshall defined a question as federal if "the title or right set up by the

---

[11]   Osborn, 22 U.S. at 817.

party may be defeated by one construction of the Constitution or law of the United States, and sustained by the opposite construction, provided the facts necessary to support the action be made out."[12] That is, a legal question is federal if the result in the suit will differ pursuant to an application of federal law. The Court then held the scope of Article III federal question jurisdiction parallel with Congress's Article I legislative power, meaning that the federal courts have constitutional federal question jurisdiction to address all federal statutes. Marshall goes further still in constructing an expansive view, holding that the federal question at issue in any suit need not create a cause of action or defense central to the case. Rather, the case will arise under federal law, for purposes of Article III of the Constitution, so long as a question of federal law "forms an ingredient of the original cause . . . [even though] other questions of fact or of law may be involved in it."[13] Moreover, as the opinion makes clear, this federal ingredient need not even be in controversy in the suit to satisfy the constitutional standard. Rather, so long as a federal ingredient could potentially arise in a suit—no matter how unlikely or peripheral to the case—the entire suit arises under federal law pursuant to Article III.

Applying this interpretation to the facts of *Osborn*, the Court found a federal ingredient sufficient to ground Article III federal question jurisdiction. The Court concluded that because the Bank was created

---

[12]   Id. at 822.

[13]   Id. at 823.

by federal statute—meaning, all of its actions could only take place because federal statute permitted it—any suit with the Bank as a party necessarily includes a federal ingredient. As such, the claim in equity against Mr. Osborn included a federal ingredient because the Bank, a federally created entity, was a party.

The companion case to *Osborn*, *Bank of the United States v. Planters' Bank of Georgia*,[14] further demonstrates the breadth of the Chief Justice's holding. In *Planters' Bank*, the Court upheld federal jurisdiction over a suit by the Bank of the United States to recover in contract (i.e., a state-law claim). The Chief Justice reasoned that a federal question formed an ingredient of the contract suit because when the Bank sues "the first question which presents itself, and which lies at the foundation of the cause, is has this legal entity a right to sue? . . . . This depends on a law of the United States. . . . [Moreover, this] important question[ ] . . . exist[s] in every possible case."[15] Further, this federal ingredient exists, the Court held, even if this capacity question is never raised by the parties or if this very question constitutes settled law. Thus, for Article III purposes, the federal question in any given suit is but the salt in the cookie dough—the smallest pinch of federal law is all that is required.

---

[14]   22 U.S. (Wheat.) 904 (1824).

[15]   *Osborn*, 22 U.S. at 823–24.

Justice Johnson offered a powerful dissent in *Osborn*.[16] He stated that, "I cannot persuade myself that the Constitution sanctions the vesting of the right of action [in federal court] . . . in any case, merely on the ground that a question might possibly be raised in it involving the Constitution or constitutionality of a law of the United States."[17] Such a rule, Justice Johnson argued, would swallow state-court jurisdiction. Under the *Osborn* rule, in Justice Johnson's estimation, the federal government could construct a federal ingredient sufficient to take Article III federal question jurisdiction over all contract claims and will contests simply by placing a stamp tax upon the paper on which the contract or will was memorialized. Similarly, Justice Johnson argued that all claims by a naturalized citizen would generate Article III federal question jurisdiction because the naturalized citizen's capacity to sue was created by federal statute. Justice Johnson, thus, aimed to illustrate that Chief Justice Marshall's construction was obviously contrary to the intention of the Framers in its federalizing jurisdiction over vast swaths of traditional state-law matters. Despite the strength of Justice Johnson's objections, the Court has consistently affirmed Marshall's broad interpretation of Article III federal question jurisdiction.[18]

---

[16]   *Osborn*, 22 U.S. at 871 (Johnson, J., dissenting).

[17]   Id. at 874.

[18]   *See Am. Nat'l Red Cross v. S.G.*, 505 U.S. 247, 264–65 (1992); *Verlinden B.V. v. Cent. Bank of Nigeria*, 461 U.S. 480, 492 (1983); *Puerto Rico v. Russell & Co.*, 288 U.S. 476, 485 (1933);

In *Verlinden B.V. v. Central Bank of Nigeria*,[19] for example, the Court reaffirmed the view that any issue of federal law will ground Article III federal question jurisdiction. *Verlinden* involved two foreign sovereigns (hence diversity jurisdiction could not arise) in a complex contract dispute to be governed by either state or Dutch law—which is to say, not federal law. The Court found a federal question, however, because all litigation in the United States that involves a foreign sovereign as a defendant invokes the Foreign Sovereign Immunities Act, 28 U.S.C. § 1330 (FSIA). The FSIA does two things. First, it creates federal jurisdiction for such suits. And second, it grants foreign-sovereign defendants broad substantive immunities to suit in the manner of affirmative defenses. The Court concluded that because these substantive, federally created defenses necessarily arise in every case with a foreign-sovereign defendant the FSIA comports with Article III federal question jurisdiction.

Osborn remains the constitutional standard. Indeed, as recently as 1992, in what was a near replay of *Osborn*, the Court in *American National Red Cross v. S.G.*,[20] upheld that federally created corporations may insist that state-law claims be heard in federal court. The Court reiterated that their federal charter presented a sufficient Article III, federal ingredient, even if this was not enough of

---

Bankers Trust Co. v. Tex. & Pac. Ry. Co., 241 U.S. 295, 305–06 (1916); *Union Pac. R.R. Co. v. Myers*, 115 U.S. 1, 11–14 (1885).

[19]   461 U.S. 480 (1983).

[20]   505 U.S. 247 (1992).

a foundation to vest statutory federal question jurisdiction under 28 U.S.C. § 1331.

3.   BEYOND THE *OSBORN* INGREDIENT TEST

In addition to this blackletter view of *Osborn* and Article III, many have argued for an even more expansive view of constitutional federal question jurisdiction. To that end, Professor Paul Mishkin famously argued that *Osborn* sanctions the "theory of protective jurisdiction." Under this approach, a mere federal jurisdictional statute, uncoupled from any substantive federal law, would provide a sufficient federal ingredient to vest Article III jurisdiction over state-law issues when the matter arises as part of an overarching federal program.[21] While individual members of the Court have flirted with this notion, a majority of the Court has never endorsed protective jurisdiction as constitutionally sound.[22] In rejecting this ultra-expansive view, most join Justice Frankfurter in concluding that " '[p]rotective jurisdiction,' once the label is discarded, cannot be justified under any view of the allowable scope to be given to Article III. . . . The theory must have as its sole justification a belief in the inadequacy of state tribunals in determining state law. The Constitution reflects such a belief in the specific situation within which the Diversity Clause was confined. The

---

[21]   Paul J. Mishkin, The Federal "Question" in the District Courts, 53 Colum. L. Rev. 157, 187–89 (1953).

[22]   See *Mesa v. California*, 489 U.S. 121, 136 (1989); *Textile Workers Union of Am. v. Lincoln Mills*, 353 U.S. 448, 460 (1957) (Burton, J., concurring); *Nat'l Mut. Ins. Co. v. Tidewater Transfer Co.*, 337 U.S. 582, 599 (1949) (Jackson, J., plurality opinion).

intention to remedy such supposed defects was exhausted in this provision of Article III."[23]

* * *

In sum, then, the Court continues to give constitutional federal question jurisdiction a sweeping interpretation. In *Osborn*, Chief Justice Marshall holds for the Court that a case may arise under constitutional federal question jurisdiction so long as any "ingredient" in the matter derives from federal law, even if that matter is not in dispute in the present suit. While scholars and jurists have flirted with even broader constructions of Article III, the Court continues to adhere to the *Osborn* rule.

B. 28 U.S.C. § 1331 FEDERAL QUESTION JURISDICTION

Recalling that most constitutional jurisdiction is not self-enacting, but requires Congress to exercise that power, we turn our attention now to 28 U.S.C. § 1331, which is the general statute that grants federal district courts with original subject matter jurisdiction over "all civil actions arising under the Constitution, laws, or treaties of the United States." Congress passed this statute into law in 1875, and the provision remains essentially unchanged today, excepting now-expired amount-in-controversy requirements. This statute currently grounds the majority of civil actions heard in federal court.

---

[23] *Lincoln Mills*, 353 U.S. 474–75 (Frankfurter, J., dissenting).

Despite the parallelism of language between the constitutional and statutory texts, and the likely original congressional intent seeking a sweeping statutory grant of jurisdiction, the Supreme Court consistently interprets § 1331 as granting a much narrower scope of federal question jurisdiction than the Constitution permits. In language that students of federal question jurisdiction should take to heart, the Court ruled that "[a]lthough the language of § 1331 parallels that of the 'Arising Under' Clause of Art. III, this Court never has held that statutory 'arising under' jurisdiction is identical to Art. III 'arising under' jurisdiction. Quite the contrary is true."[24] Thus, it is error to use the expansive construction of Article III, which is governed under the *Osborn* test, to analyze the much narrower scope of § 1331 jurisdiction and vice versa. In practice this means that showing that an exercise of jurisdiction comports with the constitutional standard for federal question jurisdiction is merely a necessary condition for the taking of federal jurisdiction. The more meaningful analysis, in most cases, will be the § 1331 one.

Under the standard account, the Court's construction of § 1331 eschews the traditional statutory-interpretation goal of divining and enforcing congressional intent. Rather, the Court generally deploys a number of self-created policy goals as interpretive guideposts when fleshing out

---

[24]   *Verlinden B.V. v. Central Bank of Nigeria*, 461 U.S. 480, 494 (1983).

§ 1331 doctrine.[25] Some matters that the Court has consistently looked to include: docket control, federalism-based concerns, institutional competency, efficiency, litigant expectations, and fundamental fairness. Keeping these broader policy goals at hand is helpful when diving into the more detailed elements of § 1331 doctrine, as it is often the balancing of these many competing ends that motivates the Court in crafting particular jurisdictional rules.

Finally, these policy goals are balanced against the backdrop of two key presumptions. First, the Court assumes that that suits arising in § 1331 jurisdiction can concurrently be heard in state courts.[26] Second, the courts also engage in the mirror image presumption. That is, the Court finds that there is a strong presumption in favor of § 1331 jurisdiction "when federal law creates a private right of action and furnishes the substantive rules of decision, . . . unless Congress [specifically] divests federal courts of their § 1331 adjudicatory authority."[27]

---

[25] David L. Shapiro, Jurisdiction and Discretion, 60 N.Y.U. L. Rev. 543, 588 (1985).

[26] *See Tafflin v. Levitt*, 493 U.S. 455, 458–59 (1990); *Gulf Offshore Co. v. Mobil Oil Corp.*, 453 U.S. 473, 478 (1981); see also Chapter 1.A.4 (discussing concurrent jurisdiction).

[27] *Mims v. Arrow Financial Services*, LLC, 132 S. Ct. 740, 748–49 (2012).

Federal Question Jurisdiction

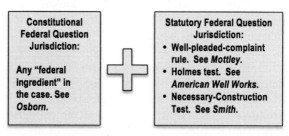

In this section, we take up the many regimes that the Court imposes upon § 1331 jurisdiction to limit its scope. First, we consider the well-pleaded complaint rule, which requires that federal issues, for § 1331 purposes, be found in the plaintiff's complaint, not in anticipated defenses. Second, we discuss the Holmes test, which mandates that the only issue in a complaint that will create a § 1331 federal question is a federally created cause of action. Third, we look to the primary exception to the Holmes test that allows courts to take § 1331 jurisdiction when a federal right is coupled with a state-law cause of action. Fourth, we address complete preemption doctrine, where the courts take § 1331 jurisdiction over erstwhile state-law claims on the theory that, in actuality, the plaintiff brings a federal cause of action. Finally, we end with a presentation of the wrinkles that declaratory judgment actions present for § 1331 jurisdiction.

1.   THE WELL-PLEADED COMPLAINT RULE

The first of these Court-fashioned rules limiting § 1331 jurisdiction lies with the "well-pleaded complaint rule." Pursuant to this rule, only federal issues raised in a plaintiff's complaint, not anticipated or actually pleaded defenses, establish statutory federal question jurisdiction. The seminal case for this rule is *Louisville & Nashville R.R. Co. v. Mottley.*[28] As such, many refer to the well-pleaded complaint rule as the *Mottley* rule.

The *Mottley* case arose after Mr. and Mrs. Mottley were injured in an 1871 train wreck in Kentucky. They settled with the railroad, accepting lifetime, unlimited, free passes on the railroad as compensation for their injuries. In 1906, Congress prohibited the issuance and honoring of all such free railroad passes. After the railroad refused to honor their contractual right to free rail travel, the Mottleys sued the railroad. Bringing the suit in federal court, the Mottleys alleged breach of contract—a state-law cause of action. They sought specific performance of their 1871 free-passes agreement.

The Mottleys, when they filed their state-law-based complaint, anticipated, as did the railroad defendant, that the 1906 federal act would be raised as an affirmative defense in the case. But the complaint itself—as is appropriate given that it is the plaintiff's document—did not raise the federal defense. Rather, the federal defense was raised in the railroad's answer. In the proceedings at trial, the

---

[28]   211 U.S. 149 (1908).

parties assumed that the presence of the federal-law defense sufficiently presented a question of federal law so as to comply with the dictates of § 1331.

The Supreme Court disagreed, raising the matter *sua sponte*. The Court ruled that plaintiff's inability to present the federal issue in the complaint constituted a § 1331 jurisdictional defect. Thus, the case was dismissed for wont of federal question jurisdiction. To be clear, the existence of the railroad's federal defense satisfied *Osborn*'s constitutional ingredient test. Nevertheless, the Court held that § 1331 presents a much narrower font of jurisdictional authority. To this end, the Court reasoned that § 1331 jurisdiction is properly tested solely in relation to the complaint. Pursuant to this rule, only federal issues lodged in the complaint itself may ground statutory federal question jurisdiction. Federal defenses, which by their very nature will not be presented in a complaint, to state-law matters will not vest § 1331 jurisdiction.

Put slightly differently, the well-pleaded complaint rule answers the question "Where?" That is to say, the rule tells litigants and courts "where" to look when seeking a federal issue that will give rise to § 1331 jurisdiction. And the answer offered is simple: Look only in the complaint.

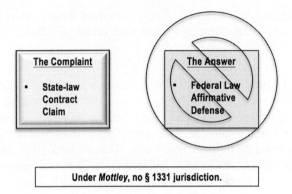

Under *Mottley*, no § 1331 jurisdiction.

Many have forcefully criticized the *Mottley* rule as unduly limiting the scope of federal question jurisdiction. The Supreme Court, however, has steadfastly adhered to it, reasoning that it responds to "the demands of reason and coherence, and the dictates of sound judicial policy."[29] While perhaps not sound in every application, there is much to be said in favor of the Court's approach. Resolving whether a court has subject matter jurisdiction as early as possible is, the majority of the time, the most efficient course. Given the scope of pre-answer-motion practice in the federal system, cases may be docketed for months or years before an answer is filed. If our system generally allowed statutory federal question jurisdiction to arise from later-in-time documents,

---

[29]   *Romero v. International Terminal Operating Co.*, 358 U.S. 354, 379 (1959).

valuable client and judicial resources would often be wasted litigating in a court that lacks jurisdiction.[30]

2.   THE HOLMES TEST

In addition to the well-pleaded complaint rule, which directs "where" one is to look to find a § 1331 federal question, the Court further restricts which matters found in the complaint will constitute statutory federal question jurisdiction. In this regard, the Court has fashioned two competing doctrines. In this section, we begin with the most prominent of the two regimes: the "Holmes test."

The Holmes test works as a complement to the well-pleaded complaint rule. While the well-pleaded complaint rule answers the question of "Where" one looks to find § 1331 federal questions (viz., the complaint), the Holmes test answers the question of "What" constitutes a federal issue. Following the Holmes test, only a federally created "cause of action" will give rise to § 1331 jurisdiction.

Operation of the Holmes test, with its focus on cause of action, requires one to distinguish between the concept of "causes of action" from other concepts, namely "rights" and "claims" in order to navigate the test. A right is a clearly stated, mandatory, judicially enforceable obligation.[31] This notion of obligation imposes a correlative duty upon a person to either refrain from interfering with, or to assist, the right

---

[30]   But see removal after later-in-time amendments discussed in Chapter 7.C.

[31]   See, e.g., *Gonzaga Univ. v. Doe*, 536 U.S. 273, 284 (2002).

holder. A cause of action is the further determination that a person falls into a class of litigants empowered to vindicate a specified right in court.[32] The concept of cause of action, then, is necessarily related to the concept of a right insofar as plaintiffs must have rights before they can be persons empowered to enforce them. But the concept of cause of action is not to be confused with the notion of a right itself. Indeed, one may have a right, yet lack the power to enforce the right. For example, an individual's rights under certain statutory schemes may only be vindicated by an administrative agency. That is, Congress may vest individuals with rights but not vest them with causes of action to enforce those rights by way of private suit. Finally, to have a federal claim, a plaintiff must: (1) assert a federal right; (2) be a member of the class of persons entitled to enforce the right (i.e., assert a cause of action); and (3) assert a transaction or occurrence that is sufficient, if true, to justify a remedy. The Courts' competing § 1331 doctrine diverge according to whether emphasis is placed upon the federal cause of action, as the Holmes test does, or upon federal right, as the *Smith* does. (The concept of claim, while at times confused as a jurisdictional matter, more properly is analyzed as a merits issue addressed pursuant to a Rule 12(b)(6) motion.)

Fortunately, in the majority of § 1331 cases, a federally created cause of action will be coupled with a federally created right and pleaded in such a manner as to present a federal claim as well. Thus

---

[32]   See *Passman v. Davis*, 442 U.S. 228, 239 n.18 (1979).

this fine-grained distinction between which aspects of the plaintiff's case raise a federal right and which raise a federal cause of action are not always of great concern for § 1331 purposes. For example, Title VII of the Civil Rights Act of 1964 both creates rights in individuals not to suffer adverse employment actions on the basis of race, color, religion, sex or national origin[33] and a private cause of action for individuals to enforce this set of rights.[34] Hence in Title VII actions, and scores upon scores of other matters where Congress has created privately enforceable federal rights, satisfying the Holmes test—and thereby taking § 1331 jurisdiction—is routine business. Plaintiffs in such cases, if pressed, need only identify the federal law creating the cause of action and the accompanying federal rights being enforced.

The rubber really meets the road for the Holmes test, however, when suits begin matching federal rights with state-law causes of action or vice versa. This often happens in situations where federal statute or regulation creates, say, a consumer-product safety rule—or put in other terms, a federal right—yet fails to create a private federal cause of action to enforce the right (i.e., fails to create the power in individuals to sue to enforce the consumer-product right). In such cases, following the basic strictures of negligence per se doctrine, plaintiffs will often couple the federal right with a state-law cause

---

[33]   42 U.S.C. § 2000e-2(a)(1).

[34]   42 U.S.C. § 2000e-2(f)(1)(A).

of action such as negligence or breach of warranty.[35] By so doing, plaintiffs aim to construct privately enforceable remedies for violations of federal rights that otherwise lack them.

Following the Holmes test, such suits—ones joining a federal right to a state-law cause of action—do not arise under § 1331 jurisdiction. Writing for the Court, Justice Holmes created his jurisdictional test in 1916 in *American Well Works Co. v. Layne & Bowler Co.*[36] Here, the plaintiff held the patent for, manufactured, and sold, what was then considered the best water pump on the market. The plaintiff contended that the defendant stated that the plaintiff's pump was a patent infringement upon the defendant's pump. Instead of bringing an infringement case, however, the plaintiff brought libel and slander (i.e., state-law) causes of action in Arkansas state court. Defendant removed to federal court.[37] This removal raised the federal question jurisdictional issue. While recognizing that the suit implicated matters of federal patent rights, Justice Holmes focused on the state-law origin of the causes of action as the essential component for the § 1331 analysis and held for the Court that a "suit arises under the law that creates the cause of action."[38] Following the Holmes approach, then, embedding a

---

[35] See, e.g., *Merrell Dow Pharmaceuticals Inc. v. Thompson*, 478 U.S. 804 (1986) (plaintiffs seek § 1331 jurisdiction by embedding federal F.D.C.A. labeling rules within state-law tort and contract causes of action).

[36] 241 U.S. 257 (1916).

[37] See Chapter 7 for a discussion of removal jurisdiction.

[38] *American Well Works*, 241 U.S. at 260.

federal matter within a state-law cause of action will never give rise to § 1331 jurisdiction. Only finding a federal cause of action on the face of the well-pleaded complaint—whether it be created by act of Congress or federal common law[39]—will vest § 1331 jurisdiction.

The Complaint

State-law Libel Cause of Action

The state-law elements include:
- **Published**
- **False (requires application of federal law)**
- **Injurious**
- **unprivileged**

Under the Holmes test, no § 1331 jurisdiction.

The Holmes test, however, does not require that plaintiffs actually establish a viable federal cause of action in order to vest § 1331 jurisdiction. This misconstruction is an error that "frequently happens where jurisdiction depends on subject matter, the question whether jurisdiction exists has been confused with the question whether the complaint states a cause of action."[40] Thus, a plaintiff need only make a so-called colorable, or arguable, assertion of a federal cause of action, as opposed to a viable

---

[39]   *Illinois v. Milwaukee*, 406 U.S. 91, 100 (1972).

[40]   *Romero v. Int'l Terminal Operating Co.*, 358 U.S. 354, 359 (1959).

presentation of a federal claim, to ground § 1331
jurisdiction.[41] As a result, the taking of § 1331
jurisdiction precedes the question of whether
plaintiff presents a viable cause of action sufficient to
survive a Rule 12(b)(6) motion. "The reason for this
is that the court must assume jurisdiction to decide
whether the allegations state a cause of action on
which the court can grant relief as well as to
determine issues of fact arising in the controversy."[42]
Put one final way, a court in cases of federal question
jurisdiction must have proper subject matter
jurisdiction to decide both successful and
unsuccessful suits on the merits.[43] Any other rule
would destroy the distinction between a dismissal for
lack of subject matter jurisdiction under Rule
12(b)(1) and a dismissal for failure to state a claim
under Rule 12(b)(6).

Thus presenting a colorable assertion to a federally
created cause of action will, in the vast majority of
instances, serve as a sufficient condition for the
grounding of § 1331 jurisdiction. This general
conclusion, however, is subject to two caveats. First,
the Court recently reaffirmed that there are some
exceptions to this view that satisfying the Holmes
test is a sufficient condition for taking § 1331
jurisdiction.[44] These exceptions to this sufficiency

---

[41]   See, e.g., *Verizon Md., Inc. v. Pub. Serv. Com'n of Md.*, 535
U.S. 635, 642–43 (2002).

[42]   *Bell v. Hood*, 327 U.S. 678, 682 (1946).

[43]   The *Fair v. Kohler Die & Specialty Co.*, 228 U.S. 2225
(1913).

[44]   *Gunn v. Minton*, 133 S. Ct. 1059, 1064 (2013).

rule are rare and thus beyond the scope of our discussion.[45]

Second, one must bear in mind that the Holmes test is merely a sufficient, not a necessary, condition for the taking of § 1331 jurisdiction. Or as the courts put it, it is a test of inclusion not of exclusion.[46] Following *Smith v. Kansas City Title & Trust Co.*,[47] the Court maintains a second and independent test for the taking of § 1331 jurisdiction, which we turn to next.

3.   THE *SMITH* TEST

Pursuant to this second blackletter test, federal question jurisdiction may lie over state-law causes of action that necessarily require construction of an embedded federal issue. As *Smith* is the Court's classic statement of this position, this line of cases is often referred to as the *Smith* test. More recent cases and commentary, however, often denominate this approach the *Grable* test in reference to a more recent application of the doctrine.[48]

In *Smith*, a stockholder sued in federal court to enjoin his corporation from purchasing bonds issued

---

[45]   See, e.g., *Shoshone Mining Co. v. Rutter*, 177 U.S. 505 (1900). For a more wide-ranging discussion of the exceptions to the Holmes test see Lumen N. Mulligan, You Can't Go Holmes Again, 107 Nw. U. L. Rev. 237 (2012).

[46]   *Gunn*, 133 S. Ct. at 1064 (borrowing Judge Friendly's language on this point); T.B. Harms Co. v. Eliscu, 339 F.2d 823, 827 (2d Cir. 1964) (Friendly, J.).

[47]   255 U.S. 180 (1921).

[48]   Grable & Sons Metal Prods., Inc. v. Darue Eng'g & Mfg., 545 U.S. 308 (2005).

pursuant to the Federal Farm Loan Act (FFLA). The plaintiff argued that such a purchase constituted a state-law breach-of-fiduciary-duty cause of action because the corporation could only purchase bonds authorized to be issued by a valid law and that the FFLA was unconstitutional. Thus the plaintiff's state-law claim necessarily required adjudication of a federal matter, the constitutionality of the FFLA. The Court, over Justice Holmes' vigorous dissent, found § 1331 jurisdiction because "it appears from the . . . statement of the plaintiff that the right to relief depends upon the construction or application of the Constitution."[49] In so doing, the Court found that a plaintiff could avail himself of a federal forum on a state-law theory of recovery under § 1331 because the plaintiff's state-law cause of action necessarily required the court to pass upon the constitutionality of a federal act.[50]

The Court engaged with this *Smith*-style approach to § 1331 jurisdiction several times in the ensuing years, culminating in 2005 with its most recent in-depth treatment of the doctrine in *Grable & Sons Metal Prods., Inc. v. Darue Engineering & Mfg.*[51] Here, the IRS seized real property belonging to Grable & Sons to satisfy a federal tax deficiency and sold the property to Darue Engineering. Five years later, Grable & Sons sued Darue Engineering in state court to quiet title, a state-law cause of action. Grable & Sons asserted that Darue Engineering's title was

---

[49] Smith, 255 U.S. at 199.

[50] See Id. at 201–02.

[51] 545 U.S. 308 (2005).

invalid because the IRS had conveyed the seizure notice to Grable & Sons in violation of provisions of the Internal Revenue Code governing such actions. The Supreme Court affirmed § 1331 jurisdiction in the case because the plaintiff's state-law cause of action necessarily depended upon a claim of a substantial federal right.

The Court elaborated on this holding, crafting a four-part test for the application of the *Smith* test. The Court nicely summarized the *Grable*, four-part test eight years later in *Gunn v. Minton*.[52] "[F]ederal jurisdiction over a state-law claim will lie if a federal issue is: (1) necessarily raised, (2) actually disputed, (3) substantial, and (4) capable of resolution in federal court without disrupting the federal-state balance approved by Congress."[53] While satisfaction of the Holmes test, then, generates a rather mechanical vesting of § 1331 jurisdiction, successful invocation of the *Smith* test rides on a more contextual analysis. This nuanced test, moreover, is designed only to act as a "special and small" exception to the Holmes test.[54] Successful invocations of the *Smith* test, as a result, are statistically rare.

---

[52]   133 S. Ct. 1059 (2013).

[53]   *Gunn*, 133 S. Ct. at 1065.

[54]   *Empire Healthchoice Assurance, Inc. v. McVeigh*, 547 U.S. 677, 699–701 (2006).

The Complaint

State-Law Quiet Title Cause of Action

The state-law elements include:
- **Proof of title**
- **Superior to others with interests in the property (requires application of federal law)**

Under *Grable & Sons* test, yes § 1331 jurisdiction.

But only if the federal issue is:
- **Necessarily raised**
- **Actually in dispute**
- **Substantial**
- **And won't disrupt state-federal dockets**

Following *Grable*, one must bear in mind, then, the narrow scope of this exception to the Holmes test. The *Smith* approach, while operating as a competing regime to the Holmes test, does not operate as an exception to the well-pleaded complaint rule. Thus even in a *Smith*-test case, the well-pleaded complaint rule requires that the federal issue be found only in the complaint. The *Smith* and *Grable* regimes merely change the "what" that must be found in the complaint from a federal cause of action, as the Holmes test requires, to an embedded federal issue in a state-law cause of action. Second, the *Grable* Court, while not overruling *Smith*, cabins the doctrine severely. Under the four-prong *Grable* test, the *Smith* approach truly is a limited exception to what is the primary rule as espoused by the Holmes test.

Jurisdiction under § 1331, to sum up, remains more limited than Article III federal question jurisdiction. First, all invocations of § 1331 require conformity with the well-pleaded complaint rule. Second, in coordination with the well-pleaded complaint rule, successful invocation of the statute requires conformity with either the Holmes test or the *Smith* test. The Holmes test, by leaps and bounds, is the more often deployed regime. Meeting the well-pleaded complaint rule and the Holmes (or the *Smith*) test, then, will result in the court taking § 1331 jurisdiction. The remaining two sections in our § 1331 discussion are but unique applications of these fundamental doctrine.

4.   COMPLETE PREEMPTION DOCTRINE

Thus far, we have thought of suits raising either federal causes of action or federal rights as defined by the plaintiff's allegations in the complaint. Indeed, the courts generally accept that a plaintiff is making a state-law cause of action if that is what his complaint states. In this section, we look to suits where the court does not accept the plaintiff's initial characterization of her claim as being grounded in state law. Pursuant to the "complete preemption doctrine," a small set of claims will arise under § 1331 jurisdiction, despite plaintiff's insistence that the suit raises only state law, because federal law so occupies the field in that area of law that any putative state-law complaint must yield to a federal construction of the claim.

Preemption doctrine falls into two categories. "Normal preemption" doctrine governs cases in which the defendant presents a federal defense to the plaintiff's state-law claim. Normal preemption, then, is but a label placed upon situations, such as was raised in *Mottley*, where the defendant presents a federal-law defense to the plaintiff's state-law claim. Because the federal issue arises as a defense in a normal preemption case, following the *Mottley* decision, § 1331 jurisdiction does not lie.[55]

"Complete preemption" cases, however, present a more complicated jurisdictional picture. In a complete-preemption case, a defendant is not merely presenting a federal defense to a state-law claim. Rather, the defendant asserts that Congress has so occupied this area of law that the plaintiff does not legally present a state-law claim, even though the complaint asserts one, and that the only possible interpretation of the plaintiff's claim is one based on federal law. Or as the Court has put the matter, "[w]hen the federal statute completely pre-empts the state-law cause of action, a claim which comes within

---

[55]   *Metropolitan Life Ins. Co. v. Taylor,* 81 U.S. 58, 63 (1987).

the scope of that cause of action, even if pleaded in terms of state law, is in reality based on federal law."[56]

Determining when a federal statute completely preempts state law is a function of statutory interpretation. Congress must direct, either explicitly or by inference, when federal law provides the exclusive cause of action in particular fields. These instances are few. Congress explicitly calls for complete preemption of nuclear-energy, catastrophic-event, state-law causes of action in the Price-Anderson Act.[57] The Court has found complete preemption by implication under only three other acts: the National Banking Act,[58] E.R.I.S.A,[59] and the Labor Management Relations Act.[60]

Jurisdictionally speaking, if the court holds that a federal statute completely preempts a state-law cause of action, then the case arises under § 1331 jurisdiction. When a "federal statute completely pre-empts . . . [a] state-law cause of action . . . that cause of action . . . is in reality based on federal law."[61] As such, when reinterpreted as a result of complete preemption, the complaint presents a federal cause of action on its face. Viewed from this vantage point, then, the completely preempted suit satisfies both the well-pleaded-complaint rule and the Holmes test.

---

[56]   *Beneficial Nat'l Bank v. Anderson*, 539 U.S. 1, 8 (2003).

[57]   42 U.S.C. § 2014(hh).

[58]   *Beneficial Nat'l Bank v. Anderson*, 539 U.S. 1 (2003).

[59]   *Metropolitan Life Ins. Co. v. Taylor*, 81 U.S. 58 (1987).

[60]   *Avco Corp. v. Machinists*, 390 U.S. 557 (1968).

[61]   *Beneficial Nat'l Bank v. Anderson*, 539 U.S. 1, 8 (2003).

From the § 1331 point of view, then, complete preemption is but a somewhat peculiar application of the now-familiar Holmes test.

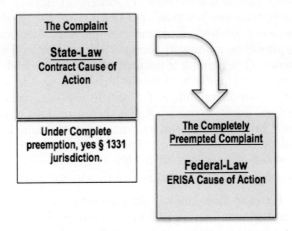

5. DECLARATORY JUDGMENT SUITS

Federal question jurisdiction suits brought under the Declaratory Judgments Act also present unique applications of Holmes test. Under the act, "[i]n a case of actual controversy within its jurisdiction, . . . any court of the United States . . . may declare the rights and other legal relations of any interested party seeking such declaration, whether or not further relief is or could be sought."[62] Under the act, then, a party need not seek monetary damages or an

---

[62]   28 U.S.C. § 2201(a).

order from the court; rather, a party need only ask the court to declare who is in the right in a given matter.

Jurisdictional quirks pop up here because often in suits in which a Declaratory Judgment Act claim is brought, the "natural" positioning of the parties becomes flipped, meaning the person who would typically be a plaintiff becomes a defendant and vice versa. This flipping of natural parties in cases where the natural defendant would have a federal defense to a state-law claim could lead to the expansion of federal question cases because the natural defendant now presents his legal arguments in the complaint instead of the answer. The Court, however, has developed an approach to thwart this jurisdictional creep. Let's explain this notion by way of examples.

Imagine that Donna, an employer, ended Paul's employment because of his disability. Paul could bring suit for damages against Donna for violations of federal law, the Americans with Disabilities Act (ADA). In this example, we would posit that Paul is the "natural" plaintiff and Donna the "natural" defendant, because in a typical suit for damages these are the roles these persons would assume.

Paul's Complaint	**Donna's Answer**
• Federal ADA Claim	• Federal Defenses

Under the Declaratory Judgment Act, however, Donna need not wait for Paul to sue her. Donna, pursuant to the act, may sue Paul for a judgment declaring that she did not violate Paul's ADA rights. In this case, notice that Donna is now plaintiff and Paul now defendant. Here Donna and Paul are not in their "natural" positions precisely because in a more typical suit for damages their roles would be reversed, as described above. The declaratory judgment act, thus, flips these natural roles.

Donna's Declaratory-Judgment Complaint	Paul's Declaratory-Judgment Answer
• Did not violate the ADA	• Donna did violate the ADA

Now in our ADA example, this flipping of the natural parties does not have § 1331 jurisdictional consequences. In the first iteration of the example, Paul presents a federal ADA claim that would satisfy both the well-pleaded-complaint rule and the Holmes test. Similarly, Donna's declaratory-judgment claim presents a federal ADA matter that would satisfy both the well-pleaded complaint rule and the Holmes test.

Let us imagine now a different suit. Senator Patty sues reporter Dan for libel. Libel is a state-law tort cause of action. Let us also posit that Dan intends to present the federal First Amendment as an affirmative defense in the suit. In the resulting law suit of *Patty v. Dan*, plaintiff Patty would bring a state-law cause of action to which defendant Dan would respond with a First Amendment (i.e., federal-law) defense. As should now be old hat, we can conclude that under the well-pleaded complaint rule § 1331 jurisdiction does not arise here because the only federal issue resides in the defense.

Patty's Complaint	Dan's Answer
• State-law Libel Claim	• Federal Defense
Under *Mottley*, no § 1331 jurisdiction.	

Now let us consider this same controversy between Patty and Dan as a suit by Dan under the Declaratory Judgment Act. Because the act allows the parties to flip their natural roles, Dan is now the plaintiff and Patty the defendant. Moreover, Dan's suit asks the court to declare that he acted with First Amendment protections when he published his story about Patty. At first blush, then, it would appear that Dan's Declaratory Judgment Act suit to resolve his First Amendment rights satisfies the well-pleaded complaint rule and the Holmes test. Hence, prima facie, this flipping of the natural parties by the Declaratory Judgment Act would seem to vest § 1331 jurisdiction in disputes that the *Mottley* rule otherwise would not allow into federal court.

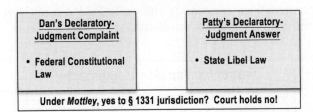

Dan's Declaratory-Judgment Complaint	Patty's Declaratory-Judgment Answer
• Federal Constitutional Law	• State Libel Law

Under *Mottley*, yes to § 1331 jurisdiction? Court holds no!

In *Franchise Tax Bd. of Cal. v. Constr. Laborers Vacation Trust*,[63] the Court held that the Declaratory Judgment Act does not expand federal question subject matter jurisdiction in this manner. Under the Court's approach, a dispute that could not obtain federal jurisdiction prior to the passage of the Declaratory Judgment Act, may not rely on the act's propensity to flip the natural roles of the parties as a basis for taking jurisdiction. In determining § 1331 jurisdiction in Declaratory Judgment Act cases, then, the courts ask: Could this case have been brought in federal court absent the existence of the Declaratory Judgment Act? Answering this question in the affirmative—as we did in our Paul and Donna ADA example—leads the court to take § 1331 jurisdiction. Answering this question in the negative—as we did in our Patty and Dan libel example—leads the court to decline § 1331 jurisdiction. Put in other words, a court can take § 1331 jurisdiction in a Declaratory Judgment Act case only if the parties, when put into their "natural" roles as if the case was a typical one

---

[63]   463 U.S. 1 (1983).

for damages, can satisfy the well-pleaded complaint rule and the Holmes (or *Smith*) test.

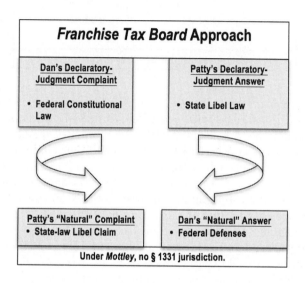

Franchise Tax Board **Approach**

Dan's Declaratory-Judgment Complaint
- **Federal Constitutional Law**

Patty's Declaratory-Judgment Answer
- **State Libel Law**

Patty's "Natural" Complaint
- **State-law Libel Claim**

Dan's "Natural" Answer
- **Federal Defenses**

Under *Mottley*, no § 1331 jurisdiction.

* * *

In this chapter, we reviewed the most commonly used basis for subject matter jurisdiction in the federal courts, federal question jurisdiction. We began with a discussion of constitutional federal question jurisdiction. Here we found that the Court gives constitutional federal question jurisdiction a sweeping interpretation following *Osborn*. Under that construction, a case may arise under constitutional federal question jurisdiction if any ingredient in the suit derives from federal law, even if that matter is not in dispute in the present suit.

We then turned to the Court's narrower construction of 28 U.S.C § 1331, the statutory basis for federal question jurisdiction. In this regard, we explored the well-pleaded complaint rule, which mandates that federal issues be found in the plaintiff's complaint, not in anticipated defenses. We then discussed the Holmes test, which mandates that the only federal issue in a complaint that will create a § 1331 federal question is a federally created cause of action. We looked also to a narrow exception to the Holmes test, the *Smith* test, that allows courts to take § 1331 jurisdiction when a federal right is coupled with a state-law cause of action. We ended with two non-standard applications of the well-pleaded complaint rule and the Holmes test: complete-preemption doctrine and declaratory-judgment actions.

CHAPTER 3

DIVERSITY JURISDICTION

"The judicial Power shall extend to . . . Controversies . . . between Citizens of different States, . . . and between a State, or the Citizens thereof, and foreign States, Citizens or Subjects."

—United States Constitution, Art. III, cl. 2

"The district courts shall have original jurisdiction of all civil actions where the matter in controversy exceeds the sum or value of $75,000, exclusive of interest and costs, and is between . . . citizens of different States; . . . citizens of a State and citizens or subjects of a foreign state . . .; citizens of different States and in which citizens or subjects of a foreign state are additional parties; and . . . a foreign state . . . as plaintiff and citizens of a State or of different States."

—28 U.S.C. § 1332(a)

Since the first Judiciary Act of 1789, opposing parties from different states have entered federal courts under "diversity jurisdiction." Unlike federal question jurisdiction, in which subject matter jurisdiction is defined in terms of the source of the law, diversity jurisdiction is bounded by the citizenship status of the parties. Under this font of jurisdiction, then, the federal courts may hear a state-law or foreign-law claim so long as the opposing parties in the suit are diverse—meaning in the Constitution's language that the case is "between

Citizens of different States, . . . [or] foreign States, Citizens or Subjects." This font of jurisdiction, which is the source of the second-most-numerous grouping of cases in the federal courts, occupies us in this chapter.

Following the Madisonian Compromise, diversity jurisdiction requires satisfaction of both constitutional and statutory bases of jurisdiction. As with federal question subject matter jurisdiction, we find that the federal courts give constitutional diversity jurisdiction an ample interpretation, while more restrictively reading 28 U.S.C. § 1332, which is the primary statutory provision for diversity jurisdiction. Because diversity jurisdiction, by definition, does not raise questions of federal law, the exercise of this ground of jurisdiction raises the sticky choice-of-law question of what bodies of law control in a diversity case, which we will deal with when we get to *Erie* doctrine in Chapter 4. In this chapter, we focus solely on the standard interpretations of Article III and § 1332 diversity jurisdiction.

A.   CONSTITUTIONAL DIVERSITY JURISDICTION

In this part, we take up the standard construction of constitutional diversity jurisdiction. First, we address the standard account of why the framers created diversity jurisdiction: namely, to provide a neutral forum for interstate civil disputes. Second, we turn to the constitutional standard for diversity jurisdiction, "minimal diversity."

1. DIVERSITY JURISDICTION'S RATIONALE

At first blush, the very existence of diversity jurisdiction seems odd—or at least redundant. Each state in the union has a functioning court system to address state-law disputes. The constitutional framers, nevertheless, saw fit to include diversity as a basis for federal-court jurisdiction. Moreover, the first Congress enacted statutory diversity jurisdiction in 1789, whereas the first long-lived general grant of federal question jurisdiction was not passed until 1875. So what is diversity all about? In short, protection for out-of-state litigants from in-state bias.

While there are competing accounts,[1] the standard view is that "the purpose of the diversity requirement . . . is to provide a federal forum for important disputes where state courts might favor, or be perceived as favoring, home-state litigants."[2] The diversity jurisdiction provision, then, aims to alleviate this concern by allowing suits between citizens of different states, or state citizens and foreign citizens, to enter the neutral federal court.

Our early sources tend to confirm that diversity jurisdiction was crafted as a response to perceived, or potential, in-state judicial bias. James Madison, for example, defended the federal courts' "cognizance of disputes between citizens of different states . . . . [as]

---

[1]   See, e.g., Stephen C. Yeazell, *Overhearing Part of a Conversation: Shutts as a Moment in a Long Dialogue*, 74 UMKC L. Rev. 781 (2006).

[2]   *Exxon Mobil Corp. v. Allapattah Servs., Inc.*, 545 U.S. 546, 553 (2005).

rather salutary. . . . It may happen that a strong prejudice may arise in some states, against the citizens of others, who may have claims against them. We know what tardy, and even defective administration of justice, has happened in some states. A citizen of another state might not chance to get justice in a state court, and at all events he might think himself injured."[3] Chief Justice Marshall confirmed this view as well. "However true the fact may be, that the tribunals of the states will administer justice as impartially as those of the nation, to parties of every description, it is not less true that the constitution itself either entertains apprehensions on this subject, or views with such indulgence the possible fears and apprehensions of suitors, that it has established national tribunals for the decision of controversies between aliens and a citizen, or between citizens of different states."[4] The *Exxon Mobil Corp. v. Allapattah Servs., Inc.* decision, in 2005, reaffirmed the contemporary Court's commitment to this reason for creating Article III diversity jurisdiction.[5]

New students of jurisdiction are reminded, that despite this in-state-bias concern, our standard principles of federal jurisdiction apply. First, the notion of concurrent jurisdiction applies in diversity jurisdiction, meaning even though the federal courts may take jurisdiction, the state courts almost always

---

[3]   3 Elliot, Debates on the Federal Constitution at 486 (1836).

[4]   *Bank of United States v. Deveaux*, 9 U.S. (5 Cranch) 61, 87 (1809).

[5]   545 U.S. at 553.

have jurisdiction as well. Second, despite the importance of this anti-bias principle, diversity jurisdiction remains under the umbrella of the Madisonian Compromise.[6] Thus this constitutional grant of jurisdiction is not self-enacting.[7] The reader is also reminded that, if there truly is an out-of-state bias in a particular locale, moving to federal court is but a partial remedy. The federal jury remains entirely composed of in-state jurors, and federal judges more often than not take the bench after years of service in the state bar where they sit. Local media remains to cover the suit. Local counsel may continue to have "insider" status that commands occasional advantages over out-of-state counsel. And so on.

2. ARTICLE III DIVERSITY

We turn now to a discussion of the standard for determining whether a suit satisfies the constitutional standard for diversity of citizenship. In order to engage with this analysis, we must deploy two terms of art: "minimal diversity" and "complete diversity." The Constitution is satisfied under the minimal diversity standard while the statute, 28 U.S.C. § 1332(a), requires satisfaction of the complete-diversity standard. We turn, then, to an explanation of these competing standards.

In a suit with only one party as plaintiff and one party as defendant, determining diversity of

---

[6]   Justice Story, contrary to the general view, believed that Congress had a duty to enact diversity jurisdiction. See *Martin v. Hunter's Lessee*, 14 U.S. (1 Wheat.) 304, 314 (1816).

[7]   *Hertz Corp. v. Friend*, 559 U.S. 77, 84 (2010).

citizenship is a straightforward analysis. The suit is diverse so long as the plaintiff and the defendant are not citizens of the same state. Thus, suit #1 below is an example of a diverse case while suit #2 below is not.

Suit #1:   π (citizen of Virginia)
v.
Δ (citizen of Delaware)

Suit #2:   π (citizen of Maryland)
v.
Δ (citizen of Maryland)

Once we have two or more parties on either side of the "v."—that is once we have more than one plaintiff or more than one defendant—determining diversity of citizenship is not as obvious. Consider suit #3.

Suit #3:   π 1 (citizen of Virginia)
π 2 (citizen of Delaware)
v.
Δ 1 (citizen of Delaware)

On the one hand, this case seems diverse because π 1 is from Virginia, while the other parties are from Delaware. On the other hand, we have Delaware citizens as opposing parties, meaning that in a sense this case lacks some elements of diverse citizenship.

More pointedly, suit #3 has some key elements of diversity of citizenship, because π 1 and Δ 1 are citizens of different states. We refer to cases that have at least one plaintiff with citizenship status that differs with that of at least one defendant as "minimally diverse." As such, suit #3 meets the standard of minimal diversity. Even if we expanded the set of plaintiffs in suit #3 to add 30 more parties from Delaware, we would still meet the minimal diversity standard because at least one plaintiff would still differ in citizenship with at least one defendant. Similarly, we could add 30 more defendants to suit #3 all from Delaware (or from any state) and the suit would remain minimally diverse because at least one plaintiff would differ in citizenship with at least one defendant.

While suit #3 is minimally diverse, from another point of view, one might argue that the case is not entirely diverse because π2 and Δ1 in that case are both citizens of Delaware. To account for this sense in which a multi-party case can be conceived of as diverse, we use the term "complete diversity." A suit is completely diverse only if no plaintiff shares a citizenship status with any defendant. Thus, suits #4 and #5 are completely diverse, because no plaintiffs share citizenship status with any defendants.

Suit #4:	π 1 (citizen of Texas)
	π 2 (citizen of Texas)
	v.
	Δ 1 (citizen of Iowa)
	Δ 2 (citizen of Iowa)

Suit #5:	π 1 (citizen of Utah)
	π 2 (citizen of California)
	v.
	Δ 1 (citizen of Maine)
	Δ 2 (citizen of Illinois)

In suit #4, there are no Texans as defendants. Or what is the same idea, there are no Iowans as plaintiffs. The fact that π1 and π2 in suit #4 are both Texans does not affect the complete diversity analysis, because it is only opposing parties that must be completely diverse from a jurisdictional point of view. Similarly, suit #5 is completely diverse because no defendants are citizens of Utah or California. Thus, both cases are completely diverse because no plaintiff in either case shares citizenship status with any defendants.

Suits #6 and #7, while minimally diverse, are not completely diverse because there is at least one plaintiff who shares citizenship status with at least one defendant.

Suit #6:	π 1 (citizen of Florida)
	π 2 (citizen of Georgia)
	v.
	Δ 1 (citizen of Alabama)
	Δ 2 (citizen of Florida)

Suit #7:	π 1 (citizen of Oregon)
	π 2 (citizen of Oregon)
	v.
	Δ 1 (citizen of Oregon)
	Δ 2 (citizen of Arizona)

Suit #6 is not completely diverse because π1 and Δ2 are both Floridians. Suit #7 is not completely diverse because π1, π2 and Δ1 are Oregonians. While both suits #6 and #7 are minimally diverse—because in each at least one plaintiff differs in citizenship from at least one defendant—they are not completely diverse because in both there is at least one plaintiff who shares citizenship status with at least one defendant.

Having this distinction between minimal and complete diversity at hand, we turn next to which standard governs Article III diversity jurisdiction. The Supreme Court did not definitively settle upon minimal diversity as the standard for Article III diversity jurisdiction until 1967. In *State Farm Fire*

& *Casualty Company v. Tashire*,[8] the Court held that an interpleader statute, 28 U.S.C. § 1335, that called for only minimal diversity among the parties was constitutional. In so holding, the Court ruled that Article III diversity jurisdiction requires only minimal diversity, even though diversity jurisdiction under the primary diversity jurisdictional statute, 28 U.S.C. § 1332(a), requires complete diversity. As the Court put it, in "*Strawbridge v. Curtiss*, . . . this Court held that the diversity of citizenship statute required 'complete diversity'. . . . But Chief Justice Marshall . . . [in *Strawbridge*] purported to construe only 'The words of the act of congress,' not the Constitution itself."[9] The Court then ruled, with little additional commentary, that minimal diversity forms the constitutional standard for diversity jurisdiction. Hence, the Court has interpreted constitutional diversity jurisdiction to be vast, giving Congress great room to employ this font of jurisdiction.

---

[8]   386 U.S. 523 (1967).

[9]   Id. at 531.

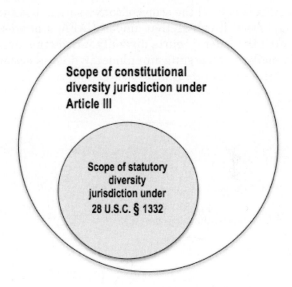

Scope of constitutional
diversity jurisdiction under
Article III

Scope of statutory
diversity
jurisdiction under
28 U.S.C. § 1332

What follows from the fact that the constitutional
standard for diversity jurisdiction requires only
minimal diversity is that Congress may choose to
enact legislation deploying minimal diversity as the
jurisdictional standard when it seeks to set an easier-
to-achieve jurisdictional requirement than what is
found under § 1332(a). To date, Congress has
exercised this power three times. Hence, parties need
only meet the minimal diversity standard under the
Interpleader Act (discussed in the *Tashire* case), the
Multiparty, Multiforum Jurisdiction Act (which is
often styled the Mass Disaster Act), and the Class
Action Fairness Act of 2005 (CAFA). Of these acts,
CAFA is likely the most consequential. A discussion

of CAFA is beyond the scope of conversation, but one should bear in mind that under CAFA, Congress granted the federal courts diversity jurisdiction over minimally diverse suits in enumerated class action suits and enumerated "mass action" suits.

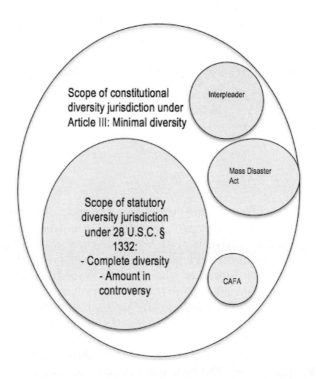

Article III diversity jurisdiction's vast scope is, however, subject to two constitutional-text-based limitations. First, despite that fact that a suit between a French plaintiff and a Mexican defendant might appear at first blush to be diverse within the meaning of Article III (insofar as the parties do not share citizenship status), the constitutional text does not embrace such a suit. Article III limits diversity suits to cases "between a State, or the Citizens thereof, and foreign States, Citizens or Subjects," making clear that diversity jurisdiction requires at least one party to the suit to be a citizen of one of the United States. The Supreme Court confirmed this plain-meaning interpretation of Article III in *Jackson v. Twentyman*.[10] Moreover, the policy implications of a contrary approach would be to open the federal courts up as a forum for all the world's international civil disputes. Following this same approach, the lower courts hold that, under *Twentyman*, Article III diversity jurisdiction requires at least one party to the suit be a citizen of a state— not merely a citizen of the United States who happens to lack state citizenship. As such, constitutional diversity jurisdiction does not arise if a party in a suit is an American citizen domiciled abroad who lacks state citizenship as a result of his or her ex-patriot domicile.

* * *

In sum, then, constitutional diversity jurisdiction was crafted to thwart bias against out-of-state litigants. Constitutional diversity jurisdiction demands only that the parties to a suit be minimally

---

[10]   27 U.S. (2 Pet.) 136 (1829).

diverse. That is to say, at least one plaintiff must differ in citizenship with at least one defendant. Finally, Article III requires that at least one party to the litigation be an American with state citizenship.

B.   28 U.S.C. § 1332 DIVERSITY JURISDICTION

Satisfying Article III jurisdiction, however, is merely a necessary—but not sufficient—condition for taking diversity jurisdiction. Because constitutional diversity jurisdiction is not self-enacting, Congress must pass a statute that exercises this Article III jurisdictional power. Any case seeking to take diversity jurisdiction must satisfy this statutory jurisdictional rule as well as the Article III minimal diversity standard. Following the Madisonian Compromise, in crafting a diversity jurisdictional statute, Congress may grant less (but not more) jurisdictional authority than the Constitution affords. In this section, we address the primary diversity jurisdiction statute, 28 U.S.C. § 1332(a)–(c), in which Congress grants a narrower scope of diversity jurisdiction than Article III provides.

Section 1332(a) sets two basic requirements for taking diversity jurisdiction. First, the statute lists categories in which parties may be deemed diverse. Second, the statute requires that "the matter in controversy exceeds the sum or value of $75,000, exclusive of interest and costs." We will address these two requirements in turn, followed by a brief discussion of other limitations upon the exercise of § 1332(a) diversity jurisdiction.

1. COMPLETE DIVERSITY

As was addressed above, diversity jurisdiction in Article III of Constitution requires only that the parties be minimally diverse (i.e., at least one plaintiff must differ in citizenship status with at least one defendant). Statutory diversity jurisdiction, however, requires that the parties be completely diverse (i.e., no plaintiffs may share citizenship status with any defendants). The Supreme Court has so held since 1806, when in the celebrated *Strawbridge v. Curtiss* case,[11] Chief Justice Marshall, writing for the Court, held that statutory diversity jurisdiction requires complete diversity, which is to say that no opposing parties may be citizens of the same state. The primary statutory diversity statute, 28 U.S.C. § 1332(a), continues to adhere to *Strawbridge*'s complete diversity requirement.

It follows from this difference in the Article III minimal diversity standard and § 1332(a)'s complete diversity standard, that the former may be satisfied while the latter is not. That is to say, because § 1332(a) imposes a more rigorous requirement than does Article III, a case may be minimally diverse yet not completely diverse. The next graphic provides an example of this interaction between the constitutional and statutory standards for diversity of citizenship.

---

[11]   7 U.S. (3 Cranch) 267 (1806).

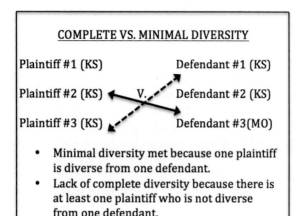

- Minimal diversity met because one plaintiff is diverse from one defendant.
- Lack of complete diversity because there is at least one plaintiff who is not diverse from one defendant.

a. Statutory Categories of Diversity

The current iteration of the statute lists four ways in which parties to a suit may satisfy the complete diversity requirement. First, § 1332(a)(1) diversity jurisdiction lies over "civil actions . . . between . . . citizens of different States." These suits, under subsection (a)(1), are straightforward cases in which all the parties are citizens of a state coupled with complete diversity of state citizenship, such as in suit #8 below.

```
┌──────────────────────────────────────────────────┐
│  Suit #8:        π 1 (citizen of Kansas)           │
│                  π 2 (citizen of California)        │
│                         v.                         │
│                  Δ 1 (citizen of New York)         │
│                  Δ 2 (citizen of Vermont)          │
└──────────────────────────────────────────────────┘
```

Pursuant to § 1332(e), citizens of the District of Columbia, the Commonwealth of Puerto Rico and other territories are treated as if they are citizens of states. As such, diversity jurisdiction lies in cases such as suit #9 under § 1332(a)(1), because the statute treats the citizen of Puerto Rico as if he were a citizen of a state.

```
┌──────────────────────────────────────────────────┐
│  Suit #9:        π 1 (citizen of Alaska)           │
│                         v.                         │
│                  Δ 1 (citizen of Puerto Rico)      │
└──────────────────────────────────────────────────┘
```

Treating non-state citizens of United States possessions as if they are state citizens for diversity jurisdiction purposes has raised some constitutional difficulties. Indeed, the Marshall Court ruled that citizens of the District of Columbia and other United States territories are not constitutionally diverse from state citizens.[12] In 1949, however, the Supreme Court in a fractured opinion found § 1332's treatment of territorial citizens as diverse from state citizens

---

[12]   *Corp. of New Orleans v. Winter*, 14 U.S. (1 Wheat.) 91 (1816); *Hepburn & Dundas v. Ellzey*, 6 U.S. (2 Cranch) 445 (1805).

constitutional in *National Mutual Insurance Co. of District of Columbia v. Tidewater Transfer Co.*[13] Two members of the Court argued that the nineteenth-century Marshall opinions should be overruled to find that District of Columbia citizens are constitutionally diverse from state citizens. Three other justices found that, although District of Columbia citizens were not citizens of a state for Article III diversity jurisdiction purposes, the diversity statute was constitutional in light of Congress's Article I general legislative authority over the District of Columbia and the territories. Four justices dissented. Despite this lack of agreement in rationale, *Tidewater* continues as good law for the proposition that, for statutory diversity jurisdiction purposes, citizens of District of Columbia and other United States territories may be treated as if they are citizens of a state.

Second, § 1332(a)(2) diversity jurisdiction lies over "civil actions . . . between . . . citizens of a State and citizens or subjects of a foreign state, except that . . . jurisdiction . . . [does not lie] between citizens of a State and citizens or subjects of a foreign state who are lawfully admitted for permanent residence in the United States and are domiciled in the same State." In § 1332(a)(2), we find two rules. The primary rule is that statutory jurisdiction lies if a state citizen faces an opposing party who is a foreign national, regardless of whether the foreign national is the plaintiff or the defendant. For example:

---

[13]   337 U.S. 582 (1949).

Suit #10:	π 1 (citizen of Minnesota)
	v.
	Δ 1 (citizen of Canada)

Suit #11:	π 1 (citizen of Brazil)
	v.
	Δ 1 (citizen of Georgia)

In both suits #10 and #11, the parties are completely diverse (i.e., no opposing parties share the same citizenship status). Further, because one of the parties is a foreign national § 1332(a)(2), not § 1332(a)(1), is the correct subsection of the statute to find diversity jurisdiction over the case. Note also that under § 1332(a)(2), which is to be contrasted with § 1332(a)(4), the foreign party's status as plaintiff or defendant is immaterial to the jurisdictional analysis.

Of course, § 1332(a)(2) jurisdiction cannot lie, as a constitutional matter, when both opposing parties are foreign nationals. Suit #12, for instance, cannot arise under § 1332(a)(2).

Suit #12:	π 1 (citizen of Mexico)
	v.
	Δ 1 (citizen of Canada)

Taking jurisdiction in suit #12 would run afoul of
Twentyman.[14] As such, § 1332(a)(2) is drafted to
require that one of the opposing parties be a citizen
of one of the United States.

Subsection 1332(a)(2) also applies to suits in which
one of the parties is a foreign national permanent
resident of the United States, but not an American
citizen. Thus, the federal district courts may take
jurisdiction in suits such as #13 below:

Suit #13:	π 1 (citizen of Minnesota)
	v.
	Δ 1 (citizen of
	Canada permanently
	residing in Hawaii)

This provision for jurisdiction over foreign
nationals permanently residing in the United States
comes with one statutory except. If the American
citizen party and the foreign national permanent
resident both reside in the same state, then § 1332(a)
diversity jurisdiction does not lie. Thus, § 1332(a)
diversity jurisdiction does not lie in suits #14 or #15.

---

[14]   27 U.S. (2 Pet.) 136 (1829).

Suit #14: π 1 (citizen of Maryland)

v.

Δ 1 (citizen of
Japan permanently residing
in Maryland)

Suit #15: π 1 (citizen of
Egypt permanently residing
in Idaho)

v.

Δ 1 (citizen of Idaho)

In these suits, even though Article III diversity jurisdiction lies and the cases could be deemed completely diverse within the meaning of *Strawbridge*, Congress decided to exempt such suits from statutory diversity jurisdiction. The primary policy rationale here is that diversity jurisdiction exists to protect an out-of-state litigant from in-state bias. A foreign national permanently residing in the same state as the opposing party, at least in Congress' judgment, is less apt to face such in-state bias because, for most intents and purposes, the party is an "in-stater." Moreover, Congress concluded that taking jurisdiction over such suits gave foreign national permanent residents easier access to the federal court system than United States citizens had, which was perceived as an unfairness. Finally,

Congress determined that these in-state, foreign-national-permanent-resident suits were inappropriately crowding the federal dockets. Thus, we have the statutory exception embodied in the latter portion of § 1332(a)(2).[15]

Third, § 1332(a)(3) diversity jurisdiction lies over "civil actions . . . between . . . citizens of different States and in which citizens or subjects of a foreign state are additional parties." Like § 1332(a)(2), § 1332(a)(3) deals with suits that include foreign nationals. Again, like § 1332(a)(2), § 1332(a)(3) is indifferent to the foreign party's status as plaintiff or defendant. But we now see that the statute introduces the notion of a foreign national as an "additional party."

What exactly constitutes an "additional party" under § 1332(a)(3) is not entirely settled. But the plain-meaning of the term "additional party" directs that that § 1332(a)(3) addresses suits in which there is at least more than one plaintiff or defendant, whereas § 1332(a)(2) addresses suits involving a foreign national and a citizen of a state in which there is but one defendant and one plaintiff. Thus, we know that if we have more than two parties as

---

[15]   Prior to the Federal Courts Jurisdiction and Venue Clarification Act of 2011, § 1332(a) used a less elegant statutory fix to the problem of foreign nationals permanently residing in the same state as the American citizen opposing party. This older statutory approach presented significant Article III challenges. See, e.g., *Saadeh v. Farouki*, 107 F.3d 52 (D.C. Cir. 1997). After 2011, however, the statutory challenges presented in cases like Saadeh no longer lay in wait for the unwary.

plaintiffs or defendants and a foreign national in the suit, § 1332(a)(3) applies.

Continuing on, it is best to approach the meaning of "additional party" from a policy perspective. Recall that *Twentyman* holds that constitutional diversity jurisdiction does not lie if all the parties to the suit are foreign nationals even if they are from differing countries. Hence there is no constitutional diversity jurisdiction over suit #16.

```
┌──────────────────────────────────────────────┐
│                                                │
│   Suit #16:     π 1 (citizen of South Africa)  │
│                         v.                     │
│                 Δ 1 (citizen of China)         │
│                                                │
└──────────────────────────────────────────────┘
```

Subsection 1332(a)(3) aims to prevent the manufacturing of diversity jurisdiction over cases such as suit #16 by merely joining an American party. Assume that our South African plaintiff and Chinese defendant in suit #16 strongly desired to litigate in federal court, but for § 1332(a)(3) (and other similar doctrine discussed below) they could enter federal court under diversity jurisdiction simply by finding an American citizen willing to join the suit as plaintiff. Subsection 1332(a)(3) prohibits this type of joinder in order to create diversity jurisdiction. Thus, § 1332(a) jurisdiction would not lie in suit #17.[16]

Suit #17:   π 1 (citizen of South Africa)
                  π 2 (citizen of Louisiana)
                              v.
                  Δ 1 (citizen of China)

The policy goal achieved by § 1332(a)(3) in barring suit #17 is to protect the integrity of the *Twentyman* ruling by prohibiting the easy manipulation of suit #16, which squarely presents a *Twentyman* problem, into an otherwise federal case by joining an "additional" American party. Thus, § 1332(a)(3) states that in suits with more than two parties as plaintiffs or defendants and at least one foreign national, the federal courts may hear the case in diversity only if the foreign national(s) are additional parties. If the American is the additional party, which is the supposition in suit #17, diversity jurisdiction does not lie.

Typically, if there are three total parties and diverse state citizens are opposing parties, the joining of a foreign national renders the foreigner the "additional party" within the meaning of § 1332(a)(3), creating diversity jurisdiction. Thus, § 1332(a)(3) diversity jurisdiction would lie in both suits #18 and #19.

---

[16]   See, e.g., *Salton, Inc. v. Philips Domestic Appliances and Personal Care B.V.*, 391 F.3d 871 (7th Cir. 2004).

Suit #18:   π 1 (citizen of South Carolina)
             π 2 (citizen of Belgium)
                         v.
             Δ 1 (citizen of Alabama)

Suit #19:   π 1 (citizen of Colorado)
                         v.
             Δ 1 (citizen of New Mexico)
             Δ 2 (citizen of Ireland)

Furthermore, assuming an authentic dispute among the completely diverse, opposing-party state citizens, joining of multiple foreign nationals on both sides of the dispute may result in the foreigners being deemed "additional" for § 1332(a)(3) purposes as well.[17] As such, § 1332(a)(3) diversity jurisdiction could be deemed to lie in suit #20.

---

[17]   See, e.g., *Transure, Inc. v. Marsh and McLennan, Inc.*, 766 F.2d 1297, 1299 (9th Cir. 1985).

Suit #20:   π 1 (citizen of Missouri)
π 2 (citizen of France)
π 3 (citizen of France)
v.
Δ 1 (citizen of New Jersey)
Δ 2 (citizen of France)

It is also worth noting that the foreign nationals need not be diverse from each other.[18]

Fourth, and finally, § 1332(a)(4) diversity jurisdiction lies over "civil actions . . . between . . . a foreign state, defined in . . . [28 U.S.C. §] 1603(a) . . . , as plaintiff and citizens of a State or of different States." This final category of statutory diversity exists, then, for cases in which a foreign nation itself—not merely a foreign national—brings suit as plaintiff. Foreign nationals, as discussed above, may take diversity jurisdiction under subsections 1332(a)(2)–(3). The text of § 1332(a)(4) limits diversity jurisdiction over foreign nations explicitly to suits in which the foreign nation is plaintiff. As an exercise of comity between nations, United States citizens wishing to bring suit in the American courts against a foreign nation as defendant may only do so under the Foreign Sovereign Immunities Act of 1976 (FSIA), which severely limits when a foreign nation may be involuntarily haled into the American courts.

---

[18]   See, e.g., *Bank of New York v. Bank of America*, 861 F. Supp. 225 (S.D. N.Y. 1994).

One must bear in mind that the FSIA defines what constitutes a foreign sovereign very broadly. For example, a commercial corporation that is majority owned by a foreign nation constitutes a foreign sovereign for purposes of the FSIA, and by cross-reference, § 1332(a)(4).[19] For example, Emirates Airlines, for jurisdictional purposes, is treated as a foreign sovereign because it is majority owned by the United Arab Emirates. Under § 1332(a)(4), then, diversity jurisdiction lies in suit #21 because the plaintiff is a foreign nation, but not under suits #22 or #23 because the defendant is a foreign nation.

Suit #21:	π 1 (the nation of Argentina)
	v.
	Δ 1 (citizen of North Dakota)

Suit #22:	π 1 (citizen of Mississippi)
	v.
	Δ 1 (the nation of Italy)

---

[19]   See 28 U.S.C. § 1603(b)(3).

Suit #23:   π 1 (citizen of Arkansas)
                     v.
                     Δ 1 (Emirates Airlines –
                     a corporation majority
                     owned by the U.A.E.)

---

b. Determining Citizenship

Having found that § 1332(a) requires that suits be completely diverse, we turn next to how the courts determine citizenship of parties and thereby make a finding that the case before them is completely diverse. After addressing a few general points, in this subsection, we briefly address how citizenship is determined for competent adult persons, persons in unique representational roles, and business entities.

A few procedural rules apply both to human parties and business-entity parties when determining the citizenship status in a diversity case. First, absent complications involving removal jurisdiction, the courts determine whether the parties are completely diverse by focusing solely upon the citizenship of the parties at the time a suit is filed.[20] Second, assuming the appropriate legal standard is applied, the citizenship of parties presents a question of fact for the trial court judge to adjudicate on a Federal Rule of Civil Procedure

---

[20]   See, e.g., *Dole Food Co. v. Patrickson*, 538 U.S. 468, 478 (2003).

12(b)(1) motion.[21] As such, most determinations of citizenship are subject to the highly deferential clearly erroneous standard of review on appeal.[22] Third, the trial court may take into evidence any relevant material in relation to determining the citizenship of parties; or, if citizenship status is uncontested, rely upon allegations in the pleadings.

Turning now to the legal standard for determining citizenship of parties, we begin with the regime that governs adult competent humans. Unlike the citizenship of corporations and humans in special representative capacities that are controlled by § 1332(c), citizenship of competent adult humans is controlled entirely by judicial construction. In this regard, the Court has long equated state citizenship, as that term is used in § 1332(a), with American citizenship coupled with domicile in a particular state.[23] Domicile, in turn, is defined as physical presence in a state coupled with an intent to remain there indefinitely.[24] Even if a person appears to reside in multiple locations, human beings, unlike corporate entities, may have citizenship in only one state at any given time.[25] Finally, the federal courts

---

[21]   See, e.g., *Sligh v. Doe*, 596 F.2d 1169, 1171 (4th Cir. 1979).

[22]   See, e.g., *Sweet Pea Marine, Ltd. v. APJ Marine, Inc.*, 411 F.3d 1242, 1247 (11th Cir. 2005).

[23]   See *Gilbert v. David*, 235 U.S. 561, 569 (1915).

[24]   *Mississippi Band of Choctaw Indians v. Holyfield*, 490 U.S. 30, 48 (1989).

[25]   *Wachovia Bank v. Schmidt*, 546 U.S. 303, 318 (2006).

define foreign citizenship in relation to that foreign nation's law.[26]

The primary test for determining citizenship of American parties, then, is to identify the party's domicile. Courts give domicile a two-part construction that measures both external phenomena (physical presence) and a mental state (intent to remain indefinitely) of the party. Domicile, furthermore, is set in the most recent state in which the party was simultaneously present and had an intent to remain indefinitely.

Most of the time, when one is dealing with competent adults, the person's current place of abode is the most recent location where the party was both present and had an intent to remain indefinitely. For example, if Ms. Smith, a competent adult, resides and works in New York City and lacks plans to move, she is almost assuredly a citizen of New York for diversity jurisdiction purposes.

---

[26]   See, e.g., *Coury v. Prot*, 85 F.3d 244 (5th Cir. 1996).

Determining Domicile for Humans

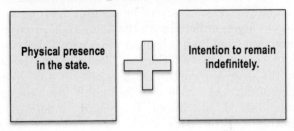

While most often the domicile question is an easy one for competent adults, the courts regularly face cases where a party's current abode is not coupled with the party's intention to remain indefinitely. Such is often the case, for instance, with members of the military, out-of-state university students, itinerant laborers, prisoners, government officials posted for only finite periods, and the like. For example, if a person from Utah moves to Massachusetts to attend a university and intends to go back home after graduation, the student's current abode in Massachusetts (where the student is currently physically present) is not coupled with an intent to remain there indefinitely. In such cases, the court determines domicile by continuing back in time until the court finds a state where the party was present and simultaneously had an intent to remain indefinitely. In our university-student example, most likely Utah would be the last place where she was both present and had an intention to remain indefinitely.

While cases involving out-of-state students tend to strike folks as intuitively correct, in other instances this analysis seems less so. For example, assume that Sargent Jones enlisted with the Army right after she graduated from high school 35 years ago. The Army, as is typical, moved Sargent Jones every 18–24 months over her career. As a result, in any given place of current abode over her adult life, Sargent Jones lacked an intent to remain indefinitely, knowing that the Army was likely to move her again in a few months. In examples such as this, the federal court may need to go all the way back to the party's childhood home to find domicile—even if it has been decades since the party resided there. Nevertheless, the childhood home in such an example would be the most recent place where the party was _both_ present and had a simultaneous intent to remain indefinitely.

In suits where human parties proceed not on their own behalf, but in a special representational capacity, the citizenship determination is controlled by § 1332(c)(2). Thus, when a party proceeds on behalf of a decedent, a minor, or an incompetent person, the party takes on the citizenship status of the decedent, minor, or incompetent person respectively. The citizenship status of the decedent, minor, or incompetent person remains subject to the two-part, American-citizenship-plus-state-of-domicile test, which in turn is defined by reference to physical presence coupled with intent to remain indefinitely. As such, if Mike, a citizen of Missouri, is the guardian of his incapacitated brother John, a citizen of Iowa, in any suit that Mike filed on John's behalf, Mike would take on John's Iowa citizenship status for diversity jurisdiction purposes.

Next, "in a class action . . . only the citizenship of the named representatives of the class is considered, without regard to whether the citizenship of other members of the class would destroy complete diversity."[27] The jurisdiction for the non-named class members will be assumed to fall under supplemental jurisdiction, 28 U.S.C. § 1367. Thus, in cases with nationwide plaintiff classes, class counsel can ensure (or defeat) diversity jurisdiction by naming appropriate parties as class representatives.

Subsection 1332(c)(1) governs the citizenship status for corporate entities. This subsection takes a two-prong approach: a general rule and a special rule for suits against insurers. As to the general rule, § 1332(c)(1) states that a corporation is a citizen of _both_ its state (or foreign nation) of incorporation and the state (or foreign nation) where it keeps its principal place of business. The rationale behind having two places of state citizenship for corporations is to (1) reflect the reality that many corporations are not incorporated in the same state as their principal place of business and (2) to reduce numbers of corporate defendants that would enter federal court in diversity if corporate citizenship were based entirely upon the state of incorporation.

State of incorporation refers to the state where the corporation filed its charter, by-laws and the like and thus created the corporate entity. Interpreting the

---

[27]   *Carden v. Arkoma Assocs.*, 494 U.S. 185, 199–200 (1990).

meaning of § 1332(c)(1)'s phrase "principal place of business" has not been as straightforward. Prior to 2010, the circuit courts were deeply split on the meaning of the phrase. Several circuits held that the corporate headquarters was the principal place of business, while others held that the location of the principal production or sales facilities constituted the principal place of business. The Supreme Court resolved this split in favor of the corporate headquarters serving as the principal place of business in *Hertz Corp. v. Friend*.[28] Corporations, then, are citizens of both their state of incorporation and their corporate headquarters for diversity purposes. For example, General Motors under this rule is a citizen of Delaware, because it is incorporated there, and a citizen of Michigan, because it is headquartered in Detroit. As a result, GM is not diverse vis-à-vis citizens of Delaware or Michigan.

Subsection 1332(c)(1) contains a special rule for insurers (both corporations and unincorporated insurers), which is designed to exclude most suits against an insurer from triggering diversity jurisdiction. This policy is premised on both docket control concerns in the federal courts and respect for the unique role that the states play in regulating insurers. Under this rule, if (a) an insurer is the defendant in a direct action, and (b) the insured is not also a party-defendant, then the corporation is a citizen of the state of its insured. A direct-action suit is one in which the plaintiff sues the insurer directly

---

[28]   559 U.S. 77 (2010).

for its own conduct, as opposed to suing only the insured with the hope of collecting from an insurer. The 1332(c)(1) rule, then, applies only in direct actions in which the insured is not a co-defendant, which pragmatically means only when the insured is suing his own insurer. Thus, in the case of an insurance corporation, it may be treated as a citizen of three states for diversity purposes: (1) its state of incorporation, (2) the state of its principal place of business, and (3) in direct actions in which the insured is not joined as a co-defendant, the insured's state of citizenship.

Lastly, it is important not to conflate 1332(c)'s rules for corporate citizenship with the rules for other non-corporate business entities. Thus, following the traditional understanding of a partnership, which views a partnership as a collection of human beings not as a separate entity, diversity is determined as if each partner was sued, or is suing, in his or her individual capacity. LLCs are similarly treated, with "every circuit that has addressed the question treat[ing] them like partnerships for the purposes of diversity jurisdiction."[29]

2.   AMOUNT IN CONTROVERSY

We turn next to § 1332(a)'s requirement that original jurisdiction in diversity jurisdiction cases may be found only when the matter in controversy exceeds $75,000. We begin this subsection with a few general remarks about the amount in controversy

---

[29]   *Johnson v. Columbia Properties Anchorage, LP*, 437 F.3d 894, 899 (9th Cir. 2006).

requirement. We turn next to a discussion of how amount in controversy is calculated in a simple one-plaintiff-brings-one-claim-against-one-defendant case. We turn next to the more difficult matter of determining amount in controversy when there are multiple parties or multiple claims. We end this section with an overview of injunction cases as these are especially difficult matters in which to determine amount in controversy.

To begin, one must remember that the amount in controversy requirement is not constitutionally mandated. Congress could entirely eliminate the requirement. Or Congress may, as it does from time to time, increase the amount in controversy requirement to a mandate that a greater sum be at issue. The purpose behind including an amount in controversy requirement is strictly one of docket control. Further, given that $75,000 is well above the median demand in either tort or contract cases, the requirement has the further effect of bringing only financially substantial cases into federal court.

Several procedural points universally apply when determining the amount in controversy. First, the party seeking federal jurisdiction has the burden to prove the amount in controversy.[30] Second, assuming the appropriate legal standard is applied, the amount in controversy presents a question of fact for the trial court judge[31] to adjudicate on a Federal Rule of Civil

---

[30]   *Buck v. Gallagher*, 307 U.S. 95, 102 (1939).

[31]   See, e.g., *Sligh v. Doe*, 596 F.2d 1169, 1171 (4th Cir. 1979).

Procedure 12(b)(1) motion.[32] As such, most determinations of the amount in controversy are subject to the highly deferential clearly erroneous standard of review on appeal.[33] If a plaintiff who originally filed in federal court wins his suit but, excluding off-sets and counterclaims, recovers less than $75,000, the court under § 1332(b) may assess the plaintiff with court fees. Finally, the statute requires that the amount in controversy *exceed* $75,000; thus, the plaintiff must be seeking at least $75,000.01 to gain statutory diversity jurisdiction.

a. Determining Amount in Simple Cases

We turn next to the process by which the amount in controversy is determined. To gain an understanding of how the district courts determine the amount in controversy, in this subsection we focus upon an easy case in which there is but one plaintiff who brings one claim against one defendant. Further, we can assume at this point that the parties are completely diverse.

In the vast majority of cases, amount in controversy is determined as a matter of pleading. To determine the amount at issue, then, the district court need only look to the face of the complaint at the outset of the suit. Absent two exceptions, the demand in the complaint controls the amount in controversy. As the Supreme Court put it, "[t]he rule governing dismissal for want of jurisdiction in cases brought in the federal court is that, unless the law

---

[32]   *Buck*, 307 U.S. at 102.

[33]   *Sligh*, 596 F.2d at 1171.

gives a different rule, the sum claimed by the plaintiff controls if the claim is apparently made in good faith."[34] Under this rule, then, a plaintiff's demand in the complaint for more than $75,000 is sufficient, unless (a) it is a legal certainty that the claim is really for less, or (b) the demand was not made in good faith.

Putting aside the two exceptions for a moment, we consider the basic rule that the demand in the complaint of more than $75,000 is enough to meet the amount in controversy requirement. A corollary to this rule is that if the plaintiff demands less than $75,000, even though he might have sought more, the amount in controversy requirement cannot be met. As such, a plaintiff, by demanding less than $75,000, can prevent the creation of diversity jurisdiction.

In looking to the face of the complaint, the district court should take the following into consideration in tabulating plaintiff's demand. The courts include all compensatory damages claimed in good faith (both economic and non-economic), punitive damages claimed in good faith, and non-discretionary attorney's fees if awarded by contract[35] or statute.[36] The district court should exclude court costs, and pre- or post-judgment interest from the demand for purposes of determining the amount in controversy.

---

[34]   *St. Paul Mercury Indemnity Co. v. Red Cab Co.*, 303 US 283, 288 (1938).

[35]   *Springstead v. Crawfordsville State Bank*, 34 S.Ct. 195 (1913).

[36]   *Missouri State Life Ins. Co. v. Jones*, 290 U.S. 199 (1933).

Next, the amount in controversy requirement must not be confused with an "expected recovery" requirement. Consider the following example. Plaintiff, a citizen of California, sues defendant, a citizen of Iowa, claiming that defendant breached her contract. Plaintiff seeks $100,000 in damages. Now let's also posit that the plaintiff has realistically a 0% chance of actually winning this suit because the statute of limitations has run. Despite the fact that the expected recovery in this case is $0, the amount in controversy remains $100,000 (as that is the amount alleged on the face of the complaint).

Many new students of jurisdiction find this distinction counter-intuitive. If we all know the plaintiff will recover $0, how then can the amount in controversy still be $100,000? For those who find this distinction troubling, try the following exercise: To determine the amount in controversy, assume that the plaintiff will win the suit, *even if this is counter to all the facts*. Now assume that the plaintiff will recover everything he requested. Is this amount over $75,000? If yes, then the amount in controversy requirement is met, even though we all know that, in fact, the plaintiff has no realistic chance of recovery. The fact that the plaintiff will almost assuredly lose his claim does not render the amount in controversy under $75,000.

We turn now to the two exceptions to the rule that amount in controversy is determined upon the face of the complaint. First, a demand for more than $75,000 may be found lacking if there is a legal certainty that the plaintiff cannot collect, even if she wins, more than $75,000. Statutory caps on recovery present ready examples. Assume that plaintiff brings suit alleging $50,000 in compensatory damages and $40,000 in punitive damages. Now ordinarily, the court should include both figures in determining the amount in controversy, which here would be $90,000. Let us now assume that the state has capped punitive damages in cases such as this one at $10,000. In such an instance, the amount in controversy would be only $50,000 and diversity jurisdiction would not lie. This example differs from the one above in which we assumed that plaintiff's suit would fall to a statute of limitations defense. Here, even assuming that plaintiff wins her case, it is a legal certainty, by operation of the state statutory cap, that she can only recover $10,000 in punitive damages plus $40,000 in compensatory damages.

The second exception covers those suits in which the demand amount is brought in bad faith. These cases are rare. What is required, usually, is a demand for recovery that, even though not barred as a legal certainty, is truly outrageous in light of the injuries alleged. For example, a plaintiff alleges false arrest at a department store that lasted for no more than 15 minutes. Plaintiff suffered no physical injuries, lost no wages, has no evidence of severe psychological trauma, yet seeks over $75,000 in damages. Only in the rare case such as this one, then, would the court seriously consider that the demand for recovery was not made in good faith.

b. Aggregating Claims

The general rule, that the good faith demands on the face of the complaint control the amount in controversy absent a legal certainty that they cannot be awarded, becomes more complicated once multiple claims or multiple parties come into the picture. In this subsection, we consider an overview of these issues, which are generally referred to as the aggregation of claims.

In the examples in Chapter 3.B.2.a above, we were contemplating the situation in which one plaintiff brought one claim against one defendant and that claim was valued at more than $75,000. Aggregation of claims becomes a concern when there are multiple claims, or counter-claims, and each individual claim is not more than $75,000, but cumulatively the claims exceed $75,000. The Court has fashioned a series of rules in this regard that sadly have little to tether each on to the other. So it would seem that one's best bet here is just to memorize the rules.

To begin, if there is one plaintiff and one defendant, Supreme Court doctrine allows for the combining of multiple claims, be they related or unrelated, by the plaintiff so as to exceed $75,000 cumulatively.[37] For example, plaintiff #1 can bring a contract claim for $35,000, a related tortious interference with contract claim for $20,000, and an unrelated trespass to property claim for $40,000

---

[37]   *Snyder v. Harris*, 394 U.S. 332, 335 (1969); *Bullard v. City of Cisco*, Tex., 290 U.S. 179, 189 (1933).

against defendant #1 and aggregate these sums so as to exceed the amount in controversy threshold.

Suit #24:
Claims by π 1
$35,000 tort claim against Δ 1
$20,000 contract claim against Δ 1
$40,000 property claim against Δ 1
$95,000

May be added to meet amount in controversy

If there is one plaintiff and one defendant, however, doctrine in most circuits does not allow for the combining of plaintiff's claims with defendant's counter-claims, even if they arise from the same transaction or occurrence. While the Supreme Court has not clearly addressed this question,[38] the majority approach embraces the above rule. For instance, plaintiff #1's $50,000 breach of contract claim may not be aggregated with defendant #1's $30,000 fraudulent inducement counter-claim to meet the amount in controversy requirement. Similarly, if plaintiff #1 brings an $80,000 contract claim, which will have jurisdiction assuming complete diversity, defendant #1 will lack § 1332 diversity jurisdiction for his $30,000 counterclaim. (Defendant will assuredly have supplemental

---

[38]   See *Horton v. Liberty Mut. Ins. Co.*, 367 U.S. 348 (1961).

jurisdiction for this counter-claim under 28 U.S.C. § 1367, however, which is addressed in Chapter 6.)

Suit #25:

$50,000 π 1's contract claim against Δ 1
$30,000 Δ1 's counter-claim against π 1
$80,000
     May **NOT** be added to meet amount
     in controversy

Cases with one plaintiff and multiple defendants present two rules based upon whether liability is sought severally or jointly. If plaintiff #1 brings two battery claims against defendant #1 for $40,000 and defendant #2 for $40,000, seeking several liability, the claims may not be aggregated so as to exceed the amount in controversy threshold.[39] On the other hand, if plaintiff #1 sues defendant #1 and defendant #2 jointly, such as in a respondent superior case, for $80,000 then the amount in controversy will be met.[40]

---

[39]   *Middle Tennessee News Co., Inc. v. Charnel of Cincinnati, Inc.*, 250 F.3d 1077, 1081 (7th Cir. 2001).

[40]   Id.

Suit #26: Seeking several liability

$40,000 π 1's battery claim against Δ 1
$40,000 π 1's battery claim against Δ 2
$80,000

> May **NOT** be added to meet amount in controversy

Suit #27: Seeking joint liability

$80,000 represents π 1's tort claim against
Δ 1 and Δ 2 jointly.

This meets amount in controversy.

Doctrine does not allow multiple plaintiffs to aggregate the value of their claims as against one defendant.[41] Thus, plaintiff #1, bringing a $40,000 breach of contract suit, and plaintiff #2, bringing an identical claim, cannot combine those figures against defendant #1 to satisfy the amount in controversy requirement. But if plaintiff #1, brought a $76,000 breach of contract suit, and plaintiff #2 brought an identical claim against defendant #1, each claim

---

[41]   *Snyder v. Harris*, 394 U.S. 332, 335 (1969).

would independently satisfy the amount in controversy requirement and, assuming diversity of citizenship, the suit would arise in diversity jurisdiction.

Suit #28:

$40,000 π 1's contract claim against Δ 1
$40,000 π 2's contract claim against Δ 1
$80,000
        May **NOT** be added to meet amount
        in controversy

This rule is subject to one exception: In cases in which two or more plaintiffs unite to enforce a single title or right in which they have a common and undivided interest, the value of the claims may be viewed cumulatively. These examples occur, for example, when property is held as tenants by the entirety. As such, a married couple, holding a putative title to Blackacre as tenants in the entirety valued at $80,000, may bring a quiet-title claim in diversity jurisdiction against defendant #1. This follows because tenants by the entirety each hold a common and undivided interest in Blackacre as a matter of property law.

Finally, class actions are subject to a different treatment. So long as one named member of the plaintiff class meets the amount in controversy requirement, all other members of the class may enter federal court pursuant to supplemental jurisdiction (a matter we turn to in Chapter 6).[42]

c. Valuing Injunctions

As our final discussion of amount in controversy, we turn to the tricky matter of placing a value on an injunction. It is well established that injunctions, just as with any other matter to arise under diversity jurisdiction, must meet the $75,000 amount in controversy requirement.[43] "Whether [the] courts, in determining the amount in controversy, are to measure the value of the . . . [injunction] solely from the plaintiff's perspective or whether they may also consider . . . the defendant's perspective is considerably less well-established."[44]

This point of view matters because, often, the value of an injunction can vary greatly depending upon whose perspective is taken. For example, assume a plaintiff brings an environmental-nuisance injunction against a defendant that owns a power plant. The plaintiff, assume, values the suit at $60,000 based on the diminished value of his real property resulting from the operation of the power plant. Defendant, however, may well value the injunction in the millions of dollars based upon either the cost of lost production from the enforcement of

---

[42]   *Exxon Mobile Corp. v. Allapattah Serv. Inc.*, 545 U.S. 546, 558–59 (2005).

[43]   *Hunt v. Wash. State Apple Adver. Comm'n,* 432 U.S. 333, 347 (1977).

[44]   *Ericsson GE Mobile Commc'ns, Inc. v. Motorola Commc'ns & Elec., Inc.*, 120 F.3d 216, 218 (11th Cir. 1997).

the injunction or the cost of installing remediation devices. Such a scenario of widely varying valuations is quite common.

Given the lack of clear Supreme Court guidance here, the circuits have devised several competing approaches to the valuation of injunctions. Several courts look strictly to the value of the injunction to the plaintiff in determining whether the case meets the amount in controversy requirement.[45] Other courts will find jurisdiction if the value of the injunction meets the amount in controversy threshold considered for either the plaintiff's or defendant's point of view.[46] Still other courts take the point of view of the party seeking federal jurisdiction as the appropriate perspective.[47]

3.   LIMITATIONS ON DIVERSITY

As we have seen, pursuant to § 1332, cases may take diversity jurisdiction if the parties are completely diverse and the amount in controversy exceeds $75,000. In this last section, we explore three limitations on the scope of this jurisdictional grant: first, 28 U.S.C. § 1359's bar on collusive joinder; second, the case-law-driven ban on family-law matters arising in diversity jurisdiction; and third, a

---

[45]   See, e.g., *Ericsson GE Mobile Commc'ns, Inc. v. Motorola Commc'ns & Elec., Inc.*, 120 F.3d 216, 219 (11th Cir. 1997).

[46]   See, e.g., In re Ford Motor Co./Citibank, 264 F.3d 952, 958 (9th Cir. 2001).

[47]   See, e.g., *Hatridge v. Aetna Cas. & Sur. Co.*, 415 F.2d 809, 814 (8th Cir. 1969).

similar judicially crafted prohibition on hearing probate issues in diversity.

a. Diversity by Collusion

Congress, by statute, prohibits jurisdiction over "a civil action in which any party, by assignment or otherwise, has been improperly or collusively made or joined to invoke the jurisdiction of such court."[48] This provision has special relevance for diversity suits, because parties could otherwise be tempted to manufacture complete diversity among themselves by assignment of claims to completely diverse third parties.

The Supreme Court heard just such a case in *Kramer v. Caribbean Mills*.[49] In *Kramer*, a Panamanian corporation and a Haitian corporation were in a dispute over the sale of the former's stock. This dispute between two alien corporations could not arise in diversity jurisdiction (see Chapter 3.A.2). To create a pathway into federal court, the Panamanian corporation, for $1 in consideration, assigned its entire interest in the stock sale by contract to Mr. Kramer, a Texas attorney. By a separate side agreement dated the same day, Kramer promised to pay 95% of any net recovery on the assigned cause of action back to the Panamanian corporation. With the suit now styled as Kramer, a Texan, suing the Haitian corporation, § 1332 jurisdiction prima facie arose. Nevertheless, the Supreme Court easily affirmed the jurisdictional

---

[48]   28 U.S.C. § 1359.

[49]   394 U.S. 823 (1969).

dismissal of the suit, finding that diversity of the parties was "improperly or collusively made" in violation of § 1359. The Court went on to hold that "[s]uch 'manufacture of Federal jurisdiction' was the very thing which Congress intended to prevent when it enacted s 1359."[50] But for § 1359, the Court went on to note, "a vast quantity of ordinary contract and tort litigation could be channeled into the federal courts at the will of one of the parties."[51] Federal Rules of Civil Procedure 19 (requiring the joinder of certain parties) and 17 (requiring that suits be brought by the real party in interest) also serve to limit the improper manufacture of diverse parties.

This is not to say that every circumstance in which a party takes advantage of changes in residency to vest diversity jurisdiction where it was previously lacking runs afoul of § 1359. In the following case, for instance, the plaintiff alleged that the defendant tortuously injured him in 1995.[52] In 1997, when both parties were citizens of Kansas, the plaintiff filed a tort claim in the state courts. In 2000, after plaintiff had permanently relocated to Oklahoma, plaintiff voluntarily dismissed the state-court action and re-filed the suit in federal court, asserting diversity jurisdiction. Because there was no evidence that the plaintiff moved to Oklahoma solely for the purpose of manufacturing diversity jurisdiction, the district court rejected a motion to dismiss. The district court

---

[50]   *Kramer*, 394 U.S. at 829.

[51]   Id. at 828–29.

[52]   *Smith v. Kennedy*, 2000 WL 575024 (D. Kan. 2000) (unpublished opinion).

found that, in what is a nice summary of many of the points we made in Chapter 1 about the strategic use of jurisdiction, "[l]itigants constantly attempt to gain . . . tactical advantages [by way of jurisdictional arguments]. . . . Defendant cites no authority for the proposition that subject matter jurisdiction is defeated if it somehow affords one party a tactical advantage. Indeed, defendant's argument that plaintiff is attempting to gain a 'tactical advantage' rings entirely hollow because defendant's argument for lack of jurisdiction appears to be nothing more than an attempt to gain his own tactical advantage— a return to state court."[53] Thus, the enlisting of completely diverse parties for the sole purpose of manufacturing diversity jurisdiction is prohibited by § 1359. Tactical use of changes in circumstances that allow for a party to invoke diversity jurisdiction is just good lawyering.

What Factors Tip this Balance?

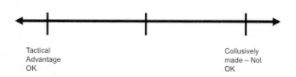

---

[53]   Id. at *2.

b. Family Law and Diversity

In addition to collusive joinder, the Supreme Court has consistently held that § 1332 does not embrace certain domestic relations matters.[54] The Court grounds this interpretation of the § 1332 on the view that the first Congress, which first passed diversity jurisdiction, intended federal equity jurisdiction to include only those matters then heard in English chancery courts, which at the time did not hear matters of divorce, alimony or child custody.[55] While not entirely discounting the Court's stated position, many commentators have argued that the domestic relations exception reflects inherent gender bias by the courts. Still others note that the exception is better grounded upon docket-control and lack-of-expertise concerns than upon the niceties of old equity practice. This controversy over the foundation of for the exception aside, the rule remains doctrinally sound.

---

[54] See *Barber v. Barber*, 62 U.S. 582, 584 (1858) (giving rise to the exception); see also *Ankenbrandt v. Richards*, 504 U.S. 689, 695 (1992) (holding that the exception is not constitutionally required).

[55] *Ankenbrant*, 504 U.S. at 699–700.

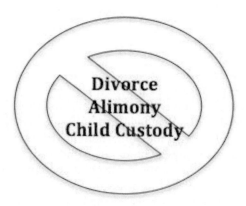

In recent years the Supreme Court has strictly limited the scope of the domestic relations exception, however, despite a general push from the lower courts to expand the breadth of the exception. In *Ankenbrandt v. Richards*, the Court ruled that the "the domestic relations exception [i]s narrowly confined to suits for divorce, alimony, or child custody decrees."[56] As such, a suit between two parents alleging that torts had been committed by the defendant father against the couple's child could be heard in diversity jurisdiction, assuming the traditional requirements of complete diversity and amount in controversy were met.

c. Probate Matters and Diversity

Mapping onto a similar template to questions of family law, the Supreme Court has long barred certain probate matters from entering federal court

---

[56]   Id. at 703.

in statutory diversity jurisdiction. In the 1940s, the Court offered a similar historical reasoning for the ban, holding that "a federal court has no jurisdiction to probate a will or administer an estate, the reason being that the equity jurisdiction conferred by the Judiciary Act of 1789 . . . , which is that of the English Court of Chancery in 1789, did not extend to probate matters."[57] The doctrine remains sound, though cabined, today.

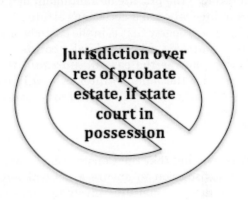

Jurisdiction over res of probate estate, if state court in possession

In 2006, the Court revisited the probate exception in *Marshall v. Marshall*.[58] There the Court noted that probate proceedings, from a personal jurisdiction perspective, treat the estate at issue as a res and thus take in rem personal jurisdiction over the estate. From this starting point, the Supreme Court held that the probate exception is but an instantiation of

---

[57] *Markham v. Allen*, 326 U.S. 490, 494 (1946).

[58] 547 U.S. 293 (2006). Marshall arose under bankruptcy jurisdiction, but the principles apply equally to diversity suits.

the "general principle that, when one court is exercising in rem jurisdiction over a res, a second court will not assume in rem jurisdiction over the same res."[59] As such, the Court held that the probate exception must be given a narrow construction. Only those matters that would attempt to take in rem personal jurisdiction of the res of the estate already under the power of a state court are to be barred by the exception. "Thus, the probate exception . . . [prohibits only] the probate or annulment of a will . . . , the administration of a decedent's estate . . . , [and] dispos[ing] of property that is in the custody of a state probate court."[60] The federal courts retain jurisdiction, as was the case in *Marshall*, to bring claims against the administrator of a will, even if those claims ultimately will be lead to recovery from estate assets.

* * *

In sum, we find that the Constitution provides for diversity jurisdiction to ensure a neutral forum to resolve state-law matters involving out-of-state litigants. Taking diversity jurisdiction requires the satisfaction of both the Article III and 28 U.S.C. § 1332 standards. Article III diversity jurisdiction is given a broad interpretation. The parties need only be minimally diverse (i.e., the case has at least one plaintiff with citizenship status that differs with that of at least one defendant) with at least one party being a state citizen.

---

[59]   Id. at 311.

[60]   Id. at 311–12.

Diversity Jurisdiction

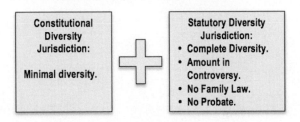

The primary diversity jurisdiction statute, § 1332, is given a narrower construction. First, the parties to the suit must be completely diverse (i.e., no plaintiff may share a citizenship status with any defendant). Section 1332(a) further delimits completely diverse parties into four statutorily acceptable classifications. Second, the courts determine state citizenship status for most American citizen adults pursuant to the simultaneous-presence-plus-indefinite-intent-to-remain test. Corporate citizenship is controlled by § 1332(c), which sets corporate citizenship at both the state of incorporation and principal place of business. Third, § 1332 requires that suits exceed $75,000 in controversy in order to enter federal court in diversity. And fourth, statutory diversity is further limited by the anti-collusion rules of 28 U.S.C. § 1359, the domestic-relations exception, and the probate exception.

CHAPTER 4

ERIE DOCTRINE

"Under the *Erie* doctrine, federal courts sitting in diversity apply state substantive law and federal procedural law."

—*Gasperini v. Center for Humanities, Inc.*, 518 U.S. 415, 427 (1996)

"The . . . twin aims of the *Erie* rule [are] discouragement of forum-shopping and avoidance of inequitable administration of the laws."

—*Hanna v. Plumer*, 380 U.S. 460, 468 (1965)

As we learned in the previous chapter, the federal courts may hear non-federal matters, if they arise within diversity jurisdiction. This begs the question: What law applies in diversity cases? Since 1938, the short answer has been that state law—be it constitutional, statutory, regulatory, or common law—controls substantive issues, while federal law governs procedural matters. This rule, known as the *Erie* Doctrine, now forms a cornerstone of American procedural law.

The Supreme Court handed down this rule in *Erie R. Co. v. Tompkins*[1] and it is deceptively simple when presented in this one-liner form. Yet *Erie*'s subtleties have bedeviled generations of law students. This chapter aims to demystify the doctrine in a six-part discussion. We begin with an introduction to *Erie*

---

[1]   304 U.S. 64 (1938).

doctrine as a species of choice of law. Second, we move to a discussion of the choice-of-law practice before *Erie*. We follow this inquiry with an analysis of the *Erie* case itself. Fourth, we turn to an overview of how the content of state law is determined under *Erie*. Fifth, we consider a three-step approach to understanding the *Erie* doctrine. And we end with some applications of this three-step approach.

A. *ERIE* AS CHOICE OF LAW

Erie problems, as we call them, are not unique. In fact, they are but a subset of a broader category of issues called choice-of-law, or synonymously labeled conflict-of-law, problems. A court faces a choice-of-law problem any time the transaction or occurrence giving rise to the lawsuit arose out of a sovereignty that is different from the court which is hearing the case. For example, assume a plaintiff, a Wyoming resident, sues a defendant, a Colorado resident, in a Colorado state court regarding an automobile accident that occurred in Wyoming. The Colorado court would face a choice-of-law problem. Should it apply Wyoming law, because it was the sovereignty where the accident occurred, or should it apply Colorado law, as it is the sovereignty that created the court? If there were differences in the laws of these states—say plaintiffs recover $100,000 under Wyoming law and $50,000 under Colorado law—the parties would vigorously argue to the court for the application of one body of law over the other. In rendering its decision, the court would look to the state's choice-of-law rules, which direct which state's law should govern. Situations such as this are run-of-the-mill matters for American courts. They are called "horizontal choice-of-law" problems because the court faces a choice among sovereignties of equal stature within our legal system (i.e., it is a choice between competing state laws).

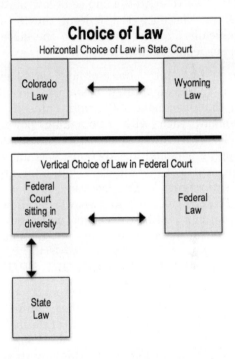

If the case above had been filed in a federal court in Colorado, as opposed to a state court, the federal court would also face a choice-of-law question because the transaction or occurrence (in our case, the car accident) giving rise to the lawsuit arose from a sovereignty different from the court's (i.e., it did not arise out of federal law). Thus the federal court faces a problem akin to the state court's: Should it apply its home sovereignty law (i.e., federal law) or should it engage in a "vertical choice of law" and apply state law? Here we refer to the choice-of-law matter as a vertical one because the federal courts sit in a hierarchically superior position to the state courts within our legal scheme.

These frequent choice-of-law problems are inherent in our federated system of government. Given that we have 50 states plus a federal government, each with rulemaking powers that interact with numerous court systems with overlapping personal jurisdictions, it is unavoidable that the courts of sovereignty X will often apply the law of sovereignty Y. *Erie* Doctrine, then, is nothing more than a method for answering how these mundane choice-of-law decisions will occur in the federal courts sitting in diversity jurisdiction.

B.   THE REGIME BEFORE *ERIE*

This choice-of-law problem inherent in our system of government was evident from the beginning. Thus, the first Congress passed the Rules of Decision Act as a provision of the Judiciary Act of 1789. This act remains largely unchanged to this day. It provides that

> The laws of the several states, except where the constitution, treaties or statutes of the United States shall otherwise require or provide, shall be regarded as rules of decisions in civil actions

in the courts of the United States in cases where they apply.[2]

The Rules of Decision Act, to a modern reader, speaks straightforwardly. If there is not a federal provision on point, apply state law regardless of whether the state law at hand derives from state constitution, state statute, or state common law.

But this straightforward, contemporary reading of the statute did not always carry the day. In 1842, the Supreme Court, in line with jurisprudential concepts reigning at the time, issued *Swift v. Tyson*.[3] Here, the Court held that the Rules of Decision Act required federal courts in diversity jurisdiction (i.e., cases where a federal rule of decision did not apply) to apply state constitutional and statutory law, but the federal courts were not bound by common law decisions of the state's highest court. Justice Story explained the Court's reasoning. "The laws of a state are more usually understood to mean the rules and enactments promulgated by the legislative authority thereof, or long-established local customs having the force of laws. . . . In the ordinary use of language it will hardly be contended that the decisions of courts constitute laws."[4]

Justice Story's position, which rings foreign to the contemporary lawyer's ear, was near universally accepted in the early nineteenth century. *Swift* expresses a form of natural-law theory, the view that

---

[2]   28 U.S.C. § 1652.

[3]   41 U.S. 1 (1842).

[4]   Id. at 18.

law is necessarily co-extensive with a moral code that exists, and is cognizable, independent from the rulings of courts. During this era, American courts regularly viewed the common law as a type of natural law. Judges at this time spoke of finding or discovering the common law, meaning that the judges did not believe they were crafting rules themselves but merely uncovering some preexisting universal norms. This view is not so much in vogue now among American lawyers. Indeed, in the early twentieth century Justice Holmes famously quipped that that "common law is not a brooding omnipresence in the sky."[5] But *Swift*'s natural-law conception reigned in 1842, and a full understanding of *Swift* (and thus *Erie,* which overrules it) requires some sympathetic engagement with this concept of common law as a natural-law entity.

Given this notion of the common law—that it is discovered by courts, not made by them—the *Swift* decision has a logic of its own. Under this view, the Rules of Decision Act does not speak to common law judicial decisions because the common law is not properly speaking the law of a state; rather, it is a universal code existing independently from the pronouncements of any given court. Moreover, given that the common law under this view is discovered by judges, not created by them, there is no reason to prefer the common law discoveries of state judges over federal judges. To the contrary, federal judges, being elevated to the federal bench from among the

---

[5]   *S. Pac. Co. v. Jensen*, 244 U.S. 205, 222 (1917) (Holmes, J., dissenting).

bar's best, may well be better discoverers of the common law than their state court colleagues—or at least this was the implicit assumption in *Swift*.

The *Swift* Court, then, held that the Rule of Decisions Act did not apply to common law, judicial pronouncements. As a result, in diversity cases, the federal courts over time discovered (or created, if you prefer) a body of common law that tended to differ from the law of the various states. Under this regime, a suit for breach of contract in the North Carolina state courts may well have been governed by rule X in regard to damages, while that very same contract case if filed in federal court under diversity jurisdiction would be subject to a very different rule Y in regard to damages. Lawyers, then, could predict whether a case would be successful or not simply by noting whether it was filed in state court or a federal court sitting in diversity. As a result, jurisdictional disputes as between a state court or a federal court sitting in diversity took on great importance, as the choice of forum (i.e., the choice of proceeding in state or federal court) also directed the choice of law.

Before *Erie*, then, choice of law in federal court proceeded as follows. A federal court would choose federal law to govern matters arising in § 1331 jurisdiction. It would follow state law as to matters of state constitutions and statutes while sitting in diversity. And, again while sitting in diversity, it would look to "general principles of law" in common law disputes, which over time became a de facto federal body of common law. Lastly, this regime for choice of substantive law was coupled with the

Conformity Act of 1872, which directed district courts to deploy the evidentiary and procedural rules of the state courts of the state in which the federal court sat.

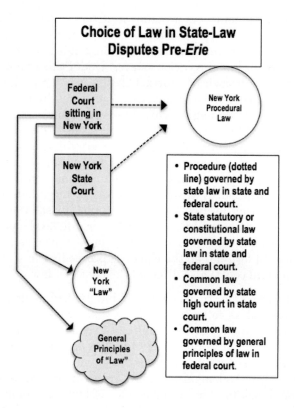

Choice of Law in State-Law Disputes Pre-*Erie*

Federal Court sitting in New York

New York Procedural Law

New York State Court

New York "Law"

General Principles of "Law"

- Procedure (dotted line) governed by state law in state and federal court.
- State statutory or constitutional law governed by state law in state and federal court.
- Common law governed by state high court in state court.
- Common law governed by general principles of law in federal court.

C. THE *ERIE* DECISION

In 1938, the federal courts experienced a sea-change in choice-of-law rules. First, 1938 was the year that the newly drafted Federal Rules of Civil Procedure came into effect. Under authority granted in the Rules Enabling Act of 1934, now codified at 28 U.S.C. § 2072, the Supreme Court drafted a set of procedural rules to be uniformly applied in all the federal district courts. These new uniform rules replaced the practice under the Conformity Act, in which each district court adopted state procedure for use in the federal court. As a result, by 1938 procedural law in federal courts switched from being controlled district-by-district under varying state law to governance under one uniform system of federal procedural law.

More to our point, the Supreme Court decided *Erie Railroad Co. v. Tompkins*[6] in 1938 as well, which changed the rules for choice of substantive law for federal courts sitting in diversity. The facts of the case are simple. The plaintiff, Mr. Tompkins, was hit by defendant Erie Railroad Company's freight train in Pennsylvania while walking near the tracks along a footpath. The parties were completely diverse, the plaintiff residing in Pennsylvania and the defendant incorporated in New York. Plaintiff exercised his right to file his state-law tort suit in diversity jurisdiction in federal district court in New York.

The parties' legal theories placed the consequences of the old *Swift* regime in sharp relief. Relying upon

---

[6]   304 U.S. 64 (1938).

Swift, the plaintiff asserted that under the general principles of the common law (i.e., federal common law) he was lawfully on the property as a licensee, and that he should recover damages because the accident resulted from the defendant's negligence. The defendant countered that Pennsylvania common law should apply. Under Pennsylvania common law, the plaintiff would be deemed a trespasser. As such, the defendant would only be liable for wanton or willful acts, not mere negligence. The district court applied *Swift* and eventually entered judgment for the plaintiff. The court of appeals affirmed.

On certiorari to the Supreme Court, the "question for decision [wa]s whether the oft-challenged doctrine of *Swift v. Tyson* shall now be disapproved."[7] The Court did just that. In so doing, it offered multiple reasons for overruling *Swift*. First, the Court held that *Swift* erred as a matter of historical legislative intent by exempting state common law rulings from the binding force of the Rules of Decision Act.[8] That is to say, the Court found that the 1789 Congress intended for state common law decisions to control in diversity suits.

Second, the Court held that that the *Swift* regime led to poor policy. Most importantly, it produced unequal application of the law, because under the *Swift* regime like cases are subject to differing substantive rules due to the happenstance of

---

[7]   Id. at 69.

[8]   Id. at 71–74.

diversity jurisdiction.[9] This unequal application of law, in turn, led parties to "forum shop" between the state and federal courts in hopes of finding the best substantive law for its side. This was the antithesis of equal application of law, in the Court's view.

Third, the Court held the *Swift* doctrine unconstitutional. Relying upon the principle that the federal government is one of limited and enumerated powers, the Court ruled that "Congress has no power to declare substantive rules of common law applicable in a state. . . . And no clause in the Constitution purports to confer such a power upon the federal courts."[10] Therefore, the Court declared that "[t]here is no federal general common law."[11] Under *Erie,* the law of a state, as referenced in the Rules of Decision Act means common law judicial decisions just as much as legislative or constitutional enactments.

The Court predicates its finding of practice under *Swift* unconstitutional upon a jurisprudential shift away from natural-law theory. *Swift*, as noted above,

---

[9]   Id. at 74–78.

[10]   Id. at 78.

[11]   Id. Many are tempted to over read this portion of *Erie* to believe that the federal courts are prohibited from creating any federal common law whatsoever. This is an erroneous conclusion. Federal common law remains alive and well after *Erie*, but only as to issues that are constitutionally within the federal government's powers and Congress has functionally delegated legislative authority to the federal courts. Some common areas of federal common law that remain viable after *Erie* include: admiralty, federal common law of foreign relations, federal common law over suits with the United States as a party, and international common law.

"rests upon the assumption that there is a transcendental body of law outside of any particular State."[12] The *Erie* Court rejects this older view of the common law. Quoting Justice Holmes, the *Erie* Court held that "law in the sense in which courts speak of it today does not exist without some definite authority behind it. The common law so far as it is enforced in a State . . . is not the common law generally but the law of that State existing by the authority of that State."[13] Thus, practice under *Swift*, because it is now seen as creating law, not discovering law, effectuated an unconstitutional transfer of legislative power from the states to the federal judiciary. Thus, the *Erie* decision not only wiped out almost a century of federal common law practice, but also completely altered the philosophical underpinnings of the legal system. Justice Frankfurter emphasized the significance of this aspect of the decision, stating that *Erie* "overruled a particular way of looking at law which [had] dominated the judicial process long after its inadequacies had been laid bare."[14]

In *Erie*, then, the Court held that in diversity cases federal courts are to apply state law to all substantive issues, which includes common law decisions issued by the state's highest court. Procedural matters, given the passage of the Rules Enabling Act of 1934, are to be governed by federal law, even when sitting in diversity. The Court summed up the general rule

---

[12] Id. at 79 (internal quotations and citations omitted).

[13] Id. (internal quotations and citations omitted).

[14] *Guaranty Trust Co. v. York*, 326 U.S. 99, 101 (1945).

well some 60 years later. "Under the *Erie* doctrine, federal courts sitting in diversity apply state substantive law and federal procedural law."[15]

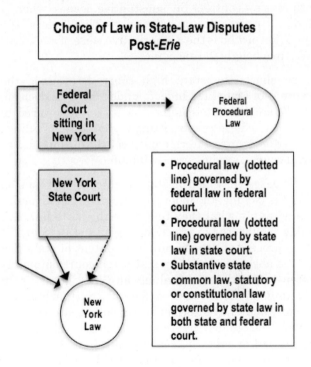

Choice of Law in State-Law Disputes Post-*Erie*

Federal Court sitting in New York → Federal Procedural Law

New York State Court

New York Law

- Procedural law (dotted line) governed by federal law in federal court.
- Procedural law (dotted line) governed by state law in state court.
- Substantive state common law, statutory or constitutional law governed by state law in both state and federal court.

---

[15]   *Gasperini v. Center for Humanities, Inc.*, 518 U.S. 415, 427 (1996).

D.   DETERMINING THE CONTENT OF STATE LAW

Erie holds that state law—be it common law or otherwise—controls on substantive issues when a federal court sits in diversity. This raises the question of who is the authoritative voice of state law. We turn briefly to this point.

In short, the state high court determines the content of state law. Indeed, under the *Erie* decision itself, only a state's highest court is empowered to bind the federal courts sitting in diversity.[16] Rulings from the state's intermediate courts of appeals, or trial courts, are not strictly binding.[17]

In cases in which a state high-court opinion on point is lacking, the federal courts sitting in diversity "must apply what they find to be the state law. . . . [as if they were,] in effect, sitting as a state court."[18] This process of determining the content of state law in the absence of binding state high-court opinion is often referred to as making an "*Erie* guess."[19] In making an *Erie* guess, a federal court, while not strictly bound by intermediate appellate state courts, should be guided by their decisions "unless it is convinced by other persuasive data that the highest court of the state would decide otherwise."[20]

---

[16]   304 U.S. at 80.

[17]   *C.I.R. v. Bosch's Estate*, 387 U.S. 456, 465 (1967).

[18]   Id.

[19]   See, e.g., *Six Flags, Inc. v. Westchester Surplus Lines Ins. Co.*, 565 F.3d 948, 954 (5th Cir. 2009).

[20]   *Bosch's Estate*, 387 U.S. at 465.

Similarly, in cases where a federal court sitting in diversity must construe a state statute or regulation without the aid of any state court decisions, the federal court must do so in light of state court rules of construction as announced by the state high court.

In addition to the *Erie* guess, federal courts in some instances may be able to certify a question directly to the state high court. Under this procedure, the federal court stays its proceedings and formally asks the state high court to answer the open question of state law. After the state high court has given an answer, then the case returns to federal court to proceed. This procedure requires that the state allow its high court to answer such questions—not all of them do. Furthermore, the certification process is often very slow and may render only vague responses that aid the federal court little. As a result, the U.S. Supreme Court holds that the decision to certify a question is within the "sound discretion of the federal court,"[21] which is appropriate only when it will "conserve the time, energy, and resources of the parties as well as of the court itself."[22]

E.   SUBSTANCE v. PROCEDURE

Having determined, then, what the content of state law is, *Erie* doctrine mandates that only substantive state law binds the federal court in diversity, while procedural law, following the Rules Enabling Act, is governed by federal law. By the term substantive

---

[21]   *Lehman Bros. v. Schein*, 416 U.S. 386, 390–91 (1974).

[22]   *Boyd Rosene & Assoc., Inc. v. Kan. Mun. Gas Agency*, 178 F.3d 1363, 1365 (10th Cir.1999).

law, *Erie* doctrine envisions issues such as the elements of state-law negligence or the availability of a state-law affirmative defense. By procedural law, *Erie* doctrine envisions matters such as the number of depositions a party may call or the means by which a party amends a pleading. In these paradigmatic examples, the distinction between substantive law and procedural law comes readily.

The Supreme Court, however, quickly realized that once it moved beyond such archetypal examples, the substance-procedure distinction was not so obviously made. We turn, then, in this section to the Court's various attempts to separate what state law should be deemed substantive, hence binding on federal courts in diversity, and what should be deemed procedural, and thus not binding upon federal courts sitting in diversity.

But seven years after issuing *Erie*, the Court concluded that "[m]atters of 'substance' and matters of 'procedure' . . . are much talked about in the books as though they defined a great divide cutting across the whole domain of law. But, of course,. . . . [e]ach implies different variables depending upon the particular problem for which it is used."[23] This is to say, the Court concluded that it matters little whether a rule is formally categorized as substantive or procedural because in any given setting a rule that is normally procedural, say, could serve functionally as a substantive one and vice versa. As such, the Court would need to devise a new methodology

---

[23]   *Guaranty Trust*, 326 U.S. at 108.

beyond the substantive or procedural label to sort out what state law binds federal courts in diversity cases. While the Court has issued numerous decisions on this question, our overview will look to three landmark decisions.

First, in *Guaranty Trust v. York*, the Court faced the question of whether a statute of limitation should be conceived of as substantive or procedural for *Erie* purposes. Mere reference to intuitive notions of what these terms mean would not resolve that matter, given that a statute of limitations can easily be conceived of as either a procedural or substantive rule. As a result, the Court crafted a new gloss on the distinction. The Court ruled that the intent of *Erie* doctrine is "to [e]nsure that, in all [diversity] cases . . . the outcome of the litigation in the federal court should be substantially the same . . . as it would be if tried in a State court."[24] Under the *Guaranty Trust* approach, then, a state law is deemed substantive, if failure to apply the state rule would substantially affect the outcome of the litigation. Conversely, a state law is deemed procedural if it concerns merely the form or mode by which a right is enforced without necessarily affecting the outcome of the suit. The *Guaranty Trust* Court was careful, however, to note that even as to rules of mere form and mode, *Erie* doctrine may require application of the state law when use of the rule bears substantially on the outcome. Under this test, the Court determined that a statute of limitation, because it has the power to completely bar recovery, is an outcome-

---

[24]   Id. at 109.

determinative rule and thus substantive (and as such binding) law for *Erie* purposes. The Court continues to deploy this outcome-determinative test.

Proper application of the test, however, requires one to determine outcome-determinativeness from the appropriate point of view, namely from the vantage point of one choosing to file a case as opposed to the perspective of one filing a motion in the midst of on-going litigation.[25] This aligns with the notion that one of the primary aims of *Erie* doctrine is to prevent forum shopping. Hence, in a tort case in which the plaintiff is partially at fault and state law would apply the old contributory negligence rule (meaning that the plaintiff would be entirely barred from recovery), the contributory negligence rule should be deemed substantive because, from the point of view of one choosing where to file the case, it is clear that application of the contributory negligence rule would determine the outcome. Conversely, assume that the federal courts allow dismissal with prejudice as a discovery-misconduct sanction, while the state courts do not. The application of this sanction most certainly will determine the outcome of the case. But from the point of view of one choosing which court to file in, the discovery sanction is not outcome determinative because discovery-misconduct sanctions would not be relevant yet; as from this hypothetical point of view, there would be no sanctions with which to contend.

---

[25] See generally *Hanna v. Plumber* 380 U.S. 460, 68–69 (1965).

In a similar vein, the outcome-determinative test stresses the determinative component. For a state-law rule to be deemed substantive, the application must be highly likely to change the result, again as seen from the point of view of one choosing where to file. Thus rules that may in some instances affect outcomes will not be deemed substantive under this approach. Hence, state-law rules on jury selection, admission of evidence, numbers of preemptory challenges, and the like—while often very important to the result of any individual case—will be deemed merely procedural under this view.

The Court revisited this substance-procedure dichotomy in our second landmark case, *Byrd v. Blue Ridge Rural Elec. Co-op., Inc.*[26] Here Mr. Byrd, who was injured while constructing overhead electrical lines, sued for damages in tort. The claim was filed in the federal district court sitting in diversity. Under South Carolina law, if the plaintiff was an employee of the defendant, his only remedy would lie under the state's workers' compensation statute, meaning his tort claim would be dismissed. But if he was an independent contractor, he would be free to bring the tort case. All agreed that these immunity rules were substantive under the outcome-determinative test and binding upon the federal court. The difficult *Erie* question arose as to who would decide whether Mr. Byrd was an employee or an independent contractor. Under South Carolina law, this factual question would be decided by the trial judge. Federal custom—influenced by, but not commanded by, the Seventh

---

[26]   356 U.S. 525 (1958).

Amendment—dictated that this factual question be decided by the jury.

The Supreme Court first determined that under *Erie*, federal courts must apply state law that is "bound up with the definition of the rights and obligations of the parties."[27] Put differently, the *Byrd* Court held that the legal elements of rights, immunities and obligations are necessarily substantive under *Erie*. Under the facts of *Byrd*, the Court ruled that the choice between a judge or jury finder of fact did not affect the very legal definition of the defendant's immunity rights. Nevertheless, the *Byrd* Court, following *Guaranty Trust*, considered that even if the choice between factfinders was merely a "form or mode of enforcing" defendant's immunity rights, it could well be outcome determinative if there is a "certainty that a different result would follow . . . or a strong possibility" that application of the rule would change the outcome.[28] Thus the Court concluded that this choice of a nominally procedural rule could be binding under *Erie*. Thus far, the case seems a rather standard application of *Guaranty Trust*.

But the Court did not end its analysis here. Even assuming that the choice between a judge or a jury as factfinder is outcome determinative, the *Byrd* Court held that the strong federal interest in maintaining the custom—again the Court was careful to note that it did not predicate its decision upon a constitutional

---

27   Id. at 535.

28   Id. at 536.

command—of sending such questions to the jury
trumped state practice. The Court reasoned that
because the state rule was not necessarily bound up
with the definition of the state-law rights at issue,
the federal interest in maintaining an independent
civil justice system with its own customs and mores,
at least in this instance, outweighed the state-law
form of fact finding—even if this constituted an
outcome-determinative difference between the state
and federal forums.

Byrd acts as a safety valve, then, within the *Erie*
doctrine. *Guaranty Trust*, and the outcome-
determinative test, aggressively treats many issues
as substantive for *Erie* purposes. *Byrd*, on the other
hand, counteracts this aggressive stance as to state-
law forms and modes of rights' enforcement by
allowing important federal interests to trump state
law in certain cases.

Hanna v. Plumber is our final landmark case in the
Court's quest to divine what state law binds under
Erie doctrine.[29] Here the plaintiff in a diversity case
served the defendant properly under the dictates of
Federal Rule of Civil Procedure 4(d)(1), which
allowed process to be left at the defendant's home in
the possession of his wife. The relevant state rule,
however, required that service of process end with in-
hand delivery to the defendant himself. The
defendant argued that the state-law rule applied
under *Guaranty Trust* because the differences
between the service rules would necessarily change

---

[29]   380 U.S. 460 (1965).

the outcome of the case in the procedural posture of a summary judgment motion to dismiss for improper service.

The Supreme Court rejected defendant's contention. It ruled that the "[o]utcome-determination analysis was never intended to serve as a talisman . . . . but rather by reference to the policies underlying the *Erie* rule," namely the prevention of forum shopping and the equitable application of law.[30] The defendant erred, the Court reminded, by failing to apply the outcome-determinative test from the point of view of one choosing where to file.[31] By properly focusing upon the perspective of choosing where to file, the Court explained, one can readily see that the application of the federal rule for service does not encourage forum shopping. Indeed, "the difference between the two rules [for service] would be of scant, if any, relevance to the choice of a forum. Petitioner, in choosing her forum, was not presented with a situation where application of the state rule would wholly bar recovery."[32] Thus the Court dispensed with the defendant's outcome-determinative analysis easily.

The reason *Hanna* stands as a landmark decision, however, lies in its further ruling that the Federal Rules of Civil Procedure hold a special status under the *Erie* doctrine. The Court determined that the "*Erie* rule has never been invoked to void a Federal

---

[30] Id. at 466–67.

[31] Id. at 468.

[32] Id. at 469.

Rule," even if the Court had narrowly interpreted some federal rules in the past so as to avoid conflict with state law.[33] Further still, the Court held the outcome-determinative test of *Guaranty Trust* inapplicable to determining the viability of the Federal Rules in diversity cases. The Court stated that in cases concerning the Federal Rules of Procedure, or any other sets of rule such as the Federal Rules of Evidence enacted under the Rules Enabling Act, the federal rule always applies unless the rule was enacted in violation of the Rules Enabling Act itself or was otherwise unconstitutional.[34] This follows because "*Erie* and its offspring cast no doubt on the long-recognized power of Congress to prescribe . . . [procedural] rules for federal courts even though some of those rules will inevitably differ from comparable state rules."[35] Following this same logic, procedural rules enacted directly by Congress, rather than through the mechanism of the Rules Enabling Act, apply in diversity cases unless the statute itself is found to be unconstitutional.

Digesting the *Erie* doctrine with these three landmark cases in mind, one can construct the substance-versus-procedure inquiry into three steps, flowing roughly in reverse chronological order. Under the first step, one asks whether a federal constitutional, statutory, treaty or formally enacted procedural rule applies? If such a federal provision

---

[33]   Id. at 470.

[34]   Id.

[35]   Id. at 473.

does not apply, then proceed to step 2. If a federal provision does apply, then under *Hanna*, the federal provision controls unless it was enacted beyond the scope of the Rules Enabling Act or the provision is otherwise unconstitutional. It is worth noting that since *Hanna*, no Rule of Civil Procedure has been found beyond the scope of the Rules Enabling Act or otherwise been held unconstitutional.[36]

Under the second step, one asks whether the choice between the federal and state law would be outcome-determinative under *Guaranty Trust*. Recall, this is to be done with an eye toward satisfying *Erie*'s twin goals of reducing forum shopping and enhancing equal application of the laws. Thus, in applying the outcome-determinative test, one must take the point of view of choosing where to file and look for very strong indicia that the outcome of the case would change with application of federal instead of state law. If under this analysis the choice of law is not outcome determinative, then apply federal law. If the choice of law is outcome determinative, go to step three.

Under step three, one must exercise the federal-interest safety valve embodied in *Byrd*. Under *Byrd*, state law that is bound up with the definition of the parties' rights and obligations necessarily applies. But recall that in some cases application of a mere state-law form or mode of enforcement may be deemed outcome determinative, and thus the state law presumptively applies. In these cases, however,

---

[36]　See *Shady Grove Orthopedic Associates, P.A. v. Allstate Ins. Co.*, 559 U.S. 393, 407 (2010).

important federal interests can outweigh the outcome-determinative factor and mandate application of the federal rule.

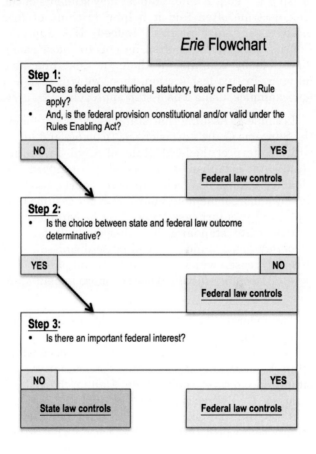

Erie Flowchart

Step 1:
• Does a federal constitutional, statutory, treaty or Federal Rule apply?
• And, is the federal provision constitutional and/or valid under the Rules Enabling Act?

NO   YES

Federal law controls

Step 2:
• Is the choice between state and federal law outcome determinative?

YES   NO

Federal law controls

Step 3:
• Is there an important federal interest?

NO   YES

State law controls   Federal law controls

F. APPLYING THE 3-STEP METHOD

While the courts themselves do not speak in terms of "step 1," "step 2" and "step 3", new students of the *Erie* doctrine often find it helpful to think of *Erie* analyses in this manner. Indeed, the Supreme Court's later cases as often as not are most easily digestible by thinking of them in this three-step manner. In this last section, then, we will review a few examples, using this 3-step approach.

Example 1: Assume that state law does not follow the Supreme Court's decisions of *Twombly* and *Iqbal*, which interpret Federal Rule of Civil Procedure 8(a)(2) to establish a plausibility standard for pleading claims. The relevant state courts, assume, deploy a more lenient standard. Further assume that a plaintiff in a tort case knows that he can meet the lenient state standard, but that he will fail the *Twombly-Iqbal* standard, leading to dismissal. In a diversity case, which standard should apply: the federal *Twombly-Iqbal* rule or the more lenient state rule?

The federal *Twombly-Iqbal* rule applies. Even though this choice between the rules appears outcome-determinative, this matter is decided at "step 1," meaning the outcome-determinative test simply does not yet apply. Under *Hanna*, the Federal Rules of Civil Procedure always apply, unless the rule is beyond the scope of the Rules Enabling Act or otherwise unconstitutional. The scope of the *Hanna* rule includes judicial opinions interpreting the Federal Rules. Given that Federal Rule 8(a)(2) is constitutional, and enacted within the Scope of the

Rules Enabling Act, the rule itself, and all judicial interpretations of it such as *Twombly* and *Iqbal*, apply in diversity cases—even if the choice of the federal rule would be outcome determinative.

The outcome would be the same if the federal rule at issue were a statute as opposed to a rule enacted under the Rules Enabling Act. Thus, in a diversity case, statutes such as 28 U.S.C. § 1404, the transfer of venue statute, apply under the *Hanna* test unless they are unconstitutional.

Example 2: Assume that the relevant state law caps recovery for punitive damages at $250,000. There is no federal rule, statute, constitutional provision or treaty addressing this matter. Pre-*Erie* federal common law, however, places no cap on punitive damages. Does the state-law cap apply in a diversity case?

The state-law cap would apply in a diversity case. As there is not an applicable federal rule, statute, constitutional provision or treaty, there is no "step-one" conflict to which the *Hanna* rule would apply. Thus, we proceed to step two. The choice here, damages cap or no damages cap, is outcome determinative within the meaning of *Guaranty Trust*, because, taking the vantage point of the time of filing, the state rule would necessarily limit the amount of damages. This effect on the outcome would encourage forum shopping as savvy plaintiffs would always choose the federal court over the state court in such a circumstance. Finally, having determined that the choice between damage caps is outcome determinative under *Guaranty Trust*, we move to the federal interest analysis under *Byrd*. Here, there are no federal interests comparable to *Byrd* that would counteract adoption of the state damages cap. As such, the damage cap should be considered substantive under the *Erie* doctrine, meaning that the state rule applies in federal courts while sitting in diversity.

Example 3: Consider next the 2010 case of *Shady Grove Orthopedic Associates, P.A. v. Allstate Ins. Co.*[37] Here, defendant Allstate refused to pay statutory interest due under New York law on plaintiff Shady Grove's insurance claim. The plaintiff filed an action in diversity and then moved, under Federal Rule of Civil Procedure 23, to certify a class action. New York law, however, prohibited the forming of class actions for the collection of statutory-interest claims such as this one. The case split the Court. The 3-step approach, however, aids in understanding the Justices' competing arguments.

The majority conceived of the case as, using our vernacular, a step-1 case. The majority viewed Federal Rule 23, the federal class action rule, as directly applicable. Further, the majority determined that Rule 23 fell within the scope of the Rules Enabling Act and was constitutional. As such, the majority, following *Hanna*, held that the federal-class-action rule applied. In so ruling, a plurality of the Court "acknowledge[d] the reality that keeping the federal-court door open to class actions that cannot proceed in state court will produce forum

---

[37]   559 U.S. 393 (2010).

shopping."[38] Nevertheless, the plurality noted that, under *Hanna*, "a Federal Rule governing procedure is valid whether or not it alters the outcome of the case in a way that induces forum shopping."[39]

The dissent viewed the case differently. The dissent interpreted Rule 23 more narrowly so as to avoid a conflict with the state-law rule.[40] As such, the dissent did not view this case as a "step-1" matter because there was not a federal rule that applied. Having overcome the step-1 hurdle, this case, in the dissent's eyes, becomes an easy analysis under step 2. The choice between the ability to certify a class action or not most certainly will be outcome determinative and, as the plurality admits, encourage forum shopping. As such, in the dissent's view, the state rule should apply under *Guaranty Trust*.

Placing the *Erie* analysis into this 3-step model, then, is helpful not only in solving *Erie* problems as they arise, but also can give a student of the doctrine a framework within which to place judicial analyses under *Erie*, which can otherwise be obtuse.

* * *

In sum, the *Erie* doctrine transformed federal practice in diversity. Under *Erie*, state law now governs substantive issues while federal law reigns over procedural matters. State law is determined as

---

[38] Id. at 415.

[39] Id. at 416.

[40] Id. at 436–37 (Ginsberg, J., dissenting).

it is announced by the state's highest court or by the process of an *Erie* guess. The separating of law into substantive, and thus controlled under state law, and procedural, and thus controlled under federal law, may be thought of in a 3-step format. First, under *Hanna*, if a federal rule, statute, constitutional provision or treaty is on point, the federal rule controls unless it was enacted beyond the scope of the Rules Enabling Act or is unconstitutional. Under step 2, if a federal provision does not apply, then if the choice between the state and federal rule is outcome determinative within the meaning of *Guaranty Trust*, state law presumptively applies. Otherwise, the federal rule controls. Finally under step 3, even if the state law presumptively applies, when there is an important federal policy at stake the federal interest may trump application of the state law under *Byrd*.

Having reviewed the two statistically most significant grounds for original federal jurisdiction—federal question and diversity—in the next chapter we turn to other bases for original federal jurisdiction that are less often deployed.

CHAPTER 5

OTHER GROUNDS FOR ORIGINAL JURISDICTION

"The judicial Power shall extend . . . to all Cases affecting Ambassadors, other public Ministers and Consuls;—to all Cases of admiralty and maritime Jurisdiction;—to Controversies to which the United States shall be a Party;—to Controversies between two or more States."

—United States Constitution, Art. III, § 2, cl. 2

"In all Cases affecting Ambassadors, other public Ministers and Consuls, and those in which a State shall be Party, the supreme Court shall have original Jurisdiction."

—United States Constitution, Art. III, § 2, cl. 3

While federal question and diversity jurisdiction cases make up the lion's share of the federal courts' civil docket, in this chapter we explore other less-numerous grounds for original federal jurisdiction. We begin with cases in which the United States is a party. Second, we address admiralty and maritime jurisdiction. Thirdly, we address matters that arise in the Supreme Court's original jurisdiction. Fourth, we briefly explore unique jurisdictional doctrine for suits against non-diverse foreign parties. Fifth, we end our discussion with a brief comment regarding original jurisdiction in habeas corpus and criminal matters. Of course, there are other important basis for federal jurisdiction, such as bankruptcy or copyright matters. As these areas of jurisdiction relate solely to specialty practices, this volume does not address them.

A.   UNITED STATES AS A PARTY

The Constitution extends the federal judicial power "to Controversies to which the United States shall be a Party." These cases, today, are the third-most-numerous civil cases on the federal docket (excluding habeas corpus). In this section, we briefly look to the jurisdictional treatment of cases in which the United States is a plaintiff and then look to the doctrine surrounding the United States as a party-defendant.

1.   UNITED STATES AS PLAINTIFF

The constitutional scope of United States-as-a-party-plaintiff jurisdiction extends to all cases in which the United States has standing to bring a civil claim,[1] which includes actions to protect uniquely sovereign interests.[2] (See Chapter 8.B discussing standing.) This grant of jurisdiction then is quite large. It extends to both common law and statutory claims that the United States might make against private parties, states, or foreign nations. The law

---

[1]   See *United States v. San Jacinto Tin Company*, 125 U.S. 273, 286 (1888) (not using the language of "standing" but listing the types of interests that correspond strongly to contemporary standing doctrine).

[2]   *Sanitary Dist. of Chicago v. U.S.*, 266 U.S. 405, 425–26 (1925).

governing such suits, typically, is federal common law.[3]

Statutory authority for jurisdiction over suits with the United States as a party-plaintiff comes from 28 U.S.C. § 1345. This grant of jurisdiction covers "all civil actions, suits or proceedings commenced by the United States, or by any agency or officer thereof expressly authorized to sue by Act of Congress." The courts uniformly interpret § 1345 as granting the full scope of constitutional authority. And, absent a few exceptions listed in other statutes, the Court holds § 1345 jurisdiction held concurrently with the state courts.[4] Thus, nearly all civil claims in which the United States has standing and is listed as a plaintiff take federal jurisdiction under § 1345. This provision includes suits against states, a font of jurisdiction that is held concurrently with the Supreme Court's original jurisdiction.[5] It also covers qui tam cases, suits brought by private parties in the name of the United States that bring some benefit to the government, and Miller Act cases, in which a party borrows the government's name to bring the functional equivalent of a mechanics lien against a government contractor.[6] Further, § 1345 provides

---

[3]   *Clearfield Trust Co. v. United States,* 318 U.S. 363, 367 (1943).

[4]   *United States v. Bank of New York & Trust Co.,* 296 U.S. 463, 479 (1936).

[5]   *United States v. State of Ill.,* 454 F.2d 297, 301 (7th Cir. 1971).

[6]   *United States Fidelity & Guaranty Company v. United States,* 204 U.S. 349, 357–58 (1907).

jurisdiction for the United States to bring third-party claims,[7] to bring counterclaims,[8] and cross-claims.[9]

The United States as Plaintiff

In most cases, the federal courts hold concurrent jurisdiction. 28 U.S.C. § 1345.

---

2.   UNITED STATES AS DEFENDANT

The treatment of jurisdiction over suits with the United States as a party-defendant differs substantially from the doctrine governing cases with the United States as a party-plaintiff. We turn first to the circuitous constitutional treatment of party-defendant cases. We turn next to the importance of sovereign immunity in these cases. We end by briefly touching upon some of the more important statutory bases for taking jurisdiction in suits with the United States as a defendant.

We turn first to Article III's scope over cases with the United States as a defendant. The Supreme Court in the early twentieth century, in conflict with its prior rulings,[10] held that suits against the federal government did not fall within Article III's grant of

---

[7]   *United States v. Hawaii*, 832 F.2d 1116 (9th Cir. 1987).

[8]   *Amoco Production Co. v. United States*, 852 F.2d 1574, 1579 (10th Cir. 1988).

[9]   *United States v. General Douglas MacArthur Senior Village, Inc.*, 508 F.2d 377, 379 (2d Cir. 1974).

[10]   *Minnesota v. Hitchcock*, 185 U.S. 373, 384 (1902).

jurisdiction over controversies in which the United States is a party.[11] The Court based this interpretation of Article III upon the text of the Judiciary Act of 1789,[12] which granted jurisdiction only for suits in which the United States was plaintiff, and Eleventh Amendment jurisprudence that constitutionalizes state sovereign immunity broadly. (The Eleventh Amendment is discussed in Chapter 9.) From this vantage point, the Court held that "controversies to which the United States may by statute be made a party defendant, at least as a general rule, lie wholly outside the scope of the judicial power vested by Art. III in the constitutional courts."[13] Reacting to this ruling, the Court issued a series of strained opinions in which it was forced to find other constitutional bases, typically federal question, for jurisdiction over defendant-party cases. By the 1960s, however, the Court reversed its position yet again, in a plurality opinion, finding that Article III embraces party-defendant suits under Article III's United States-as-a-party clause in *Glidden Co. v. Zdanok*.[14] Despite the lack of a majority opinion in *Glidden*, the lower courts agree that *Glidden* overruled *Williams*.[15]

Although *Glidden* finds that suits with the United States as a defendant may arise under Article III, the

---

[11]   *Williams v. United States*, 289 U.S. 553, 577 (1933).

[12]   Id.

[13]   *Williams*, 289 U.S. at 577.

[14]   370 U.S. 530, 564 (1962) (Harlan, J., plurality opinion).

[15]   See, e.g., *Jan's Helicopter Serv., Inc. v. FAA*, 525 F.3d 1299, 1306 n.5 (Fed. Cir. 2008).

related concept of sovereign immunity remains integral to taking jurisdiction in United States-as-a-party-defendant cases. Sovereign immunity is a legal rule that operates as a jurisdictional prohibition against any court, state or federal, "entertain[ing] the suit."[16] Successfully asserting sovereign immunity by the government defendant means that the case must be dismissed immediately. Even after *Glidden*, the federal government enjoys sovereign immunity in all cases as a default matter.[17] As a consequence, the waiver of sovereign immunity constitutes a necessary prerequisite to federal or state jurisdiction when suing the United States civilly.[18]

Only Congress may waive the United States' sovereign immunity, and it must do so unequivocally as the courts will not find a waiver by implication.[19] When Congress chooses to waive sovereign immunity, it may place limitations and conditions upon the waiver of immunity.[20] For example, Congress may refuse consent to trial by jury as part of the waiver,[21] insist upon trial before non-Article III judges as part of the waiver,[22] or invoke unique statute-of-limitation provisions as part of the waiver.[23] Finally, in the exercise of this waiver

---

[16]   *United States v. Sherwood*, 312 U.S. 584, 586 (1941).

[17]   *Dolan v. U.S. Postal Serv.*, 546 U.S. 481 (2006).

[18]   *United States v. Mitchell*, 463 U.S. 206, 212 (1983).

[19]   *United States v. Mitchell*, 445 U.S. 535, 538 (1980).

[20]   *Soriano v. United States*, 352 U.S. 270, 276 (1957).

[21]   28 U.S.C. § 2402.

[22]   28 U.S.C. § 171.

[23]   See, e.g., *United States v. Mottaz*, 476 U.S. 834, 841 (1986).

power, Congress stereotypically will only waive its immunity in federal courts, meaning that the state courts do not typically hold concurrent jurisdiction in United States-as-a-defendant cases.

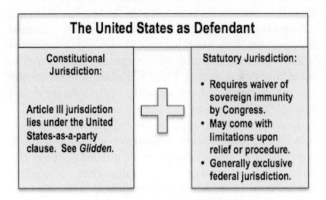

The United States as Defendant

Constitutional Jurisdiction:		Statutory Jurisdiction:
Article III jurisdiction lies under the United States-as-a-party clause. See *Glidden*.		• Requires waiver of sovereign immunity by Congress. • May come with limitations upon relief or procedure. • Generally exclusive federal jurisdiction.

A few of the more important instances in which Congress has waived sovereign immunity and created federal jurisdiction for suits against the United States are given below. The United States Court of Claims, under the Tucker Act, holds exclusive jurisdiction to hear contract claims exceeding $10,000 against the federal government,[24] and it shares concurrent jurisdiction with the district courts for contract claims for less than $10,000 against the federal government under the so-called Mini-Tucker Act.[25] The district courts have jurisdiction to hear vicarious liability suits against

---

[24]   28 U.S.C. § 1491(a)(1).

[25]   28 U.S.C. § 1346(a)(2).

the federal government for enumerated torts committed by federal employees under the Federal Tort Claims Act.[26] The district courts also hold jurisdiction to issue writs of mandamus against federal officers,[27] to hear claims for recovery of illegally collected taxes,[28] to hear Freedom of Information Act claims against the federal government,[29] to hear enumerated claims to review federal agency actions under the A.P.A.,[30] and to entertain enumerated Title VII claims against the federal government as an employer.[31] As this list demonstrates, where Congress chooses to waive immunity varies greatly as it relates to Congress' view of public policy. One final note: Congress often exercises its power to place conditions upon the waiver of sovereign immunity that leads to complicated procedural requirements, meaning that practice in all of the areas above requires specialization that goes well beyond the parameters of this introductory text.

* * *

Article III grants the federal courts jurisdiction over causes of action in which the United States is a party either as a plaintiff or a defendant. When acting as a plaintiff, federal statutory jurisdiction is typically held concurrently with the state courts and

---

[26]   28 U.S.C. § 1346(b).

[27]   28 U.S.C. § 1361.

[28]   28 U.S.C. § 1346(a)(1).

[29]   5 U.S.C. § 552(b).

[30]   5 U.S.C. § 702.

[31]   42 U.S.C. § 2000e–16.

encompasses any suit in which the United States has standing to assert a claim. When haled into court as a defendant, sovereign immunity bars jurisdiction in any court unless Congress has specifically waived it. When reviewing statutory waivers of sovereign immunity, one must carefully note any conditions or limitations that Congress has placed upon that waiver.

B.   ADMIRALTY AND MARITIME JURISDICTION

We turn next to admiralty jurisdiction, which applies maritime law to matters relating to commercially navigable waterways. Admiralty jurisdiction formed a substantial portion of the overall federal docket in the early decades of the Republic. Today, however, claims in admiralty jurisdiction take up but a small percentage of the federal civil caseload. Moreover, "[a]dmiralty and maritime law includes a host of special rights, duties, rules and procedures."[32] Given the relatively small numbers of cases and unique practices in admiralty, this volume provides only a broad overview of admiralty jurisdiction, beginning with the scope of the constitutional allocation of jurisdiction, turning next to the statutory grant of admiralty jurisdiction codified at 28 U.S.C. § 1333, and ending with a few words about choice of law in admiralty cases.

---

[32]   *Lewis v. Lewis & Clark Marine, Inc.*, 531 U.S. 438, 446 (2001).

1. CONSTITUTIONAL ADMIRALTY JURISDICTION

Article III of the Constitution extends the federal "judicial power . . . to all Cases of admiralty and maritime Jurisdiction." That the federal courts would exercise jurisdiction over maritime and admiralty claims, which often involve questions of national importance and international relations, was not much questioned during the ratification era. Furthermore, the notion of subjecting a ship and her crew to a patchwork of differing state laws as it sailed from port to port was deemed impractical at the time. Given these truly nation-wide concerns, it is not overly surprising that national jurisdiction over maritime suits predates the Constitution, with the establishment of a national appellate court of admiralty under the Articles of Confederation.[33]

Admiralty jurisdiction comes to the United States from the English legal tradition, where matters of maritime law were adjudicated in admiralty tribunals that were distinct from the common law and chancery courts. Most admiralty matters, at the time of the founding of the nation, proceeded in rem with the vessel, not the owner, being named as the defendant in the claim. This legal fiction was necessary because the owner of the vessel upon which a legal injury was centered often lived overseas, making suit against him impracticable. This reliance

---

[33] Articles of Confederation, Art. 9, § 1; see also William R. Casto, The Origins of Federal Admiralty Jurisdiction in an Age or Privateers, Smugglers, and Pirates, 37 Am. J. Legal Hist. 117, 123 (1993).

upon in rem procedures remains important today in admiralty cases. Further, suits—or libels as they are called—in admiralty were not tried to juries at the time of the ratification of the Constitution. The lack of a right to jury remains a feature of admiralty jurisdiction to this day.[34]

We turn now to which matters fall within the scope of Article III admiralty jurisdiction. England, in the time leading up to the ratification of the Constitution, had substantially limited the scope of its admiralty jurisdiction by parliamentary statute. An early constitutional question for the federal courts, then, was whether Article III's grant of admiralty jurisdiction should be interpreted as limited by those then-contemporary English statutes. The federal courts uniformly rejected the notion that the constitutional grant should be so limited. Instead, Article III admiralty jurisdiction was from the earliest American decisions given a broad interpretation based upon the "the ancient and original [admiralty] jurisdiction."[35]

Having eschewed a cramped interpretation of Article III admiralty jurisdiction, the next task for the federal courts was to set definitively the bounds for American admiralty jurisdiction. The courts at first settled upon the notion that the scope of Article III admiralty jurisdiction was fundamentally set by

---

[34]   See, e.g., *Craig v. Atlantic Richfield Co.*, 19 F.3d 472 (9th Cir. 1994).

[35]   *DeLovio v. Boit*, 7 F.Cas. 418, 2 Gall. 398, No. 3,776 (C.C.D. Mass. 1815) (Story, J.); see also *New England Mut. Marine Ins. Co. v. Dunham*, 78 U.S. 1, 15 (1870).

geography. Whether a claim fell within admiralty jurisdiction was set by reference to "character of the waters where or with reference to which the given transaction or occurrence takes place."[36] During the early ante-bellum period, the Supreme Court held that Article III admiralty jurisdiction governed only those waters that were subject to "the ebb and flow of the tide,"[37] meaning that navigation on canals, upstream rivers, and the Great Lakes was not subject to federal maritime law.

In 1845, Congress extended federal admiralty jurisdiction to the Great Lakes.[38] The Court considered whether this expansion of federal admiralty law was constitutional in *The Genesee Chief v. Fitzhugh*.[39] The Court upheld Congress's extension of admiralty jurisdiction over the Great Lakes and went on to rule that Article III admiralty jurisdiction governs all navigable waterways. The Court reasoned that "[i]f it is a public navigable water, on which commerce is carried on between different states or nations, the reason for . . . [admiralty] jurisdiction is precisely the same."[40] In the Court's view, the important national interests protected by admiralty jurisdiction, and the need to free ships and crews from sailing through a competing patchwork of state laws, can be served just

---

[36]   Grant Gilmore & Charles L. Black, The Law of Admiralty § 1–11 (2d ed. 1975).

[37]   The *Orleans*, 36 U.S. 175, 181 (1837).

[38]   Act of February 26, 1845, ch. 20, 5 Stat. 726 to 727; as amended at 28 U.S.C. § 1873.

[39]   53 U.S. 443 (1851).

[40]   Id. at 454.

as well on freshwater as it can on the world's oceans. As such, all navigable waters, not just tidal waters, became the lodestar for demarking Article III admiralty jurisdiction.

Expanding upon this navigable waterways concept, the Court in *The Montello* held that the "capability of use by the public for purposes of transportation and commerce affords the true criterion of the navigability of a river, rather than the extent and manner of that use. If . . . [the waterway] be capable in its natural state of being used for purposes of commerce, no matter in what mode the commerce may be conducted, it is navigable in fact, and becomes in law a public river or highway [subject to federal admiralty jurisdiction]."[41]

Admiralty Jurisdiction

Governs waterways that are capable of commercial navigation.

During the twentieth century, the Court continued to give Article III admiralty jurisdiction a broad construction, moving away from a strictly physical connection to a navigable waterway to a conceptual relationship to a navigable waterway. We explore this expansion by turning first to contract law. By the middle of the twentieth century it was clear that the maritime nature of a contract, and thus the

---

[41]   87 U.S. 430, 441–42 (1874).

applicability of federal admiralty jurisdiction, was "conceptual rather than spatial."[42] Following this conceptual approach, the courts do not simply "look to whether a ship or other vessel was involved in the dispute,. . . . [or] to the place of the contract's formation or performance."[43] Rather, the courts deem a contract to be maritime if "the nature and character of the contract . . . [have] reference to maritime service or maritime transactions."[44] Under this approach, then, breaching a contract to ship goods across Lake Michigan, for example, will arise in federal admiralty jurisdiction, even if there is an anticipatory breach of the agreement months before any cargo is loaded aboard the vessel, because the contract is conceptually related to services on a navigable waterway. Thus the courts find that a contract is maritime in nature anytime "the transaction relates to ships and vessels, masters and mariners, as the agents of commerce."[45]

Contracts Arise in Admiralty
If the agreement conceptually relates to navigable waters.

The courts, often following Congress' lead, have also expanded the reach of admiralty jurisdiction in tort beyond a strict injury-occurred-on-navigable-

---

[42] *Kossick v. United Fruit Co.*, 365 U.S. 731, 735 (1961).

[43] *Norfolk Southern Railway Co. v. Kirby*, 543 U.S. 14, 23 (2004) (internal citations and quotations omitted).

[44] Id. (internal quotations omitted).

[45] *Kossick*, 365 U.S. at 736.

waterways approach to a more conceptual approach. For example, part of the Jones Act extends admiralty jurisdiction to seamen seeking damages for injuries sustained during the course of their employment that occurred on land.[46] Similarly, Congress in the Extension of Admiralty Jurisdiction Act[47] expanded admiralty jurisdiction to include suits to recover damages to persons or property caused by a vessel on navigable water, "notwithstanding that such damage or injury be done or consummated on land."[48] Additionally, certain statutes ostensibly passed to regulate only watercraft have been interpreted as applicable to aircraft crashing into navigable waters.[49]

The Court reigned in this ever-expanding tendency in admiralty tort cases in the important opinion of *Executive Jet Aviation, Inc. v. City of Cleveland*.[50] In *Executive Jet*, an aircraft, scheduled for a domestic flight, took off from a Cleveland airport and immediately crashed into Lake Erie as the result of birds entering the jet's engines. The plaintiffs sought admiralty jurisdiction under a strict-locality approach, given that Lake Erie is a navigable waterway. The Supreme Court, however, found admiralty jurisdiction lacking. In so doing, it crafted a new test for admiralty tort jurisdiction: the "locality

---

[46] See *O'Donnell v. Great Lakes Dredge & Dock Company*, 318 U.S. 36 (1943).

[47] 46 U.S.C. § 30101.

[48] 46 U.S.C. § 740.

[49] See *Offshore Logistics, Incorporated v. Tallentire*, 477 U.S. 207 (1986).

[50] 409 U.S. 249 (1972).

plus maritime nexus" test. Under this test, the mere fact that an injury occurred on a navigable waterway is not sufficient for admiralty tort jurisdiction. Rather, the injury must have occurred on (or proximate to) a navigable waterway and the activities at issue must bear a significant relationship to traditional maritime activities. Thus, torts occurring on an intra-continental flight do not meet the latter portion of the test because such flights "are principally over land, the fact that an aircraft happens to fall in navigable waters, rather than on land, is wholly fortuitous."[51] A tort occurring on an inter-continental flight over the ocean, however, would invoke admiralty jurisdiction because "[a]n aircraft in that situation might be thought to bear a significant relationship to traditional maritime activity because it would be performing a function traditionally performed by waterborne vessels."[52] The courts now generally apply the *Executive Jet* test to all torts to determine the applicability of constitutional admiralty jurisdiction.

---

[51]   Id. at 271.

[52]   Id.

Torts Arise in Admiralty

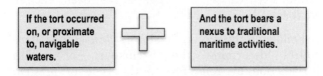

If the tort occurred on, or proximate to, navigable waters.

And the tort bears a nexus to traditional maritime activities.

2.   28 U.S.C. § 1333 ADMIRALTY JURISDICTION

In the Judiciary Act of 1789, Congress granted to the district courts original jurisdiction over admiralty and maritime matters. That act remains, functionally, unchanged today codified at 28 U.S.C. § 1333. Section 1333's scope is generally co-extensive with the constitutional grant of admiralty jurisdiction.[53]

The more pressing statutory question is whether the grant of statutory jurisdiction is exclusive to the federal courts or held concurrently with the state courts. While § 1333 states that district court admiralty jurisdiction is "exclusive," purporting to mean that the state courts are barred from hearing maritime claims, § 1331(1) includes the following clause: "saving to suitors in all cases all other remedies to which they are otherwise entitled." What this provision means, in the language of the original 1789 act, is that where plaintiffs have "the right of a common law remedy . . . [and] the common law is competent to give it" the state courts retain

---

[53]   *Swanson v. Marra Bros.*, 328 U.S. 1, 5 (1946).

concurrent jurisdiction to hear such common law claims. Thus, "[f]ederal-court jurisdiction over . . . [admiralty] cases . . . has never been entirely exclusive."[54]

Following this saving-to-suitors clause, the federal courts determine the exclusivity of federal jurisdiction by reference to the type of _personal_ jurisdiction deployed in the case. As noted above, admiralty jurisdiction, historically speaking, relied upon in rem personal jurisdiction, invoking the legal fiction of suing the vessel in lieu of the owner. Still today, many claims that a plaintiff might bring in admiralty lead to a maritime lien against the vessel at issue. As a result, these maritime lien cases take personal jurisdiction in rem by attachment of the vessel.

In these admiralty cases in which personal jurisdiction is taken in rem, subject matter jurisdiction over the case is exclusively federal. "An in rem suit against a vessel is," the Court consistently holds, "distinctively an admiralty proceeding, and is hence within the exclusive province of the federal courts."[55] As a result, the Court holds that the state courts "may not provide a remedy in rem for any cause of action within the admiralty jurisdiction."[56]

---

[54]   *Am. Dredging Co. v. Miller*, 510 U.S. 443, 446 (1994).

[55]   Id. at 446–47.

[56]   *Red Cross Line v. Atlantic Fruit Co.*, 264 U.S. 109, 124 (1924).

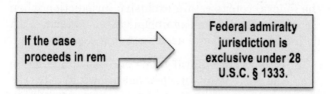

Because an in rem admiralty proceeding (and hence exclusive federal jurisdiction) must be based on attachment of a res,[57] a maritime property right that only attaches to a vessel,[58] the meaning of the term "vessel" carries substantial importance here. Vessel, as defined by 1 U.S.C. § 3, includes "every description of watercraft or other artificial contrivance used, or capable of being used, as a means of transportation on water." The Court, in *Lozman v. City of Riviera Beach*,[59] held that a floating home, which was neither capable of self-propulsion nor designed to be used as a mode of transportation, was not a vessel. In so holding, the Court refined the statutory definition of vessel generally. Following this holding, "a structure does not fall within the scope of this statutory . . . [definition of vessel] unless a reasonable observer, looking to the . . . [structure's] physical characteristics and activities, would consider it designed to a practical degree for carrying people or things over water."[60] In sum, under 28 U.S.C. § 1333,

---

[57] See The Rock Island Bridge, 73 U.S. (6 Wall) 213, 215 (1867).

[58] See 46 U.S.C. § 31342.

[59] 133 S. Ct. 735 (2013).

[60] Id. at 741.

the federal courts retain exclusive jurisdiction when a case proceeds in rem against a vessel—a term of art defined by statute and accompanying case law.

If, however, a plaintiff takes personal jurisdiction over the defendant in personam, ordinarily the common law would have provided a remedy in addition to admiralty. As such, the saving-to-suitors provision of § 1333(1) applies to preserve concurrent state-court jurisdiction.[61] For example, a plaintiff bringing a claim for breach of a maritime contract in personam against his counterparty to the contract may bring the claim in either state or federal court.

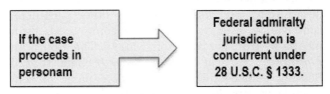

If the case proceeds in personam ⟹ Federal admiralty jurisdiction is concurrent under 28 U.S.C. § 1333.

3.   ADMIRALTY JURISDICTION AND CHOICE OF LAW

We end our discussion of admiralty law with a brief commentary on the sources of substantive law in this field. Substantive admiralty law remains, even after the *Erie* decision, predominantly governed by federal common law. As the Supreme Court holds, "Congress has largely left to this Court the responsibility for fashioning the controlling rules of admiralty law."[62]

---

[61]   Am. Dredging Co., 510 U.S. at 446.

[62]   *Fitzgerald v. United States Lines Company*, 374 U.S. 16, 20 (1963).

Thus, the Court crafts most of the maritime law of contract and tort by judicial decision.

This is not to say that Congress is precluded from legislating in areas of maritime law. Indeed, Congress' power to alter substantive maritime and admiralty law is coextensive with the constitutional boundaries of admiralty itself.[63] Three highly notable statutes merit reference here: first, the Jones Act, which grants an injured seaman the right to sue his or her employer for injuries sustained as a result of the employer's negligence; second, the Ship Mortgage Act, which allows investors to bring an action in rem to enforce a security interest in a vessel; and third, the Death on the High Seas Act, which provides widows and other beneficiaries of seamen and non-seamen remedies for deaths occurring outside the scope of employment.

Given that all of the substantive law in admiralty is federal, one could well conclude that maritime cases arises under 28 U.S.C. § 1331 as a federal question in addition to coming into federal court in admiralty jurisdiction. Such a conclusion, while tempting, is in error. The Court holds that, because admiralty was historically neither a part of common law nor equity, maritime suits are not cases "in Law and Equity, arising under this Constitution, [or] the Laws of the United States."[64] As such, federal

---

[63]   *In re Garnett,* 141 U.S. 1 (1891*).*

[64]   *Romero v. International Terminal Operating Co.*, 358 U.S. 354, 368 (1959) (internal quotations omitted).

question jurisdiction cannot be deployed as a jurisdictional basis for admiralty claims.

* * *

In closing, the courts give Article III admiralty jurisdiction a broad construction. This broad interpretation applies equally to the application of 28 U.S.C. § 1333 jurisdiction. Under these rulings, any waterway that is commercially navigable, even if not currently being used as such, may be subject to admiralty jurisdiction, as may certain structures or activities immediately proximate to such navigable waterways. Further demonstrating the wide sweep of admiralty jurisdiction, courts deem contracts as arising in admiralty so long as the agreement references maritime services or transactions. Torts arise in admiralty if the injury occurred on, or proximate to, a navigable waterway and the relevant activities at issue bear a significant relationship to a traditional maritime activity. The federal courts retain exclusive federal jurisdiction of admiralty cases that proceed in rem, while holding jurisdiction concurrently with the states over suits proceeding in personam. Finally, maritime law remains predominantly a creature of federal common law.

C.   ORIGINAL JURISDICTION IN THE SUPREME COURT

Moving from admiralty, we now consider the Supreme Court's trial, as opposed to appellate, jurisdiction. Following the Madisonian Compromise, Article III leaves the question of whether there should be original federal jurisdiction at all largely up to Congress' discretion. Indeed, the only grounds of original federal jurisdiction that Article III mandates are those matters that arise in the Supreme Court's original jurisdiction. The Constitution's grant of trial jurisdiction to the Supreme Court encompasses "all cases affecting ambassadors, other public ministers and consuls, and those in which a state shall be party." We address this quirky area of original jurisdiction in this section.

To many, original jurisdiction in the Supreme Court strikes as odd, and indeed it is given the Court's contemporary role. But this ground of jurisdiction follows from the Madisonian Compromise. Given that the compromise envisions that the Supreme Court could be the only federal court at all, if there are some matters that must be lodged in original federal jurisdiction, then the Supreme Court must have the ability to hear them. Further, housing consular and state-as-a-party litigation in the Supreme Court itself is a means of affording these unique parties respect and dignity. Thus, these matters fall with the Supreme Court's original, that is to say trial, jurisdiction under Article III.

What is more, unlike most of federal jurisdiction in which Congress retains extensive control to grant, or not, jurisdiction, the Supreme Court's original jurisdiction is largely beyond the control of Congress. Famously, the Court in *Marbury v. Madison* held that Congress may not expand the Supreme Court's original jurisdiction beyond the strict parameters set forth in Article III.[65] On the other side of the coin, Congress may not limit the Supreme Court's original jurisdiction either.[66] Thus, the Court, by direct operation of the Constitution, remains empowered to hear matters within its original jurisdiction.

There is one crack in this otherwise granite façade, however. The Court allows its original jurisdiction to be held concurrently with other federal courts. Thus, Congress in 28 U.S.C. § 1251(b) directs that the Supreme Court holds original jurisdiction concurrently with the federal district courts in all actions with foreign ambassadors or foreign consuls as parties, all suits between the United States and a state, and all suits in which a state as a plaintiff brings a claim against a citizen of another state or an alien. (The Eleventh Amendment as a general matter bars suits by private parties against states without their consent, an issue we will discuss in Chapter 9.)

Because these bases of jurisdiction are non-exclusive, the Supreme Court retains the ability to dismiss suits that fall within § 1251(b), preferring that these matter be tried in the district courts. In fact, the Supreme Court, in its entire history, has only heard three cases involving ambassadors and consuls in its original jurisdiction.[67] Additionally, the Court rarely hears suits between the United States and a state in its original jurisdiction, preferring that

---

[65]   5 U.S. (1 Cranch) 137, 174–75 (1803).

[66]   See *Arizona v. California*, 373 U.S. 546, 564 (1963); *Wisconsin v. Pelican Ins. Co.*, 127 U.S. 265, 300 (1888).

[67]   See Ex parte *Gruber*, 269 U.S. 302 (1925); *Casey v. Galli*, 94 U.S. 673 (1877); *Jones v. Le Tombe*, 3 U.S. (3 Dall.) 384 (1798).

such cases first be heard in a federal district court.[68] Similarly, the Court will only rarely entertain a suit brought by a state as a party-plaintiff against a citizen of another state or an alien.

The Court explained its reticence to hear original jurisdiction cases in *Ohio v. Wyandotte Chemicals Corp*. While "it may initially have been contemplated that this Court would always exercise its original jurisdiction . . . it seems evident to us . . . [now in 1971 that such a practice is] untenable, as a practical matter."[69] Justice Harlan went on to note that this "Court is, moreover, structured to perform as an appellate tribunal, ill equipped for the task of fact finding. . . . [and] for every case in which we might be called upon to . . . [hold a trial] we would unavoidably be reducing the attention we could give to those [appellate] matters of . . . [truly] national import."[70] As a result, suits falling into the Supreme Court's non-exclusive, original jurisdiction will almost never be tried at the Court, but rather heard in the first instance by a federal district court.

There exists, however, one area of jurisdiction that remains both original and exclusive to the Supreme Court by operation of 28 U.S.C. § 1251(a): suits between states. Thus, if California should seek to sue Arizona, the only forum for such a trial lies in the Supreme Court of the United States. As such, the Court hears a small, but consistent, series of cases

---

[68]   See, e.g., *Oregon v. Mitchell*, 400 U.S. 112 (1970)

[69]   401 U.S. 493, 497 (1971).

[70]   Id. at 498.

between the states. Many of these cases involve water rights and boundary issues resulting from the movement of rivers. The actual conducting of a trial in the Supreme Court is typically done before a "special master," who is appointed by the Court for this purpose. The master, in turn, holds hearings and produces findings of fact and conclusions of law. This report is reviewed by the Supreme Court in a procedure akin to appellate review.

D.   SUITS AGAINST NON-DIVERSE FOREIGN PARTIES

In this section, we briefly address two unique bases, not housed in diversity jurisdiction, for taking jurisdiction over non-American parties. As was discussed in Chapter 3, suits seeking to bring a foreign nation into court as a party-defendant do not arise under in diversity under 28 U.S.C. § 1332(a). Moreover, the Foreign Sovereign Immunities Act grants foreign nation states general immunity from suit in both the federal and state courts.[71] The act, however, does list several exceptions to this general immunity rule, creating exclusive jurisdiction in the federal district courts, which arise constitutionally speaking as a matter of Article III federal question jurisdiction.[72] Because the act does not exercise constitutional diversity jurisdiction, cases taking jurisdiction under the act may feature foreign plaintiffs suing foreign sovereign defendants, even if

---

[71]   28 U.S.C. § 1604.

[72]   *Verlinden B.V. v. Central Bank of Nigeria*, 461 U.S. 480, 493 (1983).

no Americans are party to the suit.[73] Pursuant to the Foreign Sovereign Immunities Act, then, jurisdiction over foreign sovereign defendants lies: (1) when immunity has been waived, (2) when the suit arises out of commercial activity carried on in the United States, (3) to recover property in the United States taken in violation of international law, (4) in matters regarding immovable property located in the United States acquired by succession or gift, (5) in enumerated vicarious liability tort claims, (6) to enforce enumerated arbitration agreements, and (7) to enforce limited matters arising in maritime law. Hence, in these situations, the federal district courts may take exclusive jurisdiction over a foreign sovereign. Special care should be given here to the definition of foreign sovereign in 28 U.S.C. § 1603, which gives this concept a broad meaning.[74]

Second, as part of the Judiciary Act of 1789, Congress passed what is now known as the Alien Tort Claims Act. Codified at 28 U.S.C. § 1350, the statute reads: "The district courts shall have original jurisdiction of any civil action by an alien for a tort only, committed in violation of the law of nations or a treaty of the United States." Constitutionally speaking, this act grants federal question jurisdiction because international law is treated as federal law in American courts.[75]

---

[73]   Id.

[74]   See Chapter 3.B.1.a discussing this point.

[75]   *The Paquete Habana*, 175 U.S. 677, 699 (1900).

The statute was long forgotten and little used until 1980 in *Filartiga v. Pena-Irala*,[76] when human-rights lawyers re-discovered the statute and used it as a means of bringing international human-rights litigation into federal court. The Supreme Court has since accepted that the Alien Tort Claim Act grants jurisdiction to hear "causes of action only for alleged violations of international law norms that are specific, universal, and obligatory."[77] The Court has been adamant, however, that only the most clearly accepted norms of international customary law, as well as treaties, will be heard under the statute.

The statute's scope is also limited in terms of who may be a party. The statute, by its plain meaning, limits jurisdiction to cases brought by foreign plaintiffs for torts in violation of international law. As such, American plaintiffs may not proceed under the act. Further, for a complex host of reasons, almost all defendants under the act will also be non-Americans. As such, cases under the Alien Tort Claim Act, while often high profile, will likely remain few in number.

E.   HABEAS CORPUS AND CRIMINAL JURISDICTION

Lastly, we review federal jurisdiction over habeas corpus claims and federal criminal prosecutions. Combined, these two areas consume substantial portions of the federal trial docket. But given that the

---

[76]   630 F.2d 876 (2d Cir. 1980).

[77]   *Kiobel v. Royal Dutch Petroleum Co.*, 133 S. Ct. 1659, 1665 (2013) (internal quotations omitted).

focus of this volume is upon civil, not criminal, jurisdiction, our discussion is truncated.[78]

The district courts, concurrently with the federal appellate courts, retain jurisdiction to issue traditional common law writs of habeas corpus under 28 U.S.C. § 2241. Habeas relief is "a writ antecedent to statute, . . . throwing its root deep into the genius of our common law,"[79] appearing in English law several centuries ago. In the pre-amended Constitution, it was the only right to receive explicit recognition, forbidding suspension of "[t]he Privilege of the Writ of Habeas Corpus . . . unless when in Cases of Rebellion or Invasion the public Safety may require it."[80] Section 2241 enacts this constitutional guarantee. It is beyond the scope of this volume to explore fully the boundaries of the Great Writ, as it is known. But it is worth noting that the scope of jurisdiction under § 2241 remains at the center of fierce debate as seen in the Antiterrorism and Effective Death Penalty Act cases[81] and the Guantanamo cases.[82]

Likely of more pragmatic importance for typical criminal offenses, the federal district courts retain jurisdiction to review final criminal convictions from

---

[78]   Of course, habeas corpus claims are technically civil actions. But for all practical purposes, they are more at home in the overall criminal-law landscape. I treat them as such here.

[79]   *Williams v. Kaiser*, 323 U.S. 471, 484, n. 2 (1945) (internal quotation marks omitted).

[80]   U.S. Const., Art. I, § 9, cl. 2.

[81]   See *Felker v. Turpin*, 518 U.S. 651 (1996).

[82]   See, e.g., *Boumediene v. Bush*, 553 U.S. 723 (2008).

both the state courts, under 28 U.S.C. § 2254, and federal courts, under 28 U.S.C. § 2255. While actions under these statutes are often referred to as habeas corpus actions, technically speaking these are congressionally crafted substitutes for common law habeas corpus review. Practice under these statutes, again, goes far afield from the scope of this text, especially once one considers the effects of the Antiterrorism and Effective Death Penalty Act of 1996. This is not meant to diminish the importance of these provisions. Indeed, in some districts nearly a quarter of the docket is filled with § 2254 and § 2255 cases, where prisoners argue that their past criminal convictions are constitutionally infirm.

Finally, the federal district courts have jurisdiction over all federal crimes. The constitutional foundation for this grant of jurisdiction comes both from Article III federal question and Article III United States-as-a-party jurisdiction. Statutory authority for federal criminal jurisdiction is housed at 18 U.S.C. § 3231, which makes federal district court jurisdiction over federal crimes exclusive.

*   *   *

While federal question and diversity jurisdiction consume the bulk of the federal civil docket, other fonts of original federal jurisdiction remain important within our legal system. These include cases in which the United States is a party; matters arising in admiralty; the Supreme Court's original jurisdiction; suits over non-diverse foreign parties; as well as habeas corpus petitions.

CHAPTER 6

SUPPLEMENTAL JURISDICTION

"[Supplemental] jurisdiction . . . [may] exist[ ] whenever there is a [federal] claim . . . and the relationship between that [federal] claim and the [additional] state claim permits the conclusion that the entire action before the court comprises but one constitutional 'case.' "

—*United Mine Workers of Am. v. Gibbs*, 383 U.S. 715, 725 (1966)

So far in this text, we have predominantly dealt with federal trial courts taking subject matter jurisdiction in suits with one claim brought by one plaintiff against one defendant. The question in such suits has been: Can the federal district court take subject matter jurisdiction over this one claim in diversity, federal question or the like? Civil suits, however, often involve many more than one claim between more than two parties. Or put more formally, the Federal Rules of Civil Procedure allow, and often require, the joinder of multiple claims and multiple parties to a civil suit.

Of note to our study is how the courts obtain subject matter jurisdiction over these additional claims and parties. Recall that subject matter jurisdiction is a claim-by-claim analysis, thus each additional claim requires a basis for taking jurisdiction. (See Chapter 1.C.) For matters in state courts of general jurisdiction, joinder of claims, typically, will not raise subject matter jurisdictional concerns, because such courts are presumed to have subject matter jurisdiction for these joined claims. In federal court, however, joinder of claims raises subject matter jurisdictional concerns as such courts are of limited jurisdiction. Thus, the fact that a federal court took subject matter jurisdiction over claim #1 under 28 U.S.C. § 1331, say, does not mean that the court will have jurisdiction over claim #2, counterclaim #3, or third-party claim #4, and so on. Each additional claim needs its own basis for subject matter jurisdiction. And when parties are joined in federal court, subject matter jurisdiction is again an issue because these courts are of limited jurisdiction, and the joinder of parties may well affect bases for taking jurisdiction by, for instance, joining a non-diverse party.[1]

Taking jurisdiction, then, over joined claims and parties is an important matter. Often, subject matter jurisdiction over joined claims vest in the normal manner under § 1331 and the like. But joined parties and claims may also take subject matter jurisdiction under "supplemental jurisdiction." We begin this chapter with an introduction of the notion of supplemental jurisdiction. We next turn to a section-by-section discussion of the supplemental jurisdictional statute, 28 U.S.C. § 1367.

---

[1]   Further, when parties are joined, be it in state or federal court, personal jurisdiction may often be a concern, which is a matter beyond the scope of this text.

A. CONCEPT OF SUPPLEMENTAL JURISDICTION

Let's begin with a simple suit. Suppose that a plaintiff, a New Yorker, sues a defendant, also a New Yorker, for gender discrimination in her employment. The claim arises under Title VII of the federal Civil Rights Act of 1964, a so-called Title VII claim. Because her cause of action is created by federal law, subject matter jurisdiction vests as a federal question under 28 U.S.C. § 1331 by satisfaction of both the well-pleaded complaint rule and the Holmes test.

Now assume that the plaintiff wishes to add a second claim under the federal Pregnancy Discrimination Act of 1978. This newly joined claim requires subject matter jurisdiction, as subject matter jurisdiction is a claim-by-claim analysis. Once again, because her second cause of action is created by federal law, subject matter jurisdiction vests again as a federal question under 28 U.S.C. § 1331 by satisfaction of both the well-pleaded complaint rule and the Holmes test.

But now suppose the plaintiff brings yet a third claim, a claim for breach of employment contract. A breach-of-contract claim arises under state law, and as such, will not normally arise under § 1331. So, federal question subject matter jurisdiction is not available for this contract claim. Diversity jurisdiction could serve as a jurisdictional basis, if the parties are completely diverse and the contract claim is for more than $75,000. But these criteria are not met here, as we are positing for this example that both parties are from New York.

In this hypothetical, which is quite common, the federal court could well be vested with jurisdiction over the Title VII and Pregnancy Discrimination claims yet lack jurisdiction over the related contract claim. The situation would be the same if the plaintiff brought the Title VII claim and the defendant brought breach of contract as a counterclaim, because the state-law counterclaim would lack jurisdiction under either § 1331 or § 1332. This leaves the quandary of what to do with such joined claims that do not arise under § 1331 or § 1332 (or some other ground for federal jurisdiction such as admiralty).

One solution to such cases would be to bifurcate the suit among the state and federal courts, leaving the claims and counterclaims with federal jurisdiction in federal court and letting the state courts hear the remaining claims. Such a solution, however, would be horribly inefficient. If all the claims arise out of the same transaction or occurrence, it would be resource preserving to have one court hear the entire matter. Another solution could be to send suits such as these entirely to state court, both the federal and non-federal claims. State courts hold general jurisdiction and thus could hear both sets of claims. This possible solution has the downside of dramatically limiting access to federal court. The third possibility, and the one the courts adopt by statute, is to take an expansive approach to federal jurisdiction in such suits so as to bring the joined non-federal claims into federal court. Thus, federal courts—in matters where § 1331 or § 1332 (or some other basis of original jurisdiction) lies over some, but not all, of the claims at issue—may exercise "supplemental jurisdiction" in an effort to collect all of the related claims together in the federal court.

The root idea of supplemental jurisdiction is that if a case—with multiple claims or parties—can acquire federal jurisdiction (either by federal question, diversity, or some other basis) over at least one claim, then the rest of the "related" claims should find federal jurisdiction as well. By allowing this supplemental jurisdiction, Congress exercises its power to grant the federal courts a broader portion of Article III constitutional jurisdiction than the standard jurisdictional statutes currently do in order to achieve efficiencies. Supplemental jurisdiction, furthermore, is designed to work hand-in-glove with the philosophy of the Federal Rules of Civil Procedure that often require the joinder of multiple claims and parties to a suit.

New students of jurisdiction often find the question of when supplemental jurisdiction applies a difficult one. The following flowchart may be a helpful starting point for determining whether supplemental subject matter jurisdiction is applicable.

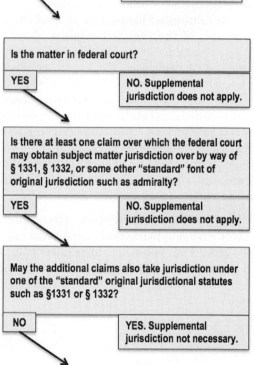

Does Supplemental Jurisdiction Apply Flowchart

Does this matter involve multiple claims or multiple parties?

YES

NO. Supplemental jurisdiction does not apply.

Is the matter in federal court?

YES

NO. Supplemental jurisdiction does not apply.

Is there at least one claim over which the federal court may obtain subject matter jurisdiction over by way of § 1331, § 1332, or some other "standard" font of original jurisdiction such as admiralty?

YES

NO. Supplemental jurisdiction does not apply.

May the additional claims also take jurisdiction under one of the "standard" original jurisdictional statutes such as §1331 or § 1332?

NO

YES. Supplemental jurisdiction not necessary.

> **Supplemental jurisdiction may apply in this matter.
> Go to an analysis of 28 U.S.C. § 1367. See flowchart
> at chapter 6.B.3.**

As this flowchart makes clear, supplemental jurisdiction is not a freestanding basis for jurisdiction. It may only be used after at least one claim has found subject matter jurisdiction in the federal court independently under § 1331, § 1332, or some other basis for original jurisdiction. As a result, one may not conclude that a claim takes supplemental jurisdiction without first concluding that a prior related claim found federal jurisdiction by some other original jurisdiction statute, which then lends a helping hand to raise the non-federal claim into federal court. Put yet another way, supplemental jurisdiction may never be exercised on its own. It may only *supplement* jurisdiction already taken under § 1331, § 1332, or the like.

Before turning to a more detailed account of 28 U.S.C. § 1367, the supplemental jurisdiction statute, we must take in a bit of jargon. Prior to the passage of § 1367, the courts developed the functional equivalent of supplemental jurisdiction via case law. The terminology and philosophy grounding this older approach remains key to understanding § 1367 as the statute in many ways codified this older practice.

This older practice distinguished between two types of supplemental jurisdiction. If the claim or claims that originally entered federal court are *not* based solely upon diversity (i.e., the claims arise at least in part upon § 1331, § 1333, etc.), the exercise of supplemental jurisdiction in such a case is deemed "pendent jurisdiction." If the claim or claims that originally entered federal court are based *solely* upon diversity, the exercise of supplemental jurisdiction in such a case is deemed "ancillary jurisdiction." This distinction mattered under the earlier approach as the courts more readily took pendent jurisdiction, while placing restrictions upon the use of ancillary jurisdiction. To this day, courts continue to use this terminology. And, as we will presently see, § 1367 continues the practice of preferring pendent jurisdiction over ancillary jurisdiction.

B. 28 U.S.C. § 1367 SUPPLEMENTAL JURISDICTION

This older practice worked well enough until, in 1989, the Supreme Court issued *Finley v. United States*,[2] which overruled much of this prior case law. In reaction, Congress passed 28 U.S.C. § 1367 in 1990 to restate, by and large, the prior regime regarding pendent jurisdiction, as laid out in *United Mine Workers of America v. Gibbs*,[3] and ancillary jurisdiction, as held in *Owen Equipment & Erection Co. v. Kroger*.[4] In this section, then, we walk through the current statute section by section. Given that the current statute largely codifies *Gibbs* and *Kroger*, the

---

[2]   490 U.S. 545 (1989).

[3]   383 U.S. 715 (1966).

[4]   437 U.S. 365 (1978).

courts often rely upon these earlier-in-time cases to interpret § 1367.

1.   ANALYSIS OF § 1367(a)

Section 1367 divides into four primary parts. All exercises of supplemental jurisdiction, be they pendent or ancillary, must first satisfy subsection (a). The text of 28 U.S.C. 1367(a) provides as follows:

> Except as provided in subsections (b) and (c) or as expressly provided otherwise by Federal statute, in any civil action of which the district courts have original jurisdiction, in **any civil action of which the district courts have original jurisdiction**, the district courts shall have supplemental jurisdiction[5] over all other **claims that are so related to claims in the action within such original jurisdiction** that they form part of the same case or controversy under Article III of the United States Constitution. Such supplemental jurisdiction shall include claims that involve the joinder or intervention of additional parties.[6]

Subsection (a) first makes clear, as discussed above, that supplemental jurisdiction must be used only as a supplement to a claim that is already found in federal jurisdiction. Secondly, as denoted by the highlighted text, subsection (a) states that supplemental jurisdiction will only extend to those additional claims that are "so related to" the original

---

[5]   That is to say, either pendent or ancillary jurisdiction.

[6]   28 U.S.C. 1367(a) (emphasis and footnote added).

claims as to form part of the same case for Article III purposes. The Supreme Court in *Gibbs* ruled that a supplemental claim is "related to" an original claim, if it "derive[s] from a common nucleus of operative fact."[7] Thus, § 1367(a) is satisfied if the original federal claim and the putative supplemental claim derive from a common nucleus of operative fact.

A few examples will help to illustrate this concept. Assume a plaintiff, from Texas, brings a federal Title VII employment discrimination suit against his former employer, a Texas corporation, for firing him due to his religion. This first claim readily takes subject matter jurisdiction as a federal question. Now assume plaintiff wishes to join a state-law claim for wrongful discharge, also alleging that the defendant-employer fired him because of his religion. The wrongful discharge claim, as a state-law cause of action, does not arise under § 1331. Further the wrongful discharge claim cannot arise under 28 U.S.C. § 1332 because the parties are not diverse. Here, however, the plaintiff could successfully argue that § 1367(a) is met because the federal Title VII claim and the state wrongful discharge tort arise out of a common nucleus of facts, namely, the alleged firing on the basis of religion.

Conveniently, this common-nucleus-of-facts test works closely with the Federal Rules of Civil Procedure's "same transaction and occurrence test." The same-transaction-and-occurrence test is ubiquitous throughout the joinder and amendment

---

[7]   383 U.S. at 725.

provisions lodged in Federal Rules 13 to 24. The test also forms the core of most common law claim preclusion, or res judicata, doctrine. As a result, the procedural rules for joinder works in coordination with the jurisdictional dictates of § 1367(a).

We return to the above example to demonstrate the point. The plaintiff's wrongful discharge claim may be permissively joined under Federal Rule of Civil Procedure 18. Moreover, per claim-preclusion doctrine, the plaintiff faces a mandatory joinder of the wrongful discharge claim here as well (i.e., the plaintiff must join the state-law claim now or lose the ability to bring it later). This is so because the two claims arise out of the same transaction or occurrence—that is, they both chiefly address the termination of employment on the basis of religion. Happily, the test under § 1367(a) tracks claim preclusion's same-transaction-and-occurrence rule. Thus, when a plaintiff would face claim preclusion for failure to join an additional claim, § 1367(a)'s nucleus-of-common-fact test will be met as well because the tests, while deploying different verbiage, lead to the same results.

Let us take a different example, one involving the joinder of a defendant's counterclaim. Assume a plaintiff, former corporate employer, sues a defendant, former CEO, for breach of a non-compete provision in the employment contract, seeking $100,000 in damages. The plaintiff is a Tennessee corporation and the defendant a Florida citizen. This suit will take federal jurisdiction handily under 28 U.S.C. § 1332 as the parties are completely diverse and more than \$75,000 is in controversy. Now let us assume that the defendant seeks to counterclaim for fraud, arguing that the non-compete provision was fraudulently inserted into the contract seeking \$50,000 in damages on the counterclaim. Because this counterclaim arises out of the same transaction as the original claim—it focuses upon the same contractual terms and their validity—it is a compulsory counterclaim under Federal Rule of Civil Procedure 13(a). But the fraud counterclaim cannot arise under § 1331, as it is a state-law claim, and it will not arise under § 1332 as it seeks less than \$75,000. The compulsory counterclaim will, however, satisfy § 1367(a), because the fraud claim arises out of a common nucleus of facts as the original non-compete claim, precisely because it focuses upon the same contractual terms and their validity. Again we see that the same-transaction-and-occurrence test of the Federal Rules of Civil Procedure works in tandem with § 1367(a)'s common-nucleus-of-operative-facts test to provide jurisdiction for the compulsory counterclaim.

Let's change this last hypothetical a bit. Now assume that the counterclaim is not for fraud, but for failure to pay bonuses three years ago. This new counterclaim does not arise out of the same transaction or occurrence as the non-complete claim, rendering the counterclaim a permissive one under Rule 13(b). Correspondingly, § 1367(a) will not be satisfied here, meaning that supplemental jurisdiction will not be available because the counterclaim for bonuses does not arise from a common nucleus of facts as the non-compete claim.

These examples aim to demonstrate that when joinder under the Federal Rules is allowed or mandated per the same-transaction-or-occurrence test—as it is under Rules 13(a), 13(g), 14, 20, and common law claim preclusion doctrine—then satisfaction of the common nucleus of fact test of § 1367(a) will invariably follow. There is a similar correspondence between the joinder tests lodged in the Federal Rules 19, 23 and 24 and § 1367(a)'s common-nucleus-of-fact test.

	Defendant	Plaintiff
Permissive claims	Rule 13(b) permissive counterclaim – no supplemental jurisdiction under § 1367(a).	Rule 18(a) permissive claim – no supplemental jurisdiction under § 1367(a).
Compulsory claims	Rule 13(a) compulsory counterclaim – supplemental jurisdiction under § 1367(a) + § 1367(b) prohibitions do not apply.	Common law res judicata – supplemental jurisdiction under § 1367(a), § 1367(b) prohibitions do not apply.

2. ANALYSIS OF § 1367(b)

Satisfaction of § 1367(a), while necessary, is not always sufficient for the vesting of supplemental jurisdiction. If a claim purports to exercise ancillary jurisdiction (i.e., the original claim arises in federal court solely on the basis of diversity), then the statute mandates an analysis under § 1367(b). Subsection (b) does not apply to additional claims arising under pendent jurisdiction (i.e., the original claims do not arise in federal court solely on the basis of diversity). As we will see shortly, subsection (b) restricts the use of ancillary supplemental jurisdiction.

The text of 28 U.S.C. § 1367(b) provides as follows:

> In any civil action of which the district courts have original jurisdiction **founded solely on section 1332** of this title, the district courts **shall not have supplemental jurisdiction** under subsection (a) **over claims by plaintiffs** against persons **made parties under Rule 14, 19, 20, or 24** of the Federal Rules of Civil Procedure, or **over claims by persons proposed to be joined as plaintiffs under Rule 19** of such rules, or seeking to intervene as plaintiffs **under Rule 24** of such rules, when exercising supplemental jurisdiction over such claims **would be inconsistent with the jurisdictional requirements of section 1332**.[8]

The first clause of the first sentence in subsection (b) states that this subsection applies only to exercises of ancillary jurisdiction. Recall, ancillary supplemental jurisdiction covers those instances in which the original case arises <u>solely</u> under § 1332 diversity jurisdiction. For example, if a plaintiff brings a Title VII suit, which arises under § 1331,

---

[8]   28 U.S.C. 1367(b) (emphasis added).

then any additional claims or counterclaims will be pendent, meaning that § 1367(b) is inapplicable. Similarly, if a plaintiff brings both a Title VII claim, arising under § 1331, and a wrongful discharge claim, arising under § 1332, then any additional claims or counterclaims remain pendent, meaning that § 1367(b) is inapplicable. This is so because the original claims are not *solely* based upon § 1332 jurisdiction. But if a plaintiff brings only state-law claims against the defendant, relying exclusively upon § 1332 for jurisdiction, then any additional supplemental claims or counterclaims will be ancillary, meaning that an analysis under § 1367(b) must be made.

Having settled that § 1367(b) applies only in exercises of ancillary supplemental jurisdiction, subsection (b) moves next to its substantive provisions. While these substantive rules embodied in subsection (b) can present a challenge, if we engage with them methodically and with an eye toward the purpose for the rule, we can come to an understanding of the operation of subsection (b).

Let us begin with the purpose for the rules codified in subsection (b), which is to preserve the integrity of the complete diversity rule. This is best explained by way of example. Imagine a plaintiff, a Kansas resident, wishes to sue four defendants, seeking $100,000 in damages from each defendant for medical malpractice in his recent heart surgery. The first defendant resides in Missouri while the other three reside in Kansas. The plaintiff here may not sue all four defendants at once in federal court as such a suit would run afoul of the complete diversity rule. Note, however, that the claims against all four defendants for medical malpractice in a heart operation arise from a common nucleus of facts. Because of this shared set of facts, a crafty plaintiff in this situation could take the option of suing just the Missouri defendant initially, thereby taking jurisdiction under § 1332. The parties would be completely diverse: the plaintiff resides in Kansas while the sole defendant resides in Missouri. Next, but for the existence of § 1367(b), our plaintiff could join the three Kansas defendants under Rule 20 and use § 1367(a) to take jurisdiction because the claims against these defendants arise from the same nucleus of facts (i.e., the same heart operation). In this hypothetical, where we imagine that § 1367 lacks a subsection (b), plaintiffs could avoid the complete diversity rule simply by suing the subset of defendants allowed under the complete diversity rule first and then using the joinder provisions of the Federal Rules and § 1367(a) to join the remaining non-diverse defendants second. Such a scheme would effectively gut the complete diversity rule.

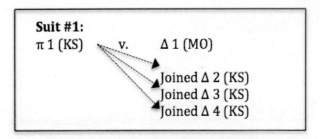

Suit #1:

π 1 (KS) v. Δ 1 (MO)

Joined Δ 2 (KS)
Joined Δ 3 (KS)
Joined Δ 4 (KS)

But for § 1367(b), joinder of defendants coupled with § 1367(a) would gut the complete diversity rule.

The same result would occur, but for subsection (b), if multiple plaintiffs sought to sue one defendant. For instance, assume three plaintiffs, the first residing in Kansas and the others in Missouri, seeking $100,000 each bring a defamation suit against one defendant, a Missouri resident. All three plaintiffs could not be original parties and take diversity jurisdiction. But for § 1367(b), however, the first plaintiff, the one residing in Kansas, could sue the Missouri defendant in federal court and take § 1332 jurisdiction. Then the additional parties could intervene under Rule 24 and take jurisdiction under § 1367(a), assuming a similar defamatory action is at issue. Again such a result would render the complete diversity rule a virtual nullity.

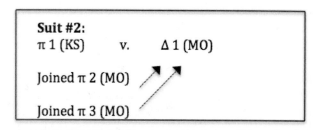

Subsection (b) aims to stop these types of "cheating" of the complete diversity rule by plaintiffs. The text states that, as to ancillary claims, even if § 1367(a) is satisfied, supplemental jurisdiction will not extend to two sets of additional claims, which correspond to our two hypotheticals above. First, ancillary supplemental jurisdiction will not extend to claims made by an original plaintiff against any party joined pursuant to Federal Rules of Civil Procedure 14, 19, 20 or 24. Thus, as to our heart-surgery hypothetical above, ancillary supplemental jurisdiction will not extend to the claims by the original plaintiff against the additional joined defendants because they were joined under Rule 20.

Second, ancillary supplemental jurisdiction will not extend to allow putative plaintiffs seeking to join a suit under Federal Rules of Civil Procedure 19 or 24 to enter the suit. Thus, as to our defamation example, ancillary supplemental jurisdiction will not extend to the claims by the putative intervening plaintiffs against the defendant because they joined the case under Rule 24. Thus, § 1367(b) preserves the integrity of the complete diversity rule by short-circuiting the ploys illustrated above.

Understanding what § 1367(b) does not bar, of course, is just as important as understanding what it docs prohibit. First, it is worth repeating that subsection (b) only applies these prohibitions to ancillary supplemental jurisdiction. As such, in a pendent jurisdiction case, a plaintiff could join a non-diverse defendant and bring a state-law claim so long as that state-law claim satisfied § 1367(a). Second, the prohibitions in ancillary jurisdiction codified in subsection (b) apply only to claims brought by plaintiffs or putative parties seeking to join as plaintiffs. Thus, defendant counterclaims, third-party actions, or cross-claims among defendants do not run afoul of § 1367(b). Third, as the last clause of § 1367(b) makes clear, subsection (b) does not prohibit the use of § 1332 when it applies. For example, a plaintiff, California resident, may not join a new defendant, an Oregon resident, and rely upon supplemental jurisdiction to support his state-law claim. Nevertheless, so long as the claim is for more than $75,000, the plaintiff could rely upon traditional § 1332 diversity jurisdiction to support the joinder.

As we have seen, § 1367(b) seeks to preserve the integrity of the complete diversity rule in cases using ancillary supplemental jurisdiction by barring the creative use of the liberal joinder philosophy of the Federal Rules of Civil Procedure and § 1367(a) jurisdiction. This fix would appear seamless. There is, however, a critical error in the drafting of § 1367(b), which creates some headaches. We turn our attention to this difficulty next.

The error lies in the clause prohibiting certain persons from joining as plaintiffs while relying upon supplemental jurisdiction. Subsection (b) states that the district courts shall not exercise § 1367(a) jurisdiction "over claims by persons proposed to be joined as plaintiffs under Rule 19 . . . , or seeking to intervene as plaintiffs under Rule 24." Rule 19, recall, is the rule for mandatory joinder of parties, and Rule 24 is the rule for intervention. Hence, § 1367(b) bars plaintiffs joined as necessary parties from using ancillary supplemental jurisdiction, and it bars plaintiffs joined as interveners from using ancillary supplemental jurisdiction. Yet, and this is the odd part, § 1367(b) does not prohibit plaintiffs permissively joined under Rule 20 from using ancillary supplemental jurisdiction. That is to say, the unadorned text of subsection (b) prohibits plaintiffs *mandatorily* joined from using ancillary supplemental jurisdiction, yet allows plaintiffs who are merely *permissively* joined under Rule 20 to rely upon supplemental jurisdiction. Such an outcome is illogical. The failure to include Rule 20 among the list of barred items in subsection (b) would appear to be an unintended drafting error.[9]

This error left the Supreme Court to craft a solution, which it did in *Exxon Mobil Corp. v.*

---

[9]   See *Exxon Mobil Corp. v. Allapattah Services, Inc.*, 545 U.S. 546, 565 (2005).

Allapattah Services, Inc.[10] The Court held that ancillary supplemental jurisdiction may vest for claims brought by plaintiffs added under Rule 20 without regard to the amount in controversy of these added claims so long as the added party does not destroy complete diversity. For example, suppose the plaintiff, a Michigan resident, sues defendant, an Ohio resident, seeking $100,000 for personal injuries resulting from a car crash. A second plaintiff could be joined under Rule 20 and seek less than $75,000 so long as that second plaintiff is not a resident of Ohio (i.e., so long as the joinder of the second plaintiff does not destroy complete diversity).

* * *

In sum, subsection (b) only applies to exercises of ancillary supplemental jurisdiction. The purpose of subsection (b) is to preserve the integrity of the complete diversity rule. To achieve this end, subsection (b) bars the exercise of ancillary supplemental jurisdiction to support additional claims brought by plaintiffs against parties joined pursuant to Rules 14, 19, 20 and 24. Similarly, subsection (b) bars the exercise of ancillary supplemental jurisdiction to support additional claims brought by putative parties seeking to be added as plaintiffs pursuant to Rules 19 and 24. Finally, per *Allopattah*, putative parties seeking to join as plaintiffs pursuant to Rule 20 may use ancillary supplemental jurisdiction to support their claims, without regard to the amount in controversy,

---

[10]   545 U.S. 546 (2005).

so long as their joinder does not destroy complete diversity.

3. ANALYSIS OF § 1367(c)

We forge ahead now to § 1367(c). All exercises of supplemental jurisdiction, be they pendent or ancillary, are subject to the dictates of subsection (c). In essence, subsection (c) constitutes a discretionary rule that allows the district court judge, on a case-by-case basis, to determine that a suit is better suited in state court. The text of 28 U.S.C. 1367(c) provides as follows:

> The district courts *may decline to exercise supplemental jurisdiction* over a claim under subsection (a) if—
>
> (1) the claim raises a *novel or complex issue* of State law,
>
> (2) the claim *substantially predominates* over the claim or claims over which the district court has original jurisdiction,
>
> (3) the district court has *dismissed all claims over which it has original jurisdiction*, or
>
> (4) in *exceptional circumstances*, there are other compelling reasons for declining jurisdiction.[11]

This rule is, thankfully, much more digestible than § 1367(b), presenting three basic fact patterns where

---

[11]   28 U.S.C. 1367(c) (emphasis added).

claims should be diverted to state court. First, in some cases the claim arising in supplemental jurisdiction will raise a question of state law that is unresolved by the state supreme court. Retaining the case in federal court, of course, deprives the state supreme court of the opportunity, absent certifying the question, to address the matter. In such cases, per § 1367(c)(1), the district court is empowered to decline jurisdiction over the additional claim. Second, in other suits the claim taking original federal jurisdiction may be insubstantial in comparison to the state-law claims. In such cases, the district court may elect not to take jurisdiction over the state-law claims. Third, if all of the original federal claims have been dismissed, the district court may dismiss the remaining supplemental claims without prejudice as well.

Subsections (a)–(c) form the core of the supplemental jurisdictional statute. The concepts we have review may also be viewed as a flow chart.

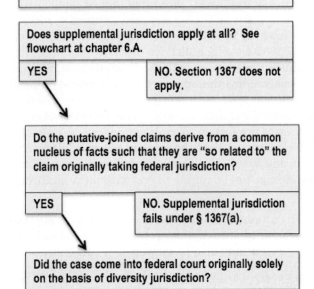

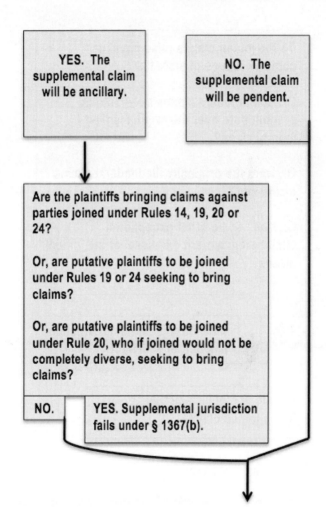

Do the joined claims raise novel or complex issues of state law?

Or, do the joined claims substantially predominate over the originally filed federal claim?

Or, were the originally filed federal claims dismissed?

Or, does some other exceptional circumstance merit dismissal of the joined claims?

NO.   YES. Supplemental jurisdiction fails under § 1367(c).

Supplemental jurisdiction applies to the joined claims.

4.   ANALYSIS OF § 1367(d)

Finally, given the complexity of the supplemental jurisdictional statute and the discretionary features of subsection (c), § 1367 provides a saving statute. A saving statute is one which extends the viability of a claim past the statute of limitations deadline when it is dismissed without prejudice. The text of § 1367(d) provides as follows:[12]

> The ***period of limitations for any claim asserted under subsection (a)***, and for any other claim in the same action that is voluntarily dismissed at the same time as or after the dismissal of the claim under subsection (a), ***shall be tolled while the claim is pending and for a period of 30 days after it is dismissed*** unless State law provides for a longer tolling period.[13]

Thus, if a claim is dismissed for lack of supplemental jurisdiction, the party bringing the claim will have at least 30 days to file the matter in the appropriate state court. The one exception to this rule lies with claims against a State or state agency as defendant.[14]

* * *

In closing, Congress grants the federal courts supplemental jurisdiction so as to allow efficient joinder of related claims in federal court. The federal courts may take supplemental jurisdiction over claims that otherwise could not arise in federal court

---

[12] The statute also includes a subsection (e), which provides that as "used in this section, the term "State" includes the District of Columbia, the Commonwealth of Puerto Rico, and any territory or possession of the United States."

[13] 28 U.S.C. § 1367(d) (emphasis added).

[14] See *Raygor v. Regents*, 534 U.S. 533 (2002).

only if a federal claim originally arises under one of the "standard" grounds for jurisdiction such as federal question or diversity. If an original claim has so arisen in federal court, then the parties, subject to the limitations of § 1367(b)-(c), may join all claims that derive from a common nucleus of fact in relation to the originally filed federal claim.

CHAPTER 7

REMOVAL JURISDICTION

"By statute 'any civil action brought in a State court of which the district courts of the United States have original jurisdiction, may be removed by the defendant or the defendants, to the [federal] district court.'"

—*Metro. Life Ins. Co. v. Taylor*, 481 U.S. 58, 63 (1987)

Up to this stage, we have envisioned suits as being originally filed in federal court, with the plaintiff making the decision at the point of filing to seek federal jurisdiction. Recall, however, that the bulk of federal jurisdiction is held concurrently with the state courts. Thus, in most cases, even if a plaintiff could have originally brought his case in federal court, he could elect to bring the suit in state court. In these instances—cases which could have been brought in federal court but the plaintiff has chosen to file in state court—the defendant is given the option to veto the choice of a state court forum and send the suit to federal court. This process is called "removal."

In this chapter, we will address the concepts necessary to operate removal of a case from state to federal court. We begin with a review of the general rule for removal as found in 28 U.S.C. § 1441. We turn second to the special rules that apply to the removal of diversity cases. Third, we address the procedural and timing aspects for removal. Fourth, we consider the relevant procedural rules that apply after a case has been removed. And we end with a brief mention of removal regimes beyond the primary § 1441 rule.

A. THE GENERAL RULE FOR REMOVAL

We turn first to the general rule for removal of cases from state to federal court. It is key to note that removal jurisdiction is entirely a creature of statute. Indeed, it is not required as a matter of constitutional law. Nevertheless, removal jurisdiction in one form or the other has been a feature of statutory jurisdictional law since the original Judiciary Act of 1789. The contemporary removal jurisdiction provisions are codified at 28 U.S.C. § 1441 et seq.

While there are many exceptions and timing nuances to delve into, the general rule for removal of an action from state court to federal court is straightforward. The statute provides that "any civil action brought in a State court of which the district courts of the United States have original jurisdiction, may be removed by the defendant."[1] This is to say, if the plaintiff could have filed the suit in federal court under any basis of jurisdiction but chose to proceed in state court, then the defendant may elect to remove the suit from state court to federal court.

Let's look to a few quick examples. First, a plaintiff, residing in Oregon, brings a 42 U.S.C. § 1983 claim against a defendant, an Ohio resident, in the Ohio state courts. Here, the defendant may

---

[1]   28 U.S.C. § 1441(a).

remove to federal court under 28 U.S.C. § 1441(a), because the plaintiff could have filed this suit in federal court under 28 U.S.C. § 1331 originally.

Plaintiff's Complaint	Defendant's Answer
• Federal-law Claim	• Federal Defense
Because π could have filed under § 1331, Δ may remove.	

Second, a plaintiff, residing in Iowa, brings a contract claim against a defendant, an Illinois resident, in the Iowa state courts for $80,000. Here, the defendant may remove to federal court under 28 U.S.C. § 1441(a), because the plaintiff could have filed this suit in federal court under 28 U.S.C. § 1332 originally.

Plaintiff's Complaint	Defendant's Answer
• Iowa resident • State-law claim for $80,000	• Illinois resident • State-law defense
Because π could have filed under § 1332, Δ may remove.	

Third, a plaintiff, residing in Texas, brings a contract claim against a defendant, an Alabama resident, in the Texas state courts for $60,000. Here, the defendant may not remove to federal court under 28 U.S.C. § 1441(a), because the plaintiff could not have filed this suit in federal court under 28 U.S.C. § 1332 originally, as it lacks a sufficient amount in controversy. Similarly, as the case does not raise a federal question, there is not § 1331 jurisdiction and as such the suit cannot be removed.

Plaintiff's Complaint	Defendant's Answer
• Texas resident • State-law claim for $60,000	• Alabama resident • State-law defense
Because π could not have filed under § 1332 (under $75,000) or § 1331 (no federal issues raised), Δ may not remove.	

Fourth, a plaintiff, residing in New York, brings a state-law libel claim against a defendant, a New York resident, in the New York state courts. The defendant asserts that the First Amendment to the federal Constitution provides an affirmative defense. Here, the defendant may not remove to federal court under 28 U.S.C. § 1441(a), because the plaintiff could not have filed this suit in federal court. Section 1331 could not provide jurisdiction here because filing in federal court runs afoul of the well-pleaded complaint rule—the only federal issue here is a defense. Similarly, the case could not arise in diversity jurisdiction because the parties are both New Yorkers.

Plaintiff's Complaint	**Defendant's Answer**
• New York resident	• New York resident
• State-law claim	• Federal-law defense

Because π could not have filed under § 1332 (parties not diverse) or § 1331 (fails the well-pleaded-complaint rule), Δ may not remove.

These examples, then, demonstrate the general rule. A defendant may remove a case to federal court if the case could have been filed in federal court in the first instance. This leaves the question, however, of which federal court is the case sent. Section 1441(a) states that cases are to be removed "to the district court of the United States for the district and division embracing the place where such action is pending." This rule, again, is quite simple. For example, if a case is removed from the New York state court in Manhattan, then it is removed to the U.S. District Court for the Southern District of New York as this federal court covers the island of Manhattan.

A few other points about this general rule are worthy of note. First, a bit of terminology. If a case is unsuccessfully removed to federal court, we deploy the term "remand" for the act of returning the suit to the state courts. This can cause confusion as appellate courts also use the term "remand" when sending a matter back to a trial court for further proceedings. But in context, the use of the term remand should not be overly vexing.

Second, in removal cases, because the defendant—as opposed to the plaintiff—invokes federal jurisdiction, the burden to establish federal jurisdiction rests upon the defendant, even though normally the burden would be on the plaintiff. So, a defendant on removal has the burden to establish that the plaintiff could have filed in federal court originally.

Third, while a successful removal to federal court will establish subject matter jurisdiction in that court, removal does not speak to personal jurisdiction. That is to say, a defendant could well remove from state to federal court and then challenge personal jurisdiction. Students are often confused on this point, likely because while removal does not affect personal jurisdiction it does affect venue. Pursuant to § 1441(a), a successful removal to federal court establishes that the federal court has venue. So a successful removal to federal court means that the federal court in question has subject matter jurisdiction and venue, but not necessarily personal jurisdiction.

Finally, a defendant may seek removal to federal court, assuming that the plaintiff could have properly filed there originally, even if the state court lacks jurisdiction. Such matters come about when a plaintiff erroneously files a matter of exclusive federal jurisdiction in a state court. For example, a plaintiff, a Georgia resident, sues a defendant, also a Georgian, in Georgia state court for copyright infringement. Copyright infringement suits belong to that small set of cases in which the federal district courts hold exclusive jurisdiction, meaning that the Georgia state courts lack subject matter jurisdiction. Despite the lack of jurisdiction in the state court, the defendant may, pursuant to 28 U.S.C. § 1441(f), rely upon § 1441(a) to remove the case to federal court. Older case law did not allow this type of removal, but Congress' addition of subsection (f) overruled those decisions.

B. REMOVAL OF CASES IN DIVERSITY JURISDICTION

While removal of federal question cases under § 1331 proceeds simply by following the general protocols of § 1441(a) outlined above, cases in which the suit would enter federal court originally "solely on the basis of the jurisdiction under section 1332(a)"[2] face an additional hurdle. The statute prohibits "home state" defendants from removing to federal court in suits solely founded upon diversity jurisdiction. We turn now to this provision.

Recall that "the purpose of . . . diversity [jurisdiction] . . . is to provide a federal forum for important disputes where state courts might favor, or be perceived as favoring, home-state litigants."[3] Diversity jurisdiction, then, alleviates this concern by taking suits between citizens of different states, or state citizens and foreign citizens, out of the state court system and into a neutral federal court.

---

[2]   28 U.S.C. § 1441(b)(2).

[3]   *Exxon Mobil Corp. v. Allapattah Servs., Inc.*, 545 U.S. 546, 553 (2005).

This policy has important implications for removal of diversity cases. Given this purpose, it makes sense that if defendants are forced to defend outside of their home states, typically in the plaintiff's home state, they should be able to remove federal court. Section 1441 allows this type of removal. By this same token, if an out-of-state plaintiff chooses to sue a defendant in the defendant's home-state courts—meaning that the out-of-state plaintiff would suffer any bias against out-of-state litigants—the general purposes supporting diversity jurisdiction would not be served by allowing the defendant to remove. Following this policy, then, § 1441(b)(2) states that suits "may not be removed if any of the . . . properly joined and served . . . defendants is a citizen of the State in which such action is brought."

Let's consider two examples. First, reconsider an example from above where we had a plaintiff, residing in Iowa, bringing a contract claim against a defendant, an Illinois resident, in the Iowa state courts for $80,000. Here, the defendant may remove to federal court under 28 U.S.C. § 1441(a), because the plaintiff could have filed this suit in federal court under 28 U.S.C. § 1332 originally. Moreover, the extra hurdle for removal of diversity cases found in § 1441(b)(2) does not apply because the Illinois defendant is being sued in an Iowa state court (i.e., not in defendant's home-state court).

Plaintiff's Complaint	**Defendant's Answer**
• Iowa resident • State-law claim for $80,000	• Illinois resident • State-law defense

Case filed in Iowa state court system. Because π could have filed under § 1332, Δ may remove. The ban upon home-state removal does not apply because Δ is not an Iowan.

Now consider a similar case. A plaintiff, residing in Florida, brings a contract claim against a defendant, a North Carolina resident, in the North Carolina state courts for $80,000. Here, § 1441(a) would allow removal because the plaintiff could have filed this suit in federal court under 28 U.S.C. § 1332 originally. But removal is not appropriate here because of the ban on home-state removals of diversity cases found in § 1441(b)(2). Because the defendant is a North Carolina resident and the case is filed in North Carolina, the suit may not be removed from state court—even though the plaintiff could have filed it in federal court in the first instance.

Plaintiff's Complaint	Defendant's Answer
• Florida resident • State-law claim for $80,000	• North Carolina resident • State-law defense

Case filed in North Carolina state court system. Because π could have filed under § 1332, Δ may presumptively remove. But because Δ resides in North Carolina, the ban upon home-state removal applies in this case.

C. PROCEDURE FOR REMOVAL

Having determined a suit eligible for removal, 28 U.S.C. § 1446 sets out the procedural regime for effectuating removal. First, pursuant to § 1446(a), a defendant seeking removal must file in the *federal* district court "a notice of removal signed pursuant to Rule 11 . . . containing a short and plain statement of the grounds for removal, together with a copy of all process, pleadings, and orders served upon such defendant." Second, under § 1446(d), the defendant seeking removal must serve a written notice of removal upon all adverse parties and file of a copy of the removal notice with the *state* court clerk's office. Filing with the state court effectuates a stay of the state court proceedings "unless and until the case is remanded."[4] Failure to file a copy of the notice of removal with the state court would result in the case continuing to proceed in both the state and federal courts. Students new to procedure tend to forget this step, erroneously believing that filing with the

---

[4]   28 U.S.C. § 1446(d).

federal court sufficient to end the state-court proceedings. So it is worth repeating that if the defendant wants the state proceedings to halt—which is why the defendant is removing in the first place—the state court must be served separately from the filing of notice in the federal court.

This leaves the question of timing. That is to say, how long does a defendant, or defendants, have from learning a case is eligible for removal to make the decision to file a notice of removal with the federal district court? Here we have a short series of rules codified at 28 U.S.C. 1446(b) and (c).

We begin with the general rule. If the originally filed complaint is eligible for removal under § 1441—meaning plaintiff could have filed the original complaint in federal court and there is no home-state bar upon removal—then, following § 1446(b)(1), the defendant has 30 days after the receipt of service of process to file notice of removal in the federal court. So, if a Title VII action is filed in state court on June 1, the defendant would have up to July 1 to remove the case to federal court. By July 2, the case is no longer eligible for removal, even though a federal question is presented. This rule applies equally for suits in diversity jurisdiction.

We move now to a slight variation on the general rule. Often the original complaint in a lawsuit filed in state court does not raise a matter eligible for federal jurisdiction but is later amended to add a claim that is amenable to federal jurisdiction. For example, a plaintiff might file a state-law wrongful discharge tort against her former employer and then some months later, after some discovery has occurred, amend the complaint to add a federal Title VII claim, which can arise under § 1331 jurisdiction. Similarly, a plaintiff, residing in Delaware, might file a state law wrongful discharge tort against her former employer, a New Jersey corporation, for $50,000 and then four months later, after some discovery has occurred, amend the complaint to add an additional $30,000 in damages, rendering the complaint eligible to arise in § 1332 diversity jurisdiction.

Section 1446(b)(3) governs these situations. It states that if the original complaint was not removable, "a notice of removal may be filed within thirty days after receipt . . . of a copy of an amended pleading, motion, order or other paper from which it may first be ascertained that the case is . . . removable." Thus in both examples above, the defendant would have 30 days from the serving of the amended complaint, which contained the claim subject to federal jurisdiction, to file a notice of removal in the federal district court.

This leads to yet another wrinkle in the timing rules. Recall that even a relatively straightforward lawsuit in a state court may go through several amended complaints. This process often takes several months or years, with the plaintiff gaining information in discovery and amending the complaint accordingly. Under § 1446(b)(3), then, the defendant gets a new thirty-day clock to file notice of removal at any time—say, in the third year of the lawsuit—once a complaint is amended to show a claim amenable to federal jurisdiction.

Section 1446(c)(1) creates an exception to this provision for suits that would be removable solely on the basis of § 1332. For such diversity suits, § 1446(c)(1) provides that the "case may not be removed . . . more than 1 year after commencement of the action, unless the district court finds that the plaintiff has acted in bad faith in order to prevent a defendant from removing the action."

Let's return to our employment examples from above to illustrate. First, assume a plaintiff files a state-law wrongful discharge tort against her former employer and then 15 months later, after some discovery has occurred, amends the complaint to add a federal Title VII claim. The addition of the Title VII claim means that the case can arise under § 1331 jurisdiction. Further, because the original complaint lacked a federal issue, the defendant would have 30 days from the filing of the amended complaint to remove to federal court. Finally, because the removal in this instance is based upon § 1331 jurisdiction, the one-year provision of 1446(c) is inapplicable.

Second, assume a plaintiff, residing in Delaware, files a state-law wrongful discharge tort against her former employer, a New Jersey corporation, for $50,000 and then 15 months later, after some discovery has occurred, amends the complaint to add $30,000 in damages. This amendment renders the complaint eligible to arise in § 1332 diversity jurisdiction—the parties are completely diverse and the amount in controversy is now met. Nevertheless, because the removal would be based solely upon diversity jurisdiction and more than a year has passed since the filing of the original complaint in state court, § 1446(c)(1) bars the removal of this case. The only way to avoid this bar upon removal is to make a showing to the federal district court that the plaintiff acted in bad faith, a tough standard to meet, in pleading the case so as to avoid § 1332 jurisdiction.

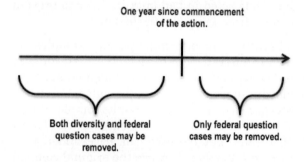

One year since commencement of the action.

Both diversity and federal question cases may be removed.

Only federal question cases may be removed.

So far, then, we have imagined cases with but one defendant. In these cases, if the original complaint is amenable to federal jurisdiction, the defendant has 30 days to file a notice of removal. If the federal issue first arises only in an amended complaint, then the defendant has 30 days from the service of the amended complaint to file a notice of removal, subject to the rule of § 1446(c) that suits arising solely upon diversity may not file a notice of removal more than one year after the commencement of the action in state court.

These three basic timing rules become a bit more complex in application when there is more than one defendant. First of all, § 1446(b)(2)(A) requires that "all defendants who have been properly joined and served must join in or consent to the removal of the action." This provision prohibits one defendant from acting alone in removal. For example, assume a plaintiff sues defendants #1 and #2 in state court, alleging a 42 U.S.C. § 1983 claim for violating his federal constitutional rights. In this example, assuming both defendants are served properly, defendant #1 could not unilaterally remove the case to federal court, even though the matter readily arises in § 1331, without first getting the consent of defendant #2. As a corollary to this rule, a lone defendant who is properly served has a functional veto over removal. For instance, assume a plaintiff sues defendants #1–#99 in state court, alleging 42 U.S.C. § 1983 violations. Assuming all the defendants are properly served, defendant #99, by refusing to consent to removal, could prevent the remaining 98 defendants from removing the case.

Further adding to timing complications in cases with multiple defendants is the fact that defendants are often served at different times. It is quite common, at the beginning of a suit, for defendant #1 to be served on, say, the fifth day after filing, while defendant #2 is served, say, on the eightieth day. Also, when dealing with joinder and amendment, a new defendant #3 may well be joined and served months or years after the previous defendants. In cases where defendants are joined and served at differing times, § 1446(b)(2)(B) states that "[e]ach defendant shall have 30 days after receipt by or service on that defendant of the . . . pleading . . . to file the notice of removal." Thus, if a defendant #1 is served on day 5, he has until day 36 to remove, while defendant #2, served on day 80, has until day 111 to remove.

These rules for service at differing times must be overlaid upon the rule in § 1446(b)(2)(A), requiring unanimity among the defendants for removal. Thus in our running example, if defendant #1 is served on day 5, and no other defendants are served until day 80, defendant #1 retains a unilateral right to remove for 30 days, up to day 36. Now assume that defendant #1 did not remove during his 30-day window. After this 30-day period closes, the case becomes no longer removable. But when defendant #2 is served on day 80, he gets his own 30-day window of opportunity to remove per § 1446(b)(2)(B). But now, because two defendants are properly served, § 1446(b)(2)(A) requires that all the defendants agree to the removal. Thus for this second 30-day window, removal may only be accomplished with the agreement of both defendants #1 and #2. Now in our hypothetical, defendant #1 chose not to remove during his initial 30-day removal window. Nevertheless, § 1446(b)(2)(C) allows that "any earlier-served defendant"—in our example defendant #1—"may consent to the removal even though that earlier-served defendant did not previously initiate or consent to removal." As such, defendant #1 is free to consent to removal during this second 30-day window even though he did not exercise the right to removal before.

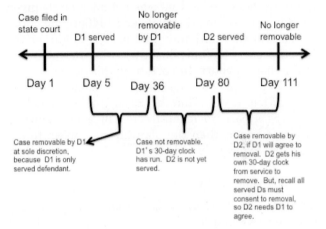

D.   PROCEDURE AFTER REMOVAL

Having found a suit amenable to removal and having timely removed it, 28 U.S.C. § 1447 governs the remaining matters in the federal district court pertaining to removal. First, § 1447(a) empowers the federal district court to bring all previously served parties before it, even if the service was effectuated by the state court, and empowers the district court to issue service to all other potential parties. Second, § 1447(b) empowers the federal district court to obtain all documents from the state court, typically with costs flowing to the removing party, either by ordering the removing party to produce the documents or by writ of certiorari directly to the state court.

Third, § 1447(c) sets a 30-day period for objections to the process of removal to be heard. That is to say, if a party believes that he was not adequately given written notice of the removal per § 1446(d), the notice of removal was untimely filed per § 1446(b), or the like, this party has only 30 days to raise this objection in the district court. Importantly, this 30-day period does not apply to objections to subject matter jurisdiction itself. That is to say, if a defendant removes a case to federal court in a procedurally proper manner, then the plaintiff may object to the lack of federal jurisdiction at any time. Only objections to the mechanics of removal are subject to a 30-day viability period.

Subsection 1447(d) is of special note. Generally speaking, when a federal district court holds that it lacks subject matter jurisdiction, this determination is appealable as a final order to the United States Circuit Courts of Appeal under 28 U.S.C. § 1291. In a removal case, however, if the district court holds that federal jurisdiction does not lie, an "order remanding a case to the State court from which it was removed is not reviewable on appeal or otherwise."[5] So while a district court's determination that federal jurisdiction does lie would eventually be appealable after final judgment, in a removal case its decision to remand to state court for lack of federal subject matter jurisdiction would not. This rule is a quirk of removal jurisdiction designed to prevent defendants from removing cases that clearly lack federal jurisdiction and then seeking appeal merely as a stalling tactic.

---

[5]   28 U.S.C. § 1447(d).

Finally, § 1447(e) allows a plaintiff in a diversity case to seek joinder of an additional party that would destroy diversity jurisdiction. The district court is granted the discretion to allow or disallow such joinder. If joinder is allowed, the case must be remanded. Hence, § 1447(e) can be used by a plaintiff as a kind of countermove to defendant's removal, deploying joinder to take the case back to the plaintiff's original choice of forum.

E.   OTHER REMOVAL REGIMES

In this chapter, we have addressed removal primarily of § 1331 and § 1332 cases pursuant to § 1441(a). Congress has provided for other types of removal that we are not covering here, but one should know that these other provisions exist. For example, 28 U.S.C. § 1442 allows for federal officers to remove from state court with but a federal affirmative defense, in violation of the well-pleaded complaint rule that governs § 1331 cases. Similarly, 28 U.S.C. § 1443 allows for the removal of enumerated civil rights claims. Congress also prohibits the removal of certain claims in 28 U.S.C. § 1445, even if they would arise in diversity jurisdiction, most notably workers' compensation claims.

* * *

In sum, removal jurisdiction allows a defendant to second-guess plaintiff's choice of a state-court forum. Subject to the myriad of exceptions and timing rules addressed above, if a state-court case could have been filed in federal court originally, a defendant may exercise his right to remove it to federal court under

§ 1441(a). This power, in turn, may incentivize plaintiffs who wish to remain in state court to craft carefully their complaints so as to avoid raising claims amenable to federal jurisdiction.

CHAPTER 8

JUSTICIABILITY

"[T]he Article III prohibition against advisory opinions [is] reflect[ed] . . . by the justiciability doctrine: Federal judicial power is limited to those disputes . . . consistent with a system of separated powers and which are traditionally thought to be capable of resolution through the judicial process."

—*Flast v. Cohen*, 392 U.S. 83, 97 (1968)

Up until this chapter, we have focused upon individual congressional grants of subject matter jurisdiction to the United States District Courts. In this chapter, we take a different focus. Here we look to subject matter jurisdictional doctrine, deriving from Article III of the Constitution, that must adhere to any case heard in federal court, regardless of which type of congressionally granted jurisdiction is deployed. This body of law is collectively labeled justiciability doctrine. Falling under this general heading, which is treated as a subject matter jurisdictional limitation upon the federal courts, we find the following doctrine: standing, mootness, ripeness, and political question. We begin our overview of this body of law with a discussion of justiciability in general, followed by a discussion of each component doctrine in turn.

A. JUSTICIABILITY DOCTRINE GENERALLY

Justiciability doctrine is the body of law that limits the subject matter jurisdiction of the federal courts regardless of which type of congressionally granted jurisdiction is at issue. That is to say, justiciability law applies equally in federal question cases, diversity cases, admiralty cases and so on. Collectively, its four component doctrine—standing, mootness, ripeness and political question—create a set of minimal requirements that every case must meet in order for the federal courts to have constitutional authority to hear to hear it. Like all subject matter jurisdictional law, justiciability determinations proceed claim-by-claim, such that a court could find claims x and y justiciable, while concluding that claim z is not.

All of justiciability doctrine purports to derive from Article III, section 2, clause 1 of the Constitution, which states that the federal courts may only resolve "cases . . . and controversies."[1] The courts, in turn, view this constitutional text as spawning two broad principles that inform justiciability law. The first of these is a ban upon advisory opinions. The second principle this volume labels as a concern for the

---

[1] Because justiciability doctrine derives from Article III of the federal Constitution, it does not directly bind state courts. State courts look to their own constitutions for questions of judicial authority. As a result, many state-court systems have very different justiciability regimes than are found in the federal courts.

counter-majoritarian difficulty.[2] Let's turn now to these principles.

1. NO ADVISORY OPINIONS

An advisory opinion is a ruling from a court that does not resolve a particular case, but rather expounds upon a legal issue in general without being in the context of a live dispute. As such, an advisory opinion almost always lacks opposing parties; rather, in an advisory opinion, one person or governmental actor seeks prospective advice from the court prior to taking action. Generally, the person seeking advice wishes to avoid later lawsuits with the force of the opinion.

At the time of the nation's founding, English courts regularly gave advisory opinions. Continuing with this tradition, the Canadian Supreme Court still issues advisory opinions from time to time as do ten state high courts.[3] Advisory opinions remain an integral part of the legal tradition in continental Europe and in several international tribunals, including the International Court of Justice. The federal courts, however, have consistently refused to engage in the practice.

---

[2] The author borrows the term from Alexander Bickel. See The Least Dangerous Branch: The Supreme Court at the Bar of Politics at 16 (Bobbs-Merril 1962).

[3] Alabama, Colorado, Delaware, Florida, Maine, Massachusetts, Michigan, New Hampshire, Rhode Island and South Dakota. See Mel A. Topf, The Jurisprudence of the Advisory Opinion Process in Rhode Island, 2 R. Williams L. Rev. 254, 256 (1997). Nevertheless, today most state attorneys general perform this advisory function by issuing formal opinion letters.

This custom dates back to the Washington administration. In the midst of an international crisis threatening to draw the newly formed United States into the war between Britain and France, President Washington sought an advisory opinion from the Supreme Court in July 1793 concerning the United States' obligations under the 1778 Franco-American Treaty. The French insisted that the treaty allowed the French ambassador to commission privateers in the United States. Washington saw this French insistence as in conflict with his recent Proclamation of Neutrality. Washington, via letter drafted by Secretary of State Thomas Jefferson, sought the Court's advice on twenty-nine issues related to the treaty.

The Court refused to enter this fray. Chief Justice Jay, on behalf of five Justices, wrote back:

> The Lines of Separation drawn by the Constitution between the three Departments of Government—their being in certain Respects checks upon each other and our being Judges of a court in the last Resort—are Considerations which afford strong arguments against the Propriety of our extra judicially deciding the questions alluded to; especially as the Power given by the Constitution to the President of calling on the Heads of Departments for opinions, seems to have been purposely as well

as expressly limited to the executive
Departments.[4]

As such, the Supreme Court instructed President
Washington to seek the advice of his attorney
general.[5] Since this letter, the federal courts have
universally held that they lack subject matter
jurisdiction to issue advisory opinions.[6] Only in the
context of a live case or controversy, then, may the
federal courts offer legal opinions.

2.   COUNTER-MAJORITARIAN PROBLEM

The second broad principle flowing from Article III
that informs justiciability doctrine is the counter-
majoritarian problem.[7] The federal courts are, by
design, mostly free of democratic accountability.
After nomination and confirmation, which in itself is
not overly accountable to the electorate, federal
judges sit for life with no reduction in salary, subject
only to impeachment for cause. By design, this
insulation protects the rights of political minorities
from ever-fickle electoral winds, acting as a counter-
majoritarian check upon governmental action.

There are many issues, however, in which the will
of the electorate, or the threat of electoral

---

[4]   3 Correspondence and Public Papers of John Jay at 488 (H.
Johnston ed. 1891).

[5]   Today this advisory function is now fulfilled in the federal
government by the Department of Justice, Office of Legal Counsel.

[6]   See, e.g., *Vieth v. Jubelirer*, 541 U.S. 267, 302 (2004)
(plurality).

[7]   See Henry P. Monaghan, Constitutional Adjudication: The
Who and When, 82 Yale L.J. 1363, 1366 (1973).

accountability, must control. For example, we now expect that after a presidential election, federal agencies will shift regulatory policy to reflect the new president's philosophy. If any one person or group, without some unique harm to himself, could thwart such regulatory changes by court injunction, democratic governance of the nation could well grind to a halt. Similarly, many other matters, such as international relations, are specifically assigned by the Constitution to the political branches of government. Again, allowing our courts to navigate the seas of diplomacy under the guise of adjudicating a law suit would undermine democratic control of an essential governmental function.

In matters such as these, justiciability doctrine acts as a bar to federal subject matter jurisdiction precisely because counter-majoritarian courts have little institutional capacity to address them. In other words, justiciability doctrine are often best understood as a unique application of separation-of-powers principles. Following these principles, the federal courts, by way of a subject matter jurisdictional ban, flatly refuse even to hear, much less rule upon, these matters better resolved by the democratically accountable branches.

As we turn to the four component doctrine, it is helpful to keep these two principles in mind as a guide. Thus, one may think of the mootness and ripeness doctrine as being applications of the no-advisory-opinions principle. Similarly, the political-question doctrine is readily conceived of as an application of the counter-majoritarian principle.

Finally, one may benefit from thinking of standing doctrine as being informed by both the no-advisory-opinions and counter-majoritarian principles.

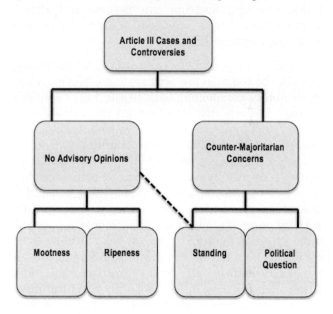

B.   STANDING DOCTRINE

Of the four component justiciability doctrine, standing has the most wide-ranging effect upon federal-court litigation. Standing law asks whether the particular plaintiff before the court has a sufficiently immediate and personal stake in the particular claim brought to render it justiciable. Standing's requirement for an immediate, as opposed to future, interest in the claim is an expression of the no-advisory-opinions principle, while the doctrine's requirement for a personal, as opposed to a public or mere taxpayer, interest in the dispute is an expression of the counter-majoritarian principle. While standing doctrine can become reticulated, keeping these two core principles in mind can help make the doctrine less opaque.

Standing as a unique body of law, while having roots in the common law writ systems, became a key justiciability component only in the mid twentieth century. Importantly, standing has its most saliency in suits for injunction against governmental actors, most typically agencies. Thus, traditional common law, or common law-like,[8] suits for monetary damages invariably have standing. It is in suits that raise the counter-majoritarian concern—e.g., suits to thwart governmental action brought by plaintiffs with no personalized, as opposed to only a political, interest—that plaintiffs tend to lack standing. It is no surprise, then, that the law of standing is now an integral feature of both constitutional and administrative law, as it is in these substantive arenas where one is most likely to find individual plaintiffs seeking to block prospective or on-going government conduct by injunction.[9] As a rule of

---

[8] By which the author means statutes creating tort-like or contract-like actions for monetary damages against non-government actors. See, e.g., *United Food and Commercial Workers Union Local 751 v. Brown Group, Inc.,* 517 U.S. 544 (1996).

[9] Suits by states against the federal government raise different concerns and are subject to loosened rules for standing, which go beyond the scope of this book. See, e.g., *Massachusetts v. E.P.A.,* 549 U.S. 497 (2007) and *American Elec. Power Co. v. Connecticut,* 131 S. Ct. 2527 (2011).

thumb, then, if a suit involves only private parties and a governmental agency's action is not otherwise at issue in the case, then standing is unlikely to be an issue.[10] On the other hand, in suits for injunction between private plaintiffs and a government agency as a defendant (or between private parties yet having implications for the enforcement of agency action), standing may well be a key concern.[11]

The Supreme Court has divided standing doctrine into two categories: (1) constitutional, or Article III, standing; and (2) prudential standing. Constitutional standing derives directly from the case-or-controversy requirement of Article III and forms an "irreducible constitutional minimum" for suits to enter federal court.[12] Prudential standing embodies "judicially self-imposed limits on the exercise of federal jurisdiction,"[13] which may be overcome by Congress. These prudential rules are more flexible than those of Article III standing, "designed to protect the courts from deciding abstract questions of wide public significance even when other

---

[10]   This is of course a rule of thumb. For example, the Court found a lack of standing in a suit between two private parties in *Steel Co. v. Citizens for a Better Environment*, 523 U.S. 83, 100 (1998). But even here, the plaintiff's claim arose by statute because the EPA had failed to act to enforce environmental disclosure rules, continuing to demonstrate the connectivity between standing doctrine and agency action or inaction.

[11]   See, e.g., *Allen v. Wright*, 468 U.S. 737 (1984) (finding no standing to enjoin the IRS).

[12]   *Lujan v. Defenders of Wildlife*, 504 U.S. 555, 560 (1992).

[13]   *United States v. Windsor*, 133 S. Ct. 2675, 2685 (2013).

governmental institutions may be more competent to address the questions."[14]

The Court further divides these two categories in sub-elements. Thus, Article III standing requires that the plaintiff present: (1) an injury-in-fact, (2) that is fairly traceable to the conduct of the defendant, (3) which is redressable by the courts via the remedy sought.[15] Prudential standing prohibits a plaintiff from bringing: (1) the claims of third parties, and (2) generalized grievances that are more properly brought to a politically accountable branch of government.[16] Prior to 2014, the Court included yet a third sub-element to prudential standing, the zone-of-interest-of-the-statute test. The Court now holds that "prudential standing is a misnomer as applied to the zone-of-interests analysis."[17] The Court currently analyzes zone of interest "using traditional tools of statutory interpretation, [to determine] whether a legislatively conferred cause of action encompasses a particular plaintiff's claim."[18]

---

[14]   Id. at 2686 (internal citation and quotations omitted).

[15]   *Lujan*, 504 U.S. at 560–61.

[16]   *Allen*, 468 U.S. at 751.

[17]   *Lexmark Int'l, Inc. v. Static Control Components, Inc.*, 134 S. Ct. 1377, 1387 (2014) (internal citations and quotations omitted).

[18]   Id.

Standing Doctrine Overview

Article III Standing
- Injury in Fact
- Traceability
- Redressability

Prudential Standing
- No Third-Party Claims
- No Generalized Grievances

"The party invoking federal jurisdiction bears the burden of establishing these elements."[19] Moreover, the level of proof needed to satisfy the elements of standing mimics the procedural posture of the case. At the pleading stage, then, factual allegations of injury resulting from the defendant's action may suffice, while at summary judgment the party invoking jurisdiction must set forth specific facts meeting the elements of standing. And at trial, those facts (if controverted) must be supported adequately by the evidence.[20] We proceed now to an element-by-element discussion of Article III standing.

1.   INJURY IN FACT

The first element of Article III standing is injury in fact, which is yet again divided into three parts. A plaintiff suffers an injury in fact if, he shows "[1] an invasion of a legally protected interest [2] which is . . .

---

[19]   *Lujan*, 504 U.S. at 561.

[20]   Id.

concrete and particularized, and . . . [3] actual or imminent."[21] Injury in fact is the heart of the standing inquiry, which links to our two broad principles animating justiciability doctrine. The injury-in-fact inquiry "serves to prevent the judicial process from being used to usurp the powers of the political branches,"[22] preserving political matters to the elected branches of government, by demanding legally cognizable interests that are actually suffered by the plaintiff—as opposed to harms to the general public welfare. At the same time, injury in fact aims to prevent issuance of advisory opinions with its actual or imminent component.

a. Legally Cognizable Interest

Under the injury-in-fact test, a plaintiff must claim an interest cognizable in court. While we cannot catalogue all of these here, one can note that the Court tends to find asserted interests with constitutional, statutory, and traditional common law origins (viz., financial, bodily, and property related injuries) cognizable, while eschewing others. A few examples suffice to make this admittedly overly broad generalization. Thus, suffering financial consequences constitutes a legally cognizable interest.[23] Changes in allocation of water rights, or other property rights, are legally cognizable.[24] On the other hand, "increases in the 'hard money' limits for

---

[21]   Id. at 560.

[22]   *Clapper v. Amnesty Int'l USA*, 133 S. Ct. 1138, 1146 (2013).

[23]   *Windsor*, 133 S. Ct. at 2686.

[24]   *Bennett v. Spear*, 520 U.S. 154, 167 (1997).

campaign contributions [that] diminished [plaintiffs'] ability to influence the election process. . . . [is] not a legally cognizable right."[25] Neither is the demand that the IRS enforce its own regulations that prohibit the granting of tax-exempt status to racially discriminatory schools, as the Court "has repeatedly held that an asserted right to have the Government act in accordance with law is not sufficient, standing alone, to confer jurisdiction."[26]

b. Concrete and Particularized

In addition to presenting a legally cognizable interest, the injury-in-fact test requires that the plaintiff's harm be concrete and particularized. The basic notion here is that the plaintiff's own legally cognizable interest must actually be negatively affected to support a lawsuit. Mere speculative assertions that an interest will be affected later, or injuries in the abstract, will not suffice.[27] Again, the Court's rulings in this regard are many and varied. Nonetheless, the closer a plaintiff can tie the damage to the cognizable interest to himself personally, the more likely it is that the Court will find the injury concrete and particularized. Thus, when the plaintiff himself is the focus of the government's conduct, "there is ordinarily little question that the action or inaction has caused him injury . . . [for purposes of standing]. When, however, . . . a plaintiff's asserted

---

[25]   *McConnell v. Federal Election Com'n*, 540 U.S. 93, 226–27 (2003).

[26]   *Allen*, 468 U.S. at 754.

[27]   See *Schlesinger v. Reservists Committee to Stop the War*, 418 U.S. 208, 216–27 (1974).

injury arises from the government's allegedly unlawful regulation (or lack of regulation) of *someone else*, much more is needed."[28]

Often this test is easily met. Claims for monetary damages for past personal, property, or contractual harms easily pass this test, as they are so obviously assertions of a unique injury to the plaintiff in which he has a "personal stake."[29] The more difficult cases come when a plaintiff seeks to enjoin an on-going or future government action. For example, the Bureau of the Census' proposed use of a sampling scheme to count residents that was demonstrated to undercount persons to such an extent as to reduce Indiana's representation in the House of Representatives after the census constituted a concrete and particularized injury to Indiana voters.[30] While the injury was perhaps slight, it did inure to each plaintiff voter personally. On the other hand, the Court has held that a pediatrician lacked standing to appeal a decision holding invalid several abortion regulations, because the doctor had "no direct stake, in the abortion process."[31] Again, this notion of personal stake in the legally cognizable interest was key to the Court's analysis.

---

[28]   *Lujan*, 504 U.S. at 561–62 (emphasis in the original).

[29]   See *Hollingsworth v. Perry*, 133 S. Ct. 2652, 2663 (2013).

[30]   *Dep't of Commerce v. U.S. House of Representatives*, 525 U.S. 316, 332 (1999).

[31]   *Diamond v. Charles*, 476 U.S. 54, 66 (1986).

c. Actual or Imminent

Finally, the injury-in-fact requirement mandates that concrete injuries to legally cognizable injuries must have happened in the past, be currently on-going, or to be on the immediate cusp of occurring. Here the no-advisory-opinions principle heavily influences the doctrine. Under this provision, monetary damages to compensate a past injury readily satisfy the rule. Similarly, an injunction to change a now-occurring course of conduct easily meets the dictates of the requirement.[32]

The difficult cases come from those suits in which the plaintiff seeks to enjoin future, but not yet occurring, conduct. On the one hand, the Court has ruled that a declared and registered, self-financed candidate for Congress who would in the near future have to comply with the campaign-finance regulation being challenged faced an imminent injury.[33] Other future injuries, however, have been found to lack this immediacy. Thus, the Court ruled that a reasonable fear that the government is likely to intercept private communications in the future "is inconsistent with . . . [the] requirement that threatened injury must be certainly impending to constitute injury in fact."[34] Similarly, an assertion that the plaintiffs have vague and non-specific intentions to return "someday" to a

---

[32]   See, e.g., *Monsanto Co. v. Geertson Seed Farms*, 130 S. Ct. 2743, 2752 (2010).

[33]   *Davis v. Fed. Election Comm'n*, 554 U.S. 724, 734–35 (2008).

[34]   *Clapper v. Amnesty Int'l USA*, 133 S. Ct. 1138, 1147 (2013) (internal quotations omitted).

habitat which will in the meantime suffer the loss of endangered species "do not support a finding of the 'actual or imminent' injury that . . . [standing-doctrine] cases require."[35]

Lastly, the notion of actual or imminent harm is tied to the type of remedy the plaintiff seeks.[36] For example, in *Los Angeles v. Lyons*, the plaintiff sued the city after suffering injuries from the illegal use of a chokehold during a traffic stop.[37] The plaintiff sought both damages and an injunction against future use of the chokehold against him. The claim for monetary damages to compensate for the injuries already sustained clearly had standing. The Court held, however, that the claim for injunctive relief—even though arising from the same set of facts as the claim for monetary damages—lacked standing. The claim for injunction lacked immediacy, the Court held, because the plaintiff was not under a credible threat of a future chokehold. The Court reasoned that "[p]ast exposure to illegal conduct does not in itself show a present case or controversy regarding injunctive relief if unaccompanied by any continuing, present adverse effects."[38]

2.   FAIRLY TRACEABLE

Having determined that the plaintiff has suffered an injury in fact, Article III standing further requires that the plaintiff's injuries be fairly traceable to the

---

[35]   *Lujan*, 504 U.S. at 564.

[36]   Cf. *Lewis v. Casey*, 518 U.S. 343, 357 (1996).

[37]   461 U.S. 95 (1983).

[38]   Id. at 102 (internal quotations omitted).

defendant's conduct. This causation element does not require a party to establish proximate causation as it is familiarly found in tort law, but only requires that the injury be "fairly traceable" to the defendant.[39] Thus, the inquiry here is to find only some minimal causal nexus between the injury complained of and the defendant before the court. [40]

Generally speaking, this loose-causation test is not especially onerous so long as the named defendant's conduct affects the plaintiff without the need to trace a causal chain through non-party actors. Conversely, the traceability test, generally speaking, is difficult to meet if the injury complained of is "th[e] result [of] the independent action of some third party not before the court."[41] For example, in *Simon v. Eastern Kentucky Welfare Rights Organization*, the plaintiffs asserted an illegal lack of access to hospital services, alleging specific occasions when they sought but were denied care solely due to their inability to pay. The Court recognized this as an injury in fact but found that this "injury at the hands of a hospital is insufficient by itself to establish a case or controversy in the context of this suit, for no hospital is a defendant. The only defendants are officials of the Department of the Treasury, and the only claims of illegal action . . . [the plaintiffs] desire the courts to adjudicate are charged to those officials," for issuing a revenue ruling allowing favorable tax treatment to

---

[39]   *Bennett*, 520 U.S. at 168–69.

[40]   Cf. *Lewis*, 518 U.S. at 357 (conceptually linking injury in fact with redressability).

[41]   *Lujan*, 504 U.S. at 560–61 (internal quotations omitted).

nonprofit hospitals that offered only emergency room service to indigents.[42] In essence, the Court ruled that the particular injuries alleged by the plaintiffs, while perhaps incentivized by the IRS, were, properly speaking, caused only by the non-party hospitals. Hence, the case lacked standing.

3. REDRESSABLE

Finally, Article III standing requires that an injury in fact, which is fairly traceable to the defendant at bar, be one that is capable of redress from the courts. Many have questioned whether the traceability and redressability requirements actually speak to unique concerns.[43] That is to say, invariably if causation is found, then the matter will be found redressable and vice versa. As such, often the very same factors that lead to a conclusion regarding traceability will speak equally to redressability. As such, the two factors can often appear as a repetitive analyses. Nevertheless, the Supreme Court adheres to this distinction, so one must address both elements.

The no-advisory-opinions principle plays a strong role in the redressability analysis. The key notion being, if the court cannot actually change the state of affairs causing the injury, any opinion offered by the court would be little more than an advisory one. Thus, federal jurisdiction is linked only to those

---

[42] *Simon v. E. Kentucky Welfare Rights Org.*, 426 U.S. 26, 40–41 (1976).

[43] See, e.g., 13A Charles A. Wright, Arthur R. Miller & Edward E. Cooper, Federal Practice & Procedure at § 3531.5 (2012).

matters in which the federal court can make some remedial difference. Further, this remedial effect corresponds to the injury claimed such that the remedy must address "the inadequacy that produced the injury-in-fact that the plaintiff has established."[44]

Once again, we see that the award of monetary damages for past injury will be found to redress such a harm adequately. Similarly, an injunctive remedy seeking to alter the defendant's direct conduct against the plaintiff will readily be found redressable.[45] The challenge for redressability, as with traceability, comes when the plaintiff seeks to enjoin the defendant at bar with the hope of influencing third parties who in turn will redress the alleged injury.

For example, in *Warth v. Seldin*, the plaintiffs sought to strike a town's zoning ordinance, asserting that the injury suffered was lack of low-income housing. The Court assumed that the ordinances had been adopted for the purpose of excluding low-income persons of color and that, if true, such an ordinance would be deemed unconstitutional. But the Court found no standing because, among other reasons, the plaintiffs could not show that they would have obtained housing in the town absent the ordinance. As a result, there was no showing that the plaintiffs "personally would benefit in a tangible way from the

---

[44]   *Lewis*, 518 U.S. at 357.

[45]   See, e.g., *Monsanto*, 130 S. Ct. at 2752.

court's intervention."[46] The claim was thus not redressable (or what is analytically the same thing, it lacked a causal nexus) because the plaintiffs would obtain housing in the defendant town only if a non-party to the suit built suitable housing after the ordinance was removed.

4. THIRD PARTY CLAIMS

Having reviewed the three requirements of constitutional standing—injury in fact, traceability, and redressability—we turn now to the two components of prudential standing. Prudential standing comprises a ban upon third-party claims and a ban upon so-called generalized grievances. We begin with the former.

The primary rule barring the bringing of claims of third parties for purposes of standing is straightforward. "In the ordinary course, a litigant must assert his or her own legal rights and interests, and cannot rest a claim to relief premised on the legal rights or interests of third parties."[47] As with so much of the law of standing, the general rule barring the presentation of third-party claims seems repetitive of the injury-in-fact requirement, which similarly requires the plaintiff to have a unique and personal stake in the litigation. Nevertheless, the Court regularly invokes the ban upon generalized grievances, but notes that the rule is merely one of prudence, meaning it can be displaced if appropriate.

---

[46]   *Warth*, 422 U.S. at 508.

[47]   *Powers v. Ohio*, 499 U.S. 400, 409–10 (1991).

We turn then to the three primary exceptions to the ban upon raising third-party claims. Under the first, the plaintiff may present the rights of others if there is (a) a close relationship between the plaintiff and third-party-right holder and (b) there is some hindrance to the third-party-right holder, preventing him from bringing the claim himself.[48] The typical examples here lie with third-parties lacking legal capacity such as when parents represent their minor children, executors represent their estates, and guardians represent those under guardianship. Other agency-type relationships fall under this exception as well; including, trustees bringing suit on behalf of beneficiaries and assignees in bankruptcy bringing claims on behalf of the debtor's estate. In each instance, the named plaintiff is borrowing the third-party's claim for standing purposes, meaning that the third party's claim, if it had been brought directly, must have standing.

Class actions form the second exception. In a class action, the named plaintiff virtually represents the unnamed class members, creating a prima facie third-party-claims problem understanding doctrine. While the issue is not entirely settled, the weight of the case law is that in a class action, so long as the class representative had standing when the class was certified, then the entire class has standing as well.[49]

---

[48]   *Kowalski v. Tesmer*, 543 US 125, 130 (2004).

[49]   See *Ortiz v. Fibreboard Corp.*, 527 U.S. 815, 831 (1999). The Court tends to address the standing issue simply by looking to the named representative. See, e.g., *Gratz v. Bollinger*, 539 U.S. 244, 251, 260 (2003).

Associational standing forms the final exception to the ban upon raising third-party claims. Under this exception, associations (e.g., the N.R.A. or Greenpeace) may bring claims without a distinct injury to the association itself, if (a) at least one member of the association would have standing to sue in his own right, (b) the interests the suit seeks to vindicate are germane to the association's purposes, and (c) neither the claim nor relief requested requires the participation of individual members in the lawsuit (i.e., no issues of mandatory joinder apply).[50] Thus, under this exception a union, say, may bring a workplace-based claim by "borrowing" the standing of one of its members so long as the member himself is not a necessary party.[51]

5. GENERALIZED GRIEVANCE

The second element of prudential standing, and last element of standing altogether, is the ban upon raising generalized grievances. The Supreme Court instructs that a plaintiff "raising only a generally available grievance about government—claiming only harm to his and every citizen's interest in proper application of the Constitution and laws, and seeking relief that no more directly and tangibly benefits him than it does the public at large—does not" have standing.[52] This rule represents an expression of the

---

[50] *Int'l Union, United Auto., Aerospace & Agr. Implement Workers of Am. v. Brock*, 477 U.S. 274, 281 (1986).

[51] See, e.g., *United Food & Commercial Workers Union Local 751 v. Brown Grp., Inc.*, 517 U.S. 544, 553 (1996).

[52] *Lujan*, 504 U.S. at 573–74.

counter-majoritarian principle. The notion is that when the injuries alleged are so broadly and equally shared by the citizenry as a whole then these "generalized grievances [are] more appropriately addressed in the representative branches."[53] Put simply, if the plaintiff's injury caused by the government is equally shared by a large class of fellow citizens, then it is a generalized grievance. The remedy for generalized grievances lies in the ballot box, not the courtroom.

Two important corollaries follow from the prohibition upon raising generalized grievances. First, the rule, based as it is upon separation-of-powers principles, applies only when there is a potential recourse to another branch of government—never in a case with a private-party defendant even if the private party caused widespread harms. Second, because the rule is one of prudential standing, Congress may choose to displace it. Congress does this by including a citizen-suit provision into an act. The inclusion of such a provision broadens the set of persons who may sue to enforce a statutory scheme, which in turn adds a layer of enforcement power. While such citizen-suit provisions abound, the Clean Water Act's clause is representative.[54]

The primary application of the ban upon bringing generalized grievances may be found in the arguments around taxpayer standing. Plaintiffs have

---

[53]   *Allen*, 468 U.S. at 751.

[54]   See 33 U.S.C. §§ 1365(a), (b)(1)(A), (g).

often argued that they are injured, for purposes of standing, as a taxpayer when the government allegedly acts illegally. The Court has not been receptive to this argument, typically on generalized-grievance grounds. In 1923, the Court held that plaintiff's status as a federal taxpayer does not establish standing because "[h]is interest in the moneys of the treasury . . . is shared with millions of others, is comparatively minute and indeterminable, and the effect upon future taxation, of any payment out of the funds, so remote, fluctuating and uncertain, that no basis is afforded for" standing.[55] The Court has found but few exceptions to this rule. The Court has allowed taxpayer standing at the municipal level, due to the greater percentage that each taxpayer holds relative to the overall tax base.[56] The Warren Court, in *Flast v. Cohen*, held that a federal taxpayer has standing in a First Amendment Establishment Clause case when Congress exercises its spending power to fund a religious entity.[57] The current Court, however, has all but overruled the *Flast* exception.[58]

* * *

Standing continues to serve as the most important of the justiciability doctrine. Following the no-advisory-opinion and counter-majoritarian-concern

---

[55]   *Massachusetts v. Mellon*, 262 U.S. 447, 487 (1923).

[56]   *Doremus v. Bd. of Education*, 342 U.S. 429 (1952).

[57]   392 U.S. 83 (1968).

[58]   See, e.g., *Arizona Christian School Tuition Org v. Winn*, 131 S. Ct. 1436 (2011); *Hein v. Freedom from Religion Foundation*, 551 U.S. 587 (2007).

principles, standing doctrine seeks to ensure, especially in suits against the government, that the plaintiff bears a unique and personal stake in the litigation. The doctrine achieves this end by the Article III requirements of injury in fact, traceability, and redressability and the prudential prohibitions upon bringing the rights of third parties and generalized grievances.

C. MOOTNESS DOCTRINE

The second of the justiciability doctrine is mootness. Mootness doctrine, as with all of justiciability law, is a rule of subject matter jurisdiction, deriving from the Article III, cases-or-controversy requirement. Moreover, mootness is primarily an expression of the no-advisory-opinions principle.

The general rule is readily summarized. A case is moot if the legal remedy sought "cannot affect the rights of the litigants in the case before [the court]."[59] Under mootness doctrine, if a court may no longer affect the interests of the parties before it, any opinion it might give would in effect be an advisory one, stripping the court of jurisdiction under Article III.

The mootness rule in many ways is repetitive of the redressability element of standing doctrine.[60] In both instances, if the federal court cannot provide a

---

[59]   *DeFunis v. Odegaard*, 416 U.S. 312, 316 (1974).

[60]   See 13A Charles A. Wright, Arthur R. Miller & Edward E. Cooper, Federal Practice & Procedure at § 3531.5 (2012).

remedy to the parties before the court, the court lacks subject matter jurisdiction. The differences in the doctrine are more of usage than of conceptual distinction. Generally speaking, if a court from the moment the case was filed could not redress the remedy, then the plaintiff will be found to lack standing for presenting an irredressable injury. If an injury was redressable when filed but becomes irredressable later in the life of the lawsuit, then mootness doctrine typically applies. Further, whereas standing generally comes to the fore in suits against the government, mootness is deployed in suits with both governmental and private-party defendants. The other difference lies in who bears the burdens on motions. The Court places the burden on the party asserting mootness, typically the defendant, to show that it is absolutely clear that the injury will not reoccur, while the party invoking federal jurisdiction, typically the plaintiff, bears the burden to establish standing.[61]

Generally, cases become moot by voluntary settlement or the passage of time that renders the requested injunctive relief irrelevant. For example, in *DeFunis v. Odegaard*,[62] the plaintiff brought a reverse-discrimination suit against the University of Washington Law School for failing to admit him. The trial court ruled for the plaintiff, and he was admitted into law school. The appeal, however, continued while he progressed in school and

---

[61]   *Friends of the Earth, Inc. v. Laidlaw Envtl. Servs., Inc.*, 528 U.S. 167, 189 (2000).

[62]   416 U.S. 312 (1974).

eventually found itself in the Supreme Court. By this time, the plaintiff was in his final semester and the school agreed that regardless of the outcome he would not be expelled. This promise, however, mooted the case. The Court reasoned that because the plaintiff "will complete his law school studies . . . regardless of any decision [the] Court might reach on the merits of this litigation . . . [it] cannot, consistently with the limitations of Art. III of the Constitution, consider the substantive constitutional issues tendered by the parties."[63]

The Court finds mootness doctrine subject to two exceptions. The first is the voluntary-cessation exception. If in the midst of a lawsuit the defendant ceases the offending conduct of his own accord, the "defendant's voluntary cessation of [the] challenged practice does not deprive a federal court of its power to determine the legality of the practice [because] [i]f it did, the courts would be compelled to leave the defendant free to return to his old ways."[64] This exception prevents a defendant from stopping his conduct just long enough to avoid a judgment, yet retaining the ability to renew the conduct later.

The second exception covers matters which are capable of repetition yet evading review. This exception covers situations that create short-term injuries, such that the courts cannot fully adjudicate them while the injury is occurring, and are capable of happening again. The archetypal example is *Roe v.*

---

[63]   Id. at 319–20.

[64]   *Friends of the Earth*, 528 U.S. at 189.

Wade.[65] There, the plaintiff challenged Texas's ban upon abortions, but her pregnancy was completed by the time the suit made it to the Supreme Court. The Court, nevertheless, did not find the case moot by employing this exception.

Three other side points are worthy of mention. First, unlike standing doctrine where the class representative is the sole determinate, under mootness doctrine, after class certification, so long as any class member's claim is not mooted, the fact that a class representative's claim becomes moot is irrelevant.[66] Second, in a habeas case in which the petitioner challenges the fact of conviction, not just the length of sentence, a petitioner's release from prison does not moot the case because of the many on-going collateral consequences of the conviction that continue, such as the moral stigma of a criminal sentence.[67] Lastly, as with all justiciability law, mootness law derives from Article III of the federal Constitution, meaning that the states are not bound by federal mootness doctrine. Many states, then, have different exceptions to mootness law than are found under the federal regime. One of the most common being "a question of public interest" exception, which allows matters of general public

---

[65]   410 U.S. 113, 125 (1973).

[66]   *Genesis Healthcare Corp. v. Symczyk*, 133 S. Ct. 1523, 1530 (2013).

[67]   *Spencer v. Kemna*, 523 U.S. 1, 8 (1998).

importance to proceed even if the named plaintiff's suit has mooted.[68]

D. RIPENESS DOCTRINE

The third justiciability doctrine is ripeness. The basic rationale of the ripeness requirement is "to prevent courts, through the avoidance of premature adjudication, from entangling themselves in abstract disagreements" with other organs of government.[69] The test is whether there is sufficient "hardship to the parties [in] withholding court consideration" until there is enforcement action.[70] In a sense, ripeness is the opposite of mootness, preventing the courts from hearing matters before an actual injury has occurred.

As should be clear, ripeness doctrine, with its focus upon whether the injury is currently occurring, is akin to the actual or imminent requirement of standing's injury-in-fact analysis. Indeed Professor Gene Nichol demonstrated that the two analyses are functionally redundant.[71] Even the Court itself has acknowledged that the two analyses tend to merge.[72]

---

[68] See, e.g., *Felzak v. Hruby*, 226 Ill.2d 382, 393, 876 N.E.2d 650 (2007).

[69] *Abbott Laboratories v. Gardner*, 387 U.S. 136, 148 (1967).

[70] Id.

[71] Gene R. Nichol, Jr., Ripeness and the Constitution, 54 U. Chi. L. Rev. 153, 178 (1987).

[72] See *MedImmune, Inc. v. Genentech, Inc.*, 549 U.S. 118, 128 n.8 (2007) ("standing and ripeness boil down to the same question in this case.").

Nevertheless, the Court insists that the two doctrine remain extant as separate doctrine.

E.   POLITICAL QUESTION DOCTRINE

The last component of the justiciability regime is political question doctrine. Whereas standing, mootness and ripeness consider factors beyond separation of powers as axioms in their analyses (e.g., timing, injury to the plaintiff, and the ban upon advisory opinions), political question doctrine focuses exclusively upon inter-branch division of authority.[73] This doctrine is purely an expression of the counter-majoritarian-concern principle. Thus, the doctrine properly applies only when the remedy envisioned would bind branches of the federal government, not private parties or states.[74] Following this notion, political question doctrine holds that legal disputes lack subject matter jurisdiction in the federal courts when resolution of the dispute may only be appropriately given from the political branches.

That some questions of law, which are otherwise ripe and have standing, would not be justiciable in the courts may strike one as odd. Indeed Chief Justice Marshall commanded, in *Marbury v. Madison* no less, that it is "emphatically the duty of the judicial department to say what the law is."[75]

---

[73]   *Baker v. Carr*, 369 U.S. 186, 217 (1962).

[74]   Id. at 210 ("it is the relationship between the judiciary and the coordinate branches of the Federal Government, and not the federal judiciary's relationship to the States, which gives rise to the 'political question.' ").

[75]   5 U.S. (1 Cranch) 137, 177 (1803).

This edict supports the notion that all matters of law should be exclusively determined by the courts. Indeed, the Court continues to give this principle its full-throated support.[76]

But there has always been a counter-trend to this *Marbury* principle. This view argues that each branch of government ought to be its own final authority, checked only by the electorate, as to the constitutionality of its conduct. Given Thomas Jefferson's early and avid advocacy of this view, it may be fair to coin this position the Jeffersonian principle. The following letter from Jefferson provides a fair summary:

> To consider the judges as the ultimate arbiters of all constitutional questions [is] a very dangerous doctrine indeed, and one which would place us under the despotism of an oligarchy. . . . The Constitution has erected no such single tribunal. . . . It has more wisely made all the departments co-equal and co-sovereign within themselves.[77]

Political question doctrine, then, may be viewed as an application of this Jeffersonian principle. Of course, the Court does not embrace his view universally. But in those instances where the

---

[76]   See, e.g., *Boumediene v. Bush*, 553 U.S. 723, 765 (2008) (citing this passage from Marbury in the Guantanamo detainee case that ordered the President and Congress to allow habeas proceedings).

[77]   Letter of Thomas Jefferson to William C. Jarvis, 1820, in The Writings of Thomas Jefferson, Memorial Edition, Vol. 15, p. 277 (Lipscomb and Bergh, eds.) (Washington, D.C., 1903–04).

political question doctrine applies, it has the effect of rendering the non-judicial branch of government the final arbiter as to the constitutionality of its own conduct.

Moving from jurisprudential principle to doctrinal rules, in *Baker v. Carr*, the Court identified six circumstances in which a suit might present a political question: (1) "a textually demonstrable constitutional commitment of the issue to a coordinate political department"; (2) "a lack of judicially discoverable and manageable standards for resolving it"; (3) "the impossibility of deciding without an initial policy determination of a kind clearly for nonjudicial discretion"; (4) "the impossibility of a court's undertaking independent resolution without expressing lack of the respect due coordinate branches of government"; (5) "an unusual need for unquestioning adherence to a political decision already made"; or (6) "the potentiality of embarrassment from multifarious pronouncements by various departments on one question."[78]

In more recent years, the Court has tended to clump these six categories into three groups. First, the Court treats constitutional textual commitments of a dispute to another branch of government as the strongest indication that a matter should be dismissed as a political question. *Marbury* itself recognized this feature of the Constitution when it held that "the president is invested with certain important political powers [, such as the veto], in the

---

[78]   *Baker v. Carr*, 369 U.S. at 217.

exercise of which he is to use his own discretion, and is accountable only to his country in his political character, and to his own conscience."[79] In keeping with this approach, the Court held nonjusticiable the Senate's impeachment procedures in light of Article I's placement in the Senate of the " 'sole Power to try all Impeachments.' "[80]

Second, the Court now tends to view the "lack of judicially manageable standards" and "requires non-judicial policy making" elements of the *Baker* list as placing similar parameters upon the courts. The key notion here is that federal judicial power is limited to issues and decision-making that are "traditional for English and American courts."[81] Thus, when the courts lack an applicable legal standard by which to resolve a case, or cannot act without making a policy determination that falls within the sphere of a political branch, the case is to be dismissed as a political question. For example, the Court during the Vietnam era dismissed a suit that sought to enjoin the use of certain training and weaponry within the National Guard on the grounds that the suit raised a political question.[82]

Finally, the Court now sees *Baker*'s "overreaching into areas controlled by other branches," "special need to defer to decision of political branches," and "potential for embarrassing multiple pronouncements on the same issue" as raising

---

[79]   *Marbury*, 5 U.S. (1 Cranch) at 166.

[80]   *Nixon v. United States*, 506 U.S. 224, 229 (1993).

[81]   *Vieth v. Jubelirer*, 541 U.S. 267, 278 (2004) (plurality).

[82]   *Gilligan v. Morgan*, 413 U.S. 1, 10 (1973).

similar concerns. The current Court tends to be more skeptical of these categories of political questions. Nevertheless, the Court will dismiss cases for lack of subject matter jurisdiction if they require the judiciary to call into question the good faith with which another branch attests to the authenticity of its internal acts.[83] Similarly, the courts will not hear matters requiring them to postpone the necessity for "attributing finality to the action of the political departments,"[84] or creating acute "risk [of] embarrassment of our government abroad, or grave disturbance at home."[85]

* * *

In close, justiciability doctrine is the body of law that limits the subject matter jurisdiction of the federal courts regardless of which type of congressionally granted jurisdiction is at issue. Collectively, these four component doctrine— standing, mootness, ripeness and political question— set a floor upon which every suit must rest in order for the federal courts to have constitutional authority to resolve them. All of justiciability doctrine derives from the cases-or-controversies requirement of the Constitution, which itself establishes two broad axioms that inform justiciability law: the ban upon advisory opinions and a separation-of-powers concern for the counter-majoritarian difficulty. Having reviewed these doctrine in detail, it is worth

---

[83]   *Field v. Clark*, 143 U.S. 649, 672–673 (1892).

[84]   *Coleman v. Miller*, 307 U.S. 433, 454 (1939).

[85]   *Baker*, 369 U.S., at 226.

recalling that in the end they all seek to ensure that the courts resolve only authentic, live disputes in which the parties have a personal stake and that the courts not co-opt the powers of the other branches of government in the name of adjudication.

CHAPTER 9

ELEVENTH AMENDMENT DOCTRINE

"The Judicial power of the United States shall not be construed to extend to any suit in law or equity, commenced or prosecuted against one of the United States by Citizens of another State, or by Citizens or Subjects of any Foreign State."

—United States Constitution, Amendment XI

"[T]he Eleventh Amendment . . . stand[s] not so much for what it says, but for the presupposition of our constitutional structure which it confirms . . . that the judicial authority in Article III is limited by . . . [State] sovereignty, and that a State will therefore not be subject to suit in federal court unless it has consented."

—*Blatchford v. Native Vill. of Noatak & Circle Vill.*, 501 U.S. 775, 779 (1991)

We move now to the Eleventh Amendment, which makes haling a state into federal court without its consent a daunting task. This Amendment is a notoriously tricky subject for new students of federal jurisdiction as this body of law raises significant and nuanced constitutional issues regarding the rights of states vis-à-vis the national government to which one could devote a lifetime of study. Fortunately, the Eleventh Amendment is not relevant in the vast majority of civil cases, as it only applies when one of the 50 states is a defendant. Given that the focus of this book is on general civil litigation, we turn to this question—jurisdiction over states as defendants—only briefly. This chapter proceeds in two broad parts. First, we explore the scope of the Eleventh Amendment's ban upon taking jurisdiction over states as non-consenting defendants. Second, we review the means by which this ban upon jurisdiction over the states may be overcome.

A.   THE ELEVENTH AMENDMENT'S BROAD SCOPE

We begin with an overview of the Eleventh Amendment's broad ban upon jurisdiction over suits in which a state is a party-defendant. First we will discuss the *Chisholm v. Georgia* decision, which was the impetus for passage of the Eleventh Amendment. Second we trace the Supreme Court's Eleventh Amendment jurisprudence, noting that its focus is upon state sovereign immunity as a broad principle as opposed to the text of the Amendment itself.

1.   THE AFTERMATH OF *CHISHOLM v. GEORGIA*

The United States Supreme Court, before Chief Justice Marshall took the bench in 1801, seldom affected the political life of the new nation. The one exception to this generalization is the 1793 opinion of *Chisholm v. Georgia*.[1] Here the plaintiff, an executor of a South Carolina decedent's estate, sued the state of Georgia in the original jurisdiction of the United States Supreme Court over payments due to the

---

[1]   2 U.S. (2 Dall.) 419 (1793).

decedent for supplies Georgia bought during the Revolutionary War. The case purported to take federal jurisdiction by diversity and original jurisdiction in the Supreme Court because a state was a party. After service upon the governor and attorney general of Georgia, the state refused to enter an appearance, relying upon the notion that the state of Georgia as a sovereign could not be compelled to appear in federal court without granting its consent. Due to the obvious importance of the question, the United States Attorney General argued the case for the plaintiff and entered a motion to compel Georgia's appearance or enter a default judgment. The issue before the Court was whether it had jurisdiction to entertain such a motion.

The Court held that it did have jurisdiction over the state of Georgia even though it had not consented to suit.[2] The majority reasoned that "the People," not the states, were sovereign in America and that the People intended to bind the states by the legislative, executive, and judicial powers of the national government. As a result, the Constitution, in the majority's view, granted jurisdiction over non-consenting states as defendants.

Justice Iredell was the lone dissenter. First he noted that the majority's construction of diversity jurisdiction was so broad as to include criminal

---

[2] Prior to Chief Justice Marshall's tenure, the Supreme Court did not deliver an opinion of the court, but rather gave the views of each justice seriatim, which is how the *Chisholm* opinion is delivered. The Court's holding is a construction of the view of the four justices in the majority.

prosecutions between a state and a citizen of another state, a result that he clearly viewed as absurd.[3] Second he believed that taking jurisdiction over a state in such a manner would, at a minimum, require statutory authority that was lacking in this case.[4] Third, common practice in all the state courts at the time was to treat the states as possessing sovereign immunity as that idea was understood at English common law.[5] Justice Iredell thus concluded that the "only remedy in a case like that before the Court . . . [lies with] a suit . . . [that could] be maintained against the crown in England."[6] Finding that no such suit could be brought against the crown, he concluded that the federal courts lacked jurisdiction as well.

The *Chisholm* opinion created quite the political uproar. The states, all fearing creditors from the war as well as the general principle of being unwillingly taken to federal court, cried foul. Congress swiftly passed the Eleventh Amendment, and the states ratified it in 1795. The Amendment is now a cornerstone of judicial federalism under American law.

2.   IMMUNITY PRINCIPLE TRUMPS TEXT

After the passage of the Eleventh Amendment, the Court has by and large imported Justice Iredell's approach to state immunity as the meaning of the Eleventh Amendment. Indeed, one way of

---

3   Id. at 431–32 (Iredell, J., dissenting).

4   Id. at 432–34.

5   Id. at 435–36.

6   Id. at 437.

conceptualizing the Supreme Court's Eleventh Amendment doctrine is to view it as an importation of the English law of immunity for the crown into American constitutional law. From this vantage, the text of the amendment is less important than is the English-style immunity principle which it represents.

A fundamental principle of English law was that the sovereign, as the authority which created the courts, could not be compelled by the courts.[7] Thus the crown enjoyed full immunity from all proceedings in the English courts. At old English common law, this rule was subject to two general exceptions well known at the time the Eleventh Amendment was ratified. First, the crown could be sued as a party-defendant only if the plaintiff sought the crown's consent to suit first, which was done under a procedure known as a petition of right.[8] Second, absent consent, writs of mandamus and prohibition were available against the King's officials who were engaged in wrongdoing under the theory that it was not a suit against the crown itself, but an individual, and that because the King does no wrong he would want such conduct to cease.[9]

This body of English law continues to serve as a rule of thumb for Eleventh Amendment

---

[7] See, e.g., *Russell v. The Men of Devon*, 100 Eng. Rep. 359 (K.B. 1788).

[8] See, e.g., *Chisholm*, 2 U.S. (2 Dall.) at 437 (Iredell, J., dissenting).

[9] See, e.g., The Case of Cardiffe Bridge, 1 Salk. 146, 91 Eng. Rep. 135 (K.B. 1701).

jurisprudence. As the Supreme Court often holds, "the sovereign immunity of the States neither derives from, nor is limited by, the terms of the Eleventh Amendment. Rather. . . the States' immunity from suit is a fundamental aspect of the sovereignty which the States enjoyed before the ratification of the Constitution, and which they retain today."[10] That is to say, the English common law of sovereign immunity remains the core principle of state immunity in federal court. Next, two of the three broad exceptions to state sovereign immunity flow from English law. First, state sovereign immunity, akin to English immunity, may be overcome by consent. Second, suits for prospective relief, much like writs of mandamus against a royal official, may be brought against state officers under the *Ex parte Young* line of cases.

After the Civil War, the Court began issuing a long series of decisions demonstrating that it is this English sovereign-immunity principle, not the text of the Amendment, that controls Eleventh Amendment jurisprudence.[11] Following this approach, the Court has ruled that the Eleventh Amendment bars federal jurisdiction when state citizens sue their own state, despite the fact that the text of the Amendment is limited to suits brought by out-of-state plaintiffs.[12]

---

[10]   *Alden v. Maine*, 527 U.S. 706, 713 (1999).

[11]   See, e.g., *Blatchford v. Native Vill. of Noatak & Circle Vill.*, 501 U.S. 775, 779 (1991) ("the Eleventh Amendment . . . stand[s] not so much for what it says, but for the presupposition of our constitutional structure which it confirms . . . that the judicial authority in Article III is limited by . . . [State] sovereignty.").

[12]   *Hans v. Louisiana*, 134 U.S. 1, 14–15 (1890).

Next, even though the Eleventh Amendment was born out of a dispute in diversity jurisdiction, the Court holds that it bars federal jurisdiction over unwilling state-party defendants in federal question jurisdiction[13] and in admiralty cases.[14] Similarly, while the text of the Amendment is limited to individuals suing states, the Supreme Court holds that the federal courts lack jurisdiction when a foreign nation sues one of the states in the union.[15] Moreover, the Court has also ruled that a state may not be forced to act as a party-defendant in its own state-court system, even though the text of the Eleventh Amendment speaks only to jurisdiction in the federal courts.[16] In this same vein, the Court holds that federal administrative tribunals, which do not exercise federal judicial power as that term is used in the text of the Eleventh Amendment, lack jurisdiction to proceed when a state is an unwilling party-defendant.[17] Thus, the Court views state sovereign immunity as a broad principle that often eclipses the very text of the Eleventh Amendment itself.

---

[13]   *Hans*, 134 U.S. at 10; *Louisiana v. Jumel*, 107 U.S. 711 (1883).

[14]   *Ex parte New York*, 256 U.S. 490, 497 (1921).

[15]   *Principality of Monaco v. Mississippi*, 292 U.S. 313, 330 (1934).

[16]   *Alden v. Maine*, 527 U.S. 706, 757 (1999).

[17]   *Fed. Mar. Comm'n v. S. Carolina State Ports Auth.*, 535 U.S. 743, 751 (2002).

B. OVERCOMING THE IMMUNITY PRINCIPLE

Having briefly explored the broad scope of the state-sovereign-immunity principle that the Eleventh Amendment represents, we turn in this section to the three mechanisms the Court recognizes for overriding state sovereign immunity. The first two mechanisms derive from the state-as-the-crown analogy. Thus we find that, consistent with old English practice, a state may consent, explicitly or implicitly, to federal court jurisdiction. The Court also allows, akin to a mandamus action against an officer of the crown, suits for injunction against state officers under the *Ex parte Young* doctrine. Finally, in a break with the analogy to immunity of the crown, Congress may abrogate a state's Eleventh Amendment immunity.

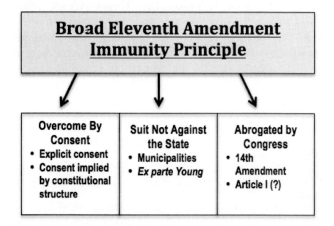

1.   STATE CONSENT

The Court divides consent to waive Eleventh Amendment immunity into two camps: (1) explicit consent and (2) implicit consent. The Court has long held that a state may waive its immunity from suit in the federal courts by explicit consent.[18] This consent may be given in a purely voluntary nature in the interest of justice and fairness. Or explicit consent to waive immunity may be given by a state as part of a bargain with the federal government for other benefits.[19] In either case, the Court insists that the State's consent be unequivocally expressed.[20]

In addition to explicit consent, the Court holds that the states have implicitly consented to waive Eleventh Amendment immunity to some types of suits by the mere fact of entering the union.[21] The notion here is that the constitutional structure demands that certain matters be amenable to federal jurisdiction lest the rule of law would be replaced by "extralegal measures," meaning that but for federal-court jurisdiction the various states and the federal government would have to resort to force of arms to resolve disputes.[22] Applying this concept, the federal courts retain jurisdiction over non-consenting state-party defendants when the United States is a party

---

[18]   See, e.g., *Clark v. Barnard*, 108 U.S. 436, 447 (1883).

[19]   Cf. *South Dakota v. Dole*, 483 U.S. 203 (1987).

[20]   See, e.g., *Edelman v. Jordan*, 415 U.S. 651, 673 (1974).

[21]   *Alden*, 527 U.S. at 755.

[22]   Id. at 756.

to the suit.[23] Similarly, the Supreme Court retains its original jurisdiction to hear suits between two states, even if the defendant state does not consent to suit.[24] Finally, the Court has long held that its power to hear appeals from the state-court systems in which the state is a party is not limited by the Eleventh Amendment.[25]

2.   *EX PARTE YOUNG*

In addition to consent, the Court holds that actions not brought against the state itself are not subject to the immunity principle of the Eleventh Amendment. Now this may seem simple enough, but the question of just who or what, exactly, constitutes the state for purposes of Eleventh Amendment immunity is not always obvious.

First, the Court concludes that subdivisions of a state are not the state itself for Eleventh Amendment-immunity purposes. Following this rule, a city or a county does not receive Eleventh Amendment immunity.[26] On the other hand, governmental entities that are an "arm of the state" do receive immunity.[27] Questions of whether a governmental unit, such as a state university or department of public health, is a non-immune

---

[23]   See, e.g., *Principality of Monaco v. State of Mississippi*, 292 U.S. 313, 329 (1934) (listing cases).

[24]   See, e.g., *Maryland v. Louisiana*, 451 U.S. 725, 745 n.21 (1981).

[25]   *Cohens v. Virginia*, 19 U.S. (6 Wheat.) 264, 412 (1821).

[26]   See *Mt. Healthy City Bd. of Ed. v. Doyle*, 429 U.S. 274, 280 (1977).

[27]   Id.

subdivision or an immune arm of the state can become quite complex and often turn upon the entity's treatment under state law.[28]

Second, and much more important, under *Ex parte Young*[29] doctrine the Eleventh Amendment does not bar suits against state officers for injunctive or declaratory relief. Also, suits for money damages for wrongful conduct fairly attributable to the officer himself, so long as the relief is sought not from the state treasury but from the officer personally, may be heard under this doctrine.

In *Ex parte Young*, the state of Minnesota passed a series of civil and criminal regulations capping railroad passenger and freight prices. The railroad shareholders sought to enjoin the enforcement of these laws, which they believed to be unconstitutional under the Due Process Clause. The plaintiff shareholders sued Minnesota State Attorney General Young to enjoin him from enforcing the regulatory regime in federal court. Mr. Young asserted Eleventh Amendment immunity, refused to submit to the authority of the federal court, and began to enforce the state regulations. The federal court, then, had Mr. Young arrested by federal marshals. Mr. Young in turn filed a habeas corpus petition with the Supreme Court for release.

In reviewing the petition, the Court first held that the state regulations at issue violated the Due

---

[28] Id.; see also *McMillian v. Monroe Cnty., Ala.*, 520 U.S. 781, 783 (1997).

[29] 209 U.S. 123 (1908).

Process Clause. The Court next held that a suit for injunction could proceed against the attorney general, not as agent of the state, but in his individual capacity. The Court reasoned—very much akin to the old English common law—that when a state official acts unconstitutionally, the official does not act as the state per se because the federal Supremacy Clause overrides the unconstitutional state law. From this point of view, the state official cannot enforce unconstitutional state law as an agent of the state because such law is by definition void. As such, the state official, because there is no valid state law to enforce, must only be acting as a private individual, not as an agent of the state. As private individuals do not receive the benefit of sovereign immunity under the Eleventh Amendment, Mr. Young could not rely upon immunity to avoid the suit for injunction. Therefore, the suit was able to proceed to judgment in federal court.

Although *Ex parte Young* does not always get recognition in the popular culture, it is likely "one of the three most important decisions the Supreme Court of the United States has ever handed down."[30] But for this decision, the Eleventh Amendment would bar all federal-court enforcement of federal constitutional rights as against the states. Indeed, most of the civil rights cases in the last century proceeded only because the Supreme Court in *Ex parte Young* adopted the "legal fiction" that state officers enforcing unconstitutional rules are not acting as the state for immunity purposes. As the

---

[30]   17 Wright & Miller, Federal Practice & Procedure § 4231.

Court put the matter, "[i]t has long been a settled principle that federal courts may enjoin unconstitutional action by state officials. See *Ex parte Young*. [While] [i]t would be superfluous to restate all the occasions on which this Court has imposed upon state officials a duty to obey the requirements of the Constitution, or compelled the performance of such duties; it may suffice to refer to *Brown v. Board of Education*."[31]

The importance of the doctrine should not overshadow the many difficulties inherent with it. For example, substantive constitutional law, pursuant to the state-action doctrine, mandates that to find law unconstitutional, one must almost always find that the offending conduct was done by the state, or national, government.[32] This is to say, excepting Thirteenth Amendment doctrine, private parties cannot commit constitutional violations. Yet at the same time, the Eleventh Amendment supposes that this very same conduct, which was the action of the government for state-action-doctrine purposes, is not state conduct for Eleventh Amendment-immunity purposes. These are tricky propositions to hold simultaneously. Similarly, the supposition that a state official, when enforcing unconstitutional state law, is not an agent of the state is tenuous at best.[33]

---

[31] *Puerto Rico v. Branstad*, 483 U.S. 219, 228 (1987).

[32] See, e.g., *Shelley v. Kraemer*, 334 U.S. 1 (1948) (holding that judicial enforcement of racial covenants to real property constituted state action under the Fourteenth Amendment).

[33] See *Pennhurst State School and Hospital v. Halderman*, 465 U.S. 89, 114, n. 25 (1984) (labeling this key proposition from *Ex parte Young* a fiction).

Nevertheless, *Ex parte Young* works well as a powerful tool to stop unconstitutional state conduct.

The many intricacies of, and developments in, *Ex parte Young* doctrine are beyond the scope of this text, but a few generalizations may be had. The doctrine avoids Eleventh Amendment immunity for suits against state officials in their personal capacity when the plaintiff seeks prospective relief, which most often is an injunction. Monetary awards can be had under *Ex parte Young* doctrine as well, but they must not be sought from the state treasury and they must be only prospective in nature—a determination that is often difficult to make.[34] Whether the relief sought is injunctive or monetary, plaintiff's attorney fees may be sought from the state itself.[35]

The Court has also carved out important limitations to *Ex parte Young* doctrine. First, *Ex parte Young* may not be used in supplemental jurisdiction as a means of enforcing state, rather than federal, law.[36] Second, *Ex parte Young* doctrine may not be used to enforce federal law when Congress by statute provides a detailed, alternative,

---

[34]   Compare *Edelman v. Jordan*, 415 U.S. 651 (1974) (finding monetary damages barred as retroactive) with *Milliken v. Bradley*, 433 U.S. 267 (1977) (finding monetary damages allowed as prospective in nature).

[35]   *Hutto v. Finney*, 437 U.S. 678 (1978).

[36]   *Pennhurst State School and Hospital v. Halderman*, 465 U.S. 89 (1984).

enforcement scheme.[37] Last, *Ex parte Young* may not be used as a means of quieting title to real property.[38]

3.   ABROGATION DOCTRINE

Moving away from analogies to the crown's immunity under old English common law, in this last section we turn to Congress' ability to override, or "abrogate" as it is termed, a state's Eleventh Amendment immunity. The *Hans v. Louisiana*[39] opinion launched the notion that the Eleventh Amendment embodies a broad immunity principle, subject only to traditional English common law exceptions. This line of cases, however, left open the possibility that in our federated system of government, in which the national government can claim supremacy, that Congress could elect to abrogate a state's immunity.

From the twentieth century forward, the Court has always assumed that Congress retains some authority to abrogate state immunity, so long as it is explicitly exercised by clear statutory language.[40] Primarily, Congress' power to abrogate a state's sovereign immunity is limited to "its power to enforce the Fourteenth Amendment—an Amendment enacted after the Eleventh Amendment and specifically designed to alter the federal-state

---

[37]   *Seminole Tribe of Fla. v. Florida*, 517 U.S. 44 (1996).

[38]   *Idaho v. Coeur d'Alene Tribe of Idaho*, 521 U.S. 261 (1997).

[39]   134 U.S. 1 (1890).

[40]   See *Quern v. Jordan,* 440 U.S. 332, 342 (1979) (requiring an unequivocal expression of congressional intent to "overturn the constitutionally guaranteed immunity of the several States.").

balance."[41] We turn the bulk of our attention, then, to this interplay of Fourteenth and Eleventh Amendments. We close this section with a brief discussion of *Central Virginia Community College v. Katz*,[42] where the Court, in a 5–4 decision, allowed Congress to use Article I—not Fourteenth Amendment—authority to abrogate a state's sovereign immunity.

a. Fourteenth Amendment Abrogation

The courts find that Congress may abrogate Eleventh Amendment immunity as a function of its expansive power under section five of the Fourteenth Amendment. The Court adopted this approach in the 1970s. Following this line of cases, the Court reasons that the Fourteenth Amendment codifies the surrender of an additional portion of state sovereignty that had been preserved under the original Constitution. This surrender includes congressional authority to allow private suits against non-consenting states.[43] Thus, because the Fourteenth Amendment "fundamentally altered the balance of state and federal power struck by the Constitution,"[44] the states must comply with federal-court jurisdiction.

---

[41]   *Coll. Sav. Bank v. Florida Prepaid Postsecondary Educ. Expense Bd.*, 527 U.S. 666, 670 (1999).

[42]   546 U.S. 356 (2006).

[43]   *Fitzpatrick v. Bitzer*, 427 U.S. 445 (1976).

[44]   *Seminole Tribe of Florida v. Florida*, 517 U.S. 44, 59 (1996).

This is not to say that Congress' power to abrogate state sovereign immunity is unbounded. Quite the contrary is the case. Congress may abrogate Eleventh Amendment immunity only by passing "appropriate legislation under § 5 [of the Fourteenth Amendment.]"[45] Thus, it is only "[w]hen Congress enacts appropriate legislation to enforce th[e] [Fourteenth] Amendment [that] federal interests are paramount and Congress may assert an authority over the States which would be otherwise unauthorized by the Constitution."[46] Absent the approach taken in *Katz* (which is discussed below), Congress may not abrogate state sovereign immunity as an exercise of its power to regulate interstate commerce or any other of its Article I powers that normally provide the constitutional foundation for legislation. Rather, Congress may only abrogate state sovereign immunity to enforce rights guaranteed by the Fourteenth Amendment; namely, the Due Process and Equal Protection Clauses.

Section five itself is a limited grant of federal power, which in turn constrains Congress' ability to abrogate state sovereign immunity. In 1997, the Court, in *City of Boerne v. Flores*,[47] established the parameters of Congress' power under section five. The Court ruled that, under the auspices of section five, Congress may not determine what constitutes a

---

[45]   *Kimel v. Florida Bd. of Regents*, 528 U.S. 62, 80 (2000).

[46]   *Alden*, 527 U.S. at 756 (internal quotations and citations omitted).

[47]   521 U.S. 507 (1997).

violation of a constitutional right,[48] Rather, Congress is limited to preventing or remedying substantive Fourteenth Amendment violations as those rights are defined by the courts.[49] In addition, the legislative remedy proposed must be congruent and proportionate to the Fourteenth Amendment injuries identified. Thus, under *City of Boerne*, Congress may pass legislation, including abrogation of state Eleventh Amendment immunity, "under § 5 . . . [only if: (1) it is] targeted at conduct transgressing the Fourteenth Amendment's substantive provisions. And [(2) the legislation demonstrates] . . . a congruence and proportionality between the injury to be prevented or remedied and the means adopted to that end."[50]

Since the mid-1990s, the Court has had several occasions to apply this two-part test. Under the first prong, if the interests furthered by the legislation under review is not recognized by the Court as protected by the Fourteenth Amendment, Congress may not constitutionally abrogate state sovereign immunity. As such, the Court concluded that Congress could not abrogate state immunity to protect either "a right to be free from a business competitor's false advertising about its own product, . . . [or] a more generalized right to be secure in one's business interests, ... [because] [n]either of these

---

[48]   Id. at 519.

[49]   Id. at 529.

[50]   *Coleman v. Court of Appeals of Maryland*, 132 S. Ct. 1327, 1333–34 (2012) (internal quotations and citations omitted).

qualifies as a property right protected by the Due Process Clause."[51]

The Court has issued several opinions under the second prong of the *City of Boerne* test as well. Here, the Court will not approve congressional abrogation of state sovereign immunity when Congress makes an insufficient finding that cognizable Fourteenth Amendment rights have been violated. Thus, the Court held the "Patent Remedy Act's indiscriminate scope . . . particularly incongruous in light of the scant support for the predicate unconstitutional conduct that Congress intended to remedy."[52]

Continuing under the second prong of *City of Boerne*, even assuming Congress can make a finding of wide-spread state violations of a cognizable Fourteenth Amendment right, not all legislation attempting to abrogate state sovereign immunity is found constitutional under section five. Rather, the constitutionality of the legislation under review tends to correlate with the level of scrutiny to which the offending state conduct is subject. Thus, if the state conduct at issue is subject to a deferential rational-basis review, the Court tends to find abrogation of state sovereign immunity unconstitutional because it is neither congruent nor

---

[51]   *Coll. Sav. Bank v. Florida Prepaid Postsecondary Educ. Expense Bd.*, 527 U.S. 666, 672 (1999).

[52]   *Florida Prepaid Postsecondary Educ. Expense Bd. v. Coll. Sav. Bank*, 527 U.S. 627, 647 (1999).

proportional to the injuries identified.[53] On the other hand, when the state conduct at issue is subject to a more rigorous standard of view, such as intermediate or strict scrutiny, then it more readily finds that abrogation of state sovereign immunity is constitutionally congruent and proportionate to the injuries suffered.[54]

* * *

In sum, Congress can abrogate Eleventh Amendment state sovereign immunity under the Fourteenth Amendment. To do so, Congress must unequivocally express its intent. And it must comply with the *City of Boerne* two-part test for use of section five of the Fourteenth Amendment. As such, to abrogate state immunity Congress can only act to prevent, or to remedy, the violation of rights protected by the Fourteenth Amendment. Moreover, the abrogation of state immunity must be found congruent and proportionate to the injurious conduct identified.

b. Article I Abrogation

In addition to abrogation by way of the Fourteenth Amendment, the courts have at times found Congress empowered to override Eleventh Amendment immunity as a function of its Article I

---

[53] See, e.g., *Bd. of Trustees of Univ. of Alabama v. Garrett*, 531 U.S. 356, 368 (2001); *Kimel v. Florida Bd. of Regents*, 528 U.S. 62, 82–83 (2000).

[54] See, e.g., *Tennessee v. Lane*, 541 U.S. 509, 522–23 (2004); *Nevada Dept. of Human Resources v. Hibbs*, 538 U.S. 721, 728–729 (2003).

powers. As with Fourteenth Amendment abrogation, such an approach requires Congress clearly to state an intention to waive immunity. This approach, if generally allowed, would have wide-ranging implications for state immunity and federal power, given that any ordinary legislation would be able to trump constitutionalized state immunity.

The Supreme Court seemed, at least to some observers, to have adopted this sweeping view in *Pennsylvania v. Union Gas Co.*[55] The issue for the Court in *Union Gas Co.* was whether Congress in the Comprehensive Environmental Response, Compensation and Liability Act had abrogated the states' sovereign immunity. In a fractured opinion, the Justices concluded that Congress had abrogated state immunity. The further question of whether Congress had used its Article I or Fourteenth Amendment powers to pass such an abrogation also split the Justices. There was, however, at least a plurality of the Court who would have allowed Congress to abrogate state immunity pursuant to its Article I power to regulate interstate commerce.[56]

This newly born expansion of congressional abrogation power was short lived, however. The Court authoritatively overruled *Union Gas Co.* seven years later in *Seminole Tribe of Florida v. Florida.*[57] "The Eleventh Amendment," the Court held,

---

[55]   491 U.S. 1 (1989).

[56]   Id. at 57 (White, J., concurring in part dissenting in part) (noting that he did "not agree with much of [the plurality's] reasoning.").

[57]   517 U.S. 44 (1996).

"restricts the judicial power under Article III, and Article I cannot be used to circumvent the constitutional limitations placed upon federal jurisdiction."[58]

Nevertheless, but ten years after *Seminole Tribe*, the Court once again ruled that Congress may use Article I power to abrogate state immunity. In *Katz*, the Court held, pursuant to the Article I power to legislate in bankruptcy, that Congress can assign the federal courts jurisdiction to proceed with non-consenting states as defendants in bankruptcy cases.[59] The Court offered two main justifications for its holding. First, the Court reasoned that because "[b]ankruptcy jurisdiction, as understood today and at the time of the framing, is principally in rem jurisdiction. . . . , [meaning that] the court's [personal] jurisdiction is premised on the debtor and his estate, and not on the creditors [who in this case are arms of the state]. . . . , its exercise does not, in the usual case, interfere with state sovereignty."[60] Thus, *Katz* allowed an Article I-based abrogation of state immunity. Secondly, the Court concluded that "[i]nsofar as orders ancillary to the bankruptcy courts' in rem jurisdiction . . . implicate States' sovereign immunity from suit, the States agreed in the plan of the Convention not to assert that immunity."[61] This second rationale, which fits more

---

[58]   Id. at 72–73.

[59]   Katz, 546 U.S. at 375.

[60]   Id. at 369–70 (internal citations and quotations omitted).

[61]   Id. at 373.

comfortably in the implied-consent camp, tends to soften the Article I-based rationale offered above.

Katz should not be over read, however. Signaling an unwillingness to return to the expansive *Union Gas Co.* approach, the Court stressed that the "scope of this consent was limited"[62] and that bankruptcy proceedings are unique in their taking of personal jurisdiction not over states per se but the debtors' estates. All this is to say, it is hard to imagine another Article I power that would squarely fall within the ambit of the *Katz* decision. But, then again, a future expansion of *Katz* could find another Article I power to be similarly unique so as to justify abrogation of state sovereign immunity. Nevertheless as a matter of current blackletter law, abrogation by way of the Fourteenth Amendment remains the primary means at Congress' disposal to overcome the state-sovereign-immunity principle embodied in the Eleventh Amendment.

* * *

Synthesizing this morass of case law, especially in brief, is demanding. Nevertheless, one can construct an "Eleventh Amendment Annotated"[63] in which the text of the Amendment itself and the key cases are presented together as a summary of Eleventh Amendment doctrine. The following is such an exercise:

---

[62] Id. at 378.

[63] Dean Evan Caminker first introduced this exercise of an Annotated Eleventh Amendment to the author.

[Absent consent[64] or Congressional abrogation,[65] t]he Judicial power of the United States[, the Article I administrative power of the United States,[66] and the Judicial power of the various State courts[67]—excepting the appellate jurisdiction of Supreme Court,[68] suits between two States,[69] suits in which the United States is a party,[70] and bankruptcy suits[71]—]shall not be construed to extend to any suit in law or equity [(including suits arising under federal question jurisdiction[72]) or in admiralty[73]], commenced or prosecuted against one of the United States by [Citizens of the defending-party State,[74]] Citizens of another State, or by Citizens or Subjects of any Foreign State [or Foreign Nations.[75] The term State does not include

---

[64]   See, e.g., *Clark v. Barnard*, 108 U.S. 436, 447 (1883).

[65]   See, e.g., *Coll. Sav. Bank v. Florida Prepaid Postsecondary Educ. Expense Bd.*, 527 U.S. 666, 670 (1999).

[66]   *Fed. Mar. Comm'n v. S. Carolina State Ports Auth.*, 535 U.S. 743, 751 (2002).

[67]   *Alden v. Maine*, 527 U.S. 706, 757 (1999).

[68]   *Cohens v. Virginia*, 19 U.S. (6 Wheat.) 264, 412 (1821).

[69]   See, e.g., *Maryland v. Louisiana*, 451 U.S. 725, 745 n.21 (1981).

[70]   See, e.g., *Principality of Monaco v. State of Mississippi*, 292 U.S. 313, 329 (1934) (listing cases).

[71]   *Cent. Virginia Cmty. Coll. v. Katz*, 546 U.S. 356, 375 (2006).

[72]   *Hans v. Louisiana*, 134 U.S. 1, 10 (1890); *Louisiana v. Jumel*, 107 U.S. 711 (1883).

[73]   Ex parte *New York*, 256 U.S. 490, 497 (1921).

[74]   *Hans v. Louisiana*, 134 U.S. 1, 14–15 (1890).

[75]   *Principality of Monaco v. Mississippi*, 292 U.S. 313, 330 (1934).

governmental officers[76] or political subdivisions[77] within the meaning of this Amendment.]

---

[76]   *Ex parte Young*, 209 U.S. 123 (1908).

[77]   See *Mt. Healthy City Bd. of Ed. v. Doyle*, 429 U.S. 274, 280 (1977).

CHAPTER 10

ABSTENTION DOCTRINE

"[T]his longstanding public policy against federal court interference with state court proceedings. . . . , is referred to by many as 'Our Federalism.'. . . . It should never be forgotten that this slogan, 'Our Federalism,' born in the early struggling days of our Union of States, occupies a highly important place in our Nation's history and its future. . . . [Thus,] the normal thing to do when federal courts are asked to enjoin pending proceedings in state courts is not to issue such injunctions."

—*Younger v. Harris*, 401 U.S. 37, 43–45 (1971)

In this final chapter, we address abstention doctrine. Abstention is a "judge-made doctrine . . . , first fashioned in 1941 in *Railroad Commission of Texas v. Pullman Co.*,"[1] which directs that a federal court that is otherwise fully vested with constitutional and statutory subject matter jurisdiction must nevertheless "abstain" from hearing a dispute. Abstention doctrine is rooted in federalism concerns and comes in five types, each named for the case from which it arose: *Pullman*,[2]

---

[1]   *Zwickler v. Koota*, 389 U.S. 241, 248 (1967).

[2]   *Railroad Comm'n of Tex. v. Pullman Co.*, 312 U.S. 496 (1941).

Burford,[3]   *Thibodaux*,[4]   *Colorado*   *River*,[5]   and *Younger*.[6] After a brief general introduction to abstention doctrine, we will discuss each of the abstention doctrine in turn, spending the majority of our time with *Younger* abstention.

A.   ABSTENTION DOCTRINE GENERALLY

Abstention doctrine represents a series of rules in which the federal courts decline to proceed with a case, even though they have constitutional and statutory subject matter jurisdiction. While each of the abstention doctrine have unique nuances, they share many common aspects. We turn now to these uniform features.

Abstention doctrine represents an exception to the general rule that if a federal court has jurisdiction it must proceed with the suit. The Supreme Court has long held that it has "no more right to decline the exercise of jurisdiction which is given, than to usurp that which is not given."[7] Indeed, "the federal courts' obligation to adjudicate claims within their jurisdiction . . . [is] virtually unflagging."[8] Thus one must bear in mind that while abstention doctrine

---

[3]   *Burford v. Sun Oil Co.*, 319 U.S. 315 (1943).

[4]   *Louisiana Power & Light Co. v. City of Thibodaux*, 360 U.S. 25 (1959).

[5]   *Colorado River Water Conservation Dist. v. United States*, 424 U.S. 800 (1976).

[6]   *Younger v. Harris*, 401 U.S. 37 (1971).

[7]   *Cohens v. Virginia*, 19 U.S. (6 Wheat.) 264, 404 (1821).

[8]   *New Orleans Pub. Serv., Inc. v. Council of City of New Orleans*, 491 U.S. 350, 359 (1989).

plays an important role, it remains "the exception, not the rule."[9]

The Court, in light of this status as an exception to the norm of hearing all suits that fall within a federal court's subject matter jurisdiction, limits application of abstention doctrine substantially. These limiting principles arises from the fact that judicial federalism drives abstention doctrine. Following these foundational principles, the Court finds abstention doctrine justified only when it ensures that "unclear issues of state law . . . are . . . referred to the state courts"[10] for resolution or when proceeding with the federal suit would lead to an "undue interference with state proceedings."[11] As a result, abstention doctrine does not apply to suits in federal court lacking this essential link to either unclear state law or interference with state proceedings.

Even if a federal suit requires the determination of unclear state law or will interfere with state proceedings, abstention doctrine does not automatically apply. The Court "locate[s] the power to abstain in the historic discretion exercised by federal courts sitting in equity."[12] As such, federal actions in equity—because the relief itself is

---

[9]   *Colorado River*, 424 U.S. at 813.

[10]   *Pennhurst State Sch. & Hosp. v. Halderman*, 465 U.S. 89, 122 (1984).

[11]   *New Orleans Pub. Serv.*, 491 U.S. at 359.

[12]   *Quackenbush v. Allstate Ins. Co.*, 517 U.S. 706, 718 (1996) (internal quotations omitted); see also *Pullman*, 312 U.S. at 500–01.

discretionary and because the history of equity
practice comports with the notion of abstaining from
the exercise of jurisdiction—form the core of cases in
which abstention doctrine applies. Abstention
doctrine also applies with equal force to federal suits
for declaratory relief as such relief is also
discretionary in nature.[13] Moreover, in these "cases
where the relief being sought is equitable . . . or
otherwise discretionary, [as is the case in
declaratory-judgment suits,] federal courts . . . [can]
decline to exercise jurisdiction altogether by either
dismissing the suit or remanding it to state court."[14]
Thus, a federal court may outright dismiss a case, or
issue a stay, pursuant to abstention doctrine only if:
(1) it is one seeking equitable or declaratory relief,
and (2) the suit requires the determination of unclear
state law or will interfere with state proceedings.

Following the above rule, suits at law for monetary
damages do not constitute the core application of
abstention doctrine. Nevertheless, abstention
doctrine may apply to such suits.[15] The Court,
however, restricts application of abstention doctrine
in suits at law to those matters that are "intimately
involved with [the State's] sovereign prerogative,"
such that "[t]he considerations that prevail[ ] in
conventional equity suits for avoiding the hazards of
serious disruption by federal courts of state
government or needless friction between state and

---

[13]   See *Samuels v. Mackell*, 401 U.S. 66, 69–70, 72–73 (1971).

[14]   *Quackenbush*, 517 U.S. at 721.

[15]   Id. at 720.

federal authorities are similarly appropriate."[16] Thus, your run-of-the-mill suit for damages will not likely fall within the ambit of abstention doctrine because most cases do not strike at state sovereign prerogatives. Moreover, even in those rare actions where a suit at law may be subject to abstention doctrine, the federal court is only empowered to issue a stay of the federal proceeding, it may not dismiss the suit entirely as it can with claims for equitable or declaratory relief.[17] Thus, abstention may justify only a stay of federal proceedings if: (1) it is a suit at law, (2) the suit strikes at sovereign prerogatives, and (3) the suit requires the determination of unclear state law or will interfere with state proceedings.

Abstention doctrine also interacts with state sovereign immunity under the Eleventh Amendment. Recall that pursuant to *Ex parte Young* a plaintiff may seek to bar unconstitutional state conduct primarily by seeking equitable injunctive relief from a state officer. Such suits, as noted above, are the primary means of exercising federal judicial authority to curb unconstitutional state conduct. Federal suits for injunctive relief, however, form the heartland of abstention doctrine when the federal suit requires the determination of unclear state law or will interfere with state proceedings. Plaintiffs in such civil-rights cases must avoid, usually, suits for damages for fear of Eleventh Amendment difficulties; yet at the same time they must craft their equitable relief in such a manner as to avoid abstention

---

16   *Thibodaux*, 360 U.S. at 28.

17   *Quackenbush*, 517 U.S. at 721.

doctrine. Plaintiffs in suits against state officials, then, must carefully set a course that avoids both of these jurisdictional incarnations of Scylla and Charybdis, which can be a challenge.

* * *

In close, abstention doctrine directs that a federal court that is otherwise in full possession of subject matter jurisdiction nevertheless must decline to hear the suit in enumerated circumstances. The doctrine forms an exception to the general rule that federal courts must exercise jurisdiction assigned to them. Abstention doctrine, which is motivated entirely out of concerns for judicial federalism, applies only when the federal court must make a determination of unclear state law or when its adjudication will interfere with state proceedings. The heartland of the doctrine lies in federal suits for equitable or declaratory relief. Abstention doctrine empowers the federal courts to dismiss or stay such cases. Finally, abstention doctrine may, in rarer cases that strike at a state's sovereign prerogatives, apply to suits at law for monetary damages. In such cases, however, the federal court is not empowered to dismiss the case, but may only stay the federal proceeding.

Abstention Doctrine

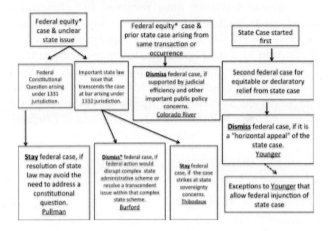

N.B.: "Equity*" as used in the flowchart should be read as including declaratory relief as well as suits at law for damages when allowed under abstention doctrine. "Dismiss*" denotes that most, but not all, instances of *Burford* abstention lead to dismissal.

B. UNCLEAR STATE LAW AND ABSTENTION DOCTRINE

Abstention doctrine first developed as a means of dealing with state-law issues in federal court where the content of state law was unsettled in the 1940s and 1950s. These doctrine, while still extant and deployed at times, came into being before the federal courts had the ability to certify a question of unclear state law to a state high court.[18] As the Supreme Court has noted, this certification process covers most of the territory once reserved for abstention based upon unclear state law.[19] Nevertheless, not every state allows for certified questions, making abstention the only game in town in those states. Further, *Burford* abstention applies not only to avoid federal adjudication of cases with unclear state law, but to avoid federal disruption of complex state administrative schemes. As such, *Pullman*, *Burford*, and *Thibodaux* abstention retain relevance.

1.   CONSTITUTIONAL AVOIDANCE UNDER *PULLMAN*

The Court first crafted abstention doctrine in *Railroad Commission of Texas v. Pullman Co.*[20] Here, the Court held that federal courts must abstain from hearing suits for injunction in federal question jurisdiction when difficult and unsettled points of state law must be resolved before a substantial federal constitutional issue can be decided. Let's turn now to the facts of the case.

In Texas at the time, it was the practice among the railroads to assign a Pullman conductor, who was invariably a white man, to trains with two or more sleeping cars, while trains with only one sleeping car were left under the supervision of a Pullman porter,

---

[18]   For a discussion of this certification procedure see Chapter 4.D above.

[19]   See *Arizonans for Official English v. Arizona*, 520 U.S. 43, 76 (1997) (discussing Pullman abstention).

[20]   312 U.S. 496 (1941).

who at the time was invariably an African-American man. The Texas Railroad Commission ordered this practice changed such that a Pullman conductor (i.e., a white man) would staff all trains, even those with but one sleeper car. The Pullman porters, among others, challenged the regulation as unconstitutional racial discrimination, seeking an injunction in federal court.

The federal constitutional question in *Pullman*, however, was predicated upon a determination of unsettled state law. It was not clear under Texas law whether the Railroad Commission was empowered to issue orders regarding the staffing of sleeper cars. Moreover, this uncertainty affected the federal constitutional question. If the commission lacked such staffing authority, the racially discriminatory regulation could be found void as a matter of state administrative law. Only if the commission was found as a matter of state law to have authority over staffing of sleeper cars would the federal court need to take up the constitutionality of the commission's regulation.

Given this ambiguity in state law and its relationship to the federal constitutional question, the Court held that the district court must stay its proceedings. Moreover, the district court was to order the parties to proceed in the state courts to find an answer to this unsettled state administrative law question. If after engaging in this state litigation the federal constitutional matter remained, then the parties would be free to return to federal court, remove the stay, and seek injunction. The Supreme

Court reasoned that by abstaining in such cases, the federal courts would avoid both unnecessary adjudication of federal constitutional questions and "needless friction with state policies."[21]

The Court, erring against application of *Pullman* abstention in later cases, holds that a state law must be exceptionally unclear to trigger *Pullman* abstention. The Court has "frequently emphasized that abstention is not to be ordered unless . . . [state law] is of an uncertain nature, and is obviously susceptible of a limiting construction."[22] As a general course, the federal courts should use tools of construction and interpretation available to the state courts, much like an *Erie* guess,[23] to construct unclear state law if at all possible.[24]

The usual situation when *Pullman*-type abstention applies is where the unclear issue of state law may make it unnecessary to decide a federal constitutional question. Typically these matters arise as part of a civil-rights case. Although the certification procedure now dominates over abstention in suits where a question of unsettled state law forms a necessary precursor to a constitutional question, federal courts retain the power to stay their proceedings to allow the parties

---

[21]   Id. at 500.

[22]   *Zwickler v. Koota*, 389 U.S. 241, 251 & n. 14 (1967).

[23]   See Chapter 4.D.

[24]   See *Hawaii Hous. Auth. v. Midkiff*, 467 U.S. 229, 236 (1984).

to seek a resolution of the state-law issue in such cases.

2.   DISRUPTION OF COMPLEX STATE ADMINISTRATIVE SCHEMES UNDER *BURFORD*

Two years after *Pullman*, the Court, in another case from Texas, decided *Burford v. Sun Oil Co.*[25] Here the Supreme Court held that federal courts sitting in diversity jurisdiction must dismiss federal suits for injunction that would disrupt state administration of complex matters. We turn first to the facts of the case.

Texas law at the time mandated that all oil wells be permitted by a state agency. The law generally mandated that each well be spaced at least a certain distance from adjacent wells. The state agency, however, took the position that it could grant exceptions to this minimum-spacing requirement. The agency granted Mr. Burford well permits without mandating that he comply with the normal well-spacing rules pursuant to its power to grant exceptions. Sun Oil sought to enjoin the use of these permits on two grounds: (1) in diversity jurisdiction, arguing that the spacing exception was not valid under Texas law, and (2) under federal question jurisdiction, arguing that they suffered a due process violation.

The Court held that the federal suit for injunction must be dismissed. First, the Court noted that the

---

[25]   319 U.S. 315 (1943).

federal issues raised in the suit were relatively insignificant, while it raised several issues of unsettled state law that bore greatly upon Texas' future ability to regulate the in-state oil industry.[26] Second, the Court noted that Texas law provided a thorough administrative process coupled with a probing and consolidated judicial review of the permitting process. Third, the Court found that the state judicial scheme was unique such that "the Texas courts are working partners with the . . . Commission in the business of creating a regulatory system for the oil industry."[27] Fourth, in this context, the Court held that to permit federal judicial review of the state agency's orders would lead only to "[d]elay, misunderstanding of local law, and needless federal conflict with the State policy."[28] As such, the Court ruled that the federal case should be dismissed.

The Court has since summed up contemporary application of the doctrine as follows. "Where timely and adequate state court review is available, a federal court sitting in equity must decline to interfere with the proceedings or orders of state administrative agencies: (1) when there are difficult questions of state law bearing on policy problems of substantial public import whose importance transcends the result in the case at bar; or (2) where the exercise of federal review of the question in a case and in similar cases would be disruptive of state

---

[26]   Id. at 331 & 331 n.28.

[27]   Id. at 326.

[28]   Id. at 327.

efforts to establish a coherent policy with respect to a matter of substantial public concern."[29] The Court will also allow *Burford* abstention in suits at law, but there only to seek a stay of federal proceedings.[30] Nevertheless, the Court continues to assert that *Burford* abstention must not be invoked too readily. "While *Burford* is concerned with protecting complex state administrative processes from undue federal influence, it does not require abstention whenever there exists such a process, or even in all cases where there is a potential for conflict with state regulatory law or policy."[31]

3. *THIBODAUX* ABSTENTION

The last abstention doctrine to deal with unsettled state law arises out of the *Louisiana Power & Light Co. v. City of Thibodaux* opinion.[32] Under this line of cases, a federal court must stay its proceedings in the face of unsettled state law when the matter at bar strikes at important sovereign prerogatives of the state. Moving first to the facts of the case.

Thibodaux presented a state-law eminent-domain issue, arising in federal court under diversity jurisdiction. Moreover, the suit was not for injunction, but a suit at law, with the Power companying seeking to forbid the city from expropriating its property.[33] The relevant state law

---

29   *New Orleans Public Service, Inc.*, 491 U.S. at 361.

30   *Quackenbush*, 517 U.S. at 721.

31   Id. at 727 (internal citations and quotations omitted).

32   360 U.S. 25 (1959).

33   Id. at 28.

was deemed confused, with an old state statute seeming to allow the taking of the property while a more contemporary opinion of the state attorney general seemed to deny such a power.[34] The district court stayed the case, pending resolution of the state-law matter in the state system. The Court affirmed. It justified this ruling by focusing upon "the special nature of eminent domain" proceedings, which are both akin to actions for injunction and "intimately involved with sovereign prerogative."[35]

Thus, in unique cases, like eminent domain, where the sovereign interest of a state are at risk, a federal court sitting in diversity may stay its proceedings to allow for the state system to resolve the relevant state-law ambiguity. Parties seeking to deploy *Thibodaux* abstention, as the Court's companion opinion of *County of Allegheny v. Frank Mashuda Co.* makes clear, may only stay the federal proceeding, not dismiss it.[36] Finally, as with other matters in which the federal courts abstain in the face of unsettled state law, abstention remains a choice of last resort. Engaging in an *Erie* guess or certification procedure is often the better course.[37]

---

[34]   Id. at 30.

[35]   Id. at 28.

[36]   360 U.S. 185 (1959) (reversing when district court in an eminent domain case dismissed the federal action in the face of unsettled state law).

[37]   See *Lehman Bros. v. Schein*, 416 U.S. 386, 392–95 (1974) (Rehnquist, J., concurring).

C.   PREVENTION OF PARALLEL
LITIGATION UNDER *COLORADO RIVER*

While the three doctrine dealing with abstention
in the face of unclear state law may now often be
avoided by the certification process or an *Erie* guess,
the final two abstention doctrine have not been so
superseded by more recent procedural innovations.
In both *Colorado River* and *Younger* abstention, the
Supreme Court mandates abstention, not to avoid
deciding unsettled issues of state law, but rather to
avoid interference with state judicial processes. We
turn in this section to the *Colorado River Water
Conservation Dist. v. United States* opinion,[38] where
the Court held that a district court must abstain
when the same matter before it is pending in the
state courts if doing so is supported both by the
dictates of judicial efficiency and other identifiable
federal policy goals.

The *Colorado River* case began when the United
States, suing on its own behalf and as trustee for
Indian tribes, filed a claim in federal court against
nearly 1,000 water users for a declaration of the
federal government's water rights in Colorado, in
particular Water District 7. The Water Districts,
under Colorado law, also operated water-rights
courts, which continuously adjudicated water-right
claims within their physical territory. Unhappy with
the federal forum, one of the defendants in the
federal action filed an application to have the United
States joined to the Division 7 water-rights

---

[38]   424 U.S. 800 (1976).

proceedings, where all claimants to Division-7 water could adjudicate both state and federal claims. This joinder was allowed because the federal McCarran Amendment permitted the United States to litigate over water rights in state courts. Having joined the United States to the state water-court action, the federal defendant's moved the federal district court to dismiss the federal action.

The Supreme Court held that dismissal of the federal suit was the proper course. Generally speaking, as between state and federal courts, the rule is that "the pendency of an action in the state court is no bar to proceedings concerning the same matter in the Federal court having jurisdiction."[39] The Court found the *Colorado River* case presented exceptional circumstances to justify deviation from this general rule on two main grounds. First, it held that "for reasons of wise administration" federal courts may abstain from engaging in parallel litigation if doing so furthers judicial efficiency.[40] Second, and more importantly, the Court held that abstention to prevent litigation in parallel with a state court case justified when, as was evidenced by the McCarran Amendment in relation to water rights, federal policy clearly favors consolidated resolution of disputes in a state court.[41]

Since the *Colorado River* opinion, the Court has highlighted that the balancing of these factors is

---

[39]   *Donovan v. City of Dallas*, 377 U.S. 408, 412 (1964).

[40]   *Colorado River*, 424 U.S. at 817–18.

[41]   Id. at 819.

"heavily weighted in favor of the exercise of [federal] jurisdiction."[42] In furtherance of this preference against abstention, the Court has formulated factors to be weighed in addition to efficiency and federal policy in considering whether abstention to avoid parallel state litigation applies. District courts are to consider: (1) the geographic (in)convenience of the federal court to the parties,[43] (2) the order in which the competing courts first took jurisdiction,[44] (3) the progress that has been made (and would therefore be for naught) in the federal court,[45] (4) the benefits of avoiding piecemeal litigation in the present context,[46] (5) whether federal law provides the rule of decision on the merits,[47] and (6) whether the state-court proceedings are adequate to protect the litigant's rights.[48] Applying these principles, the Court has held that *Colorado River* abstention does not apply when there is no jurisdiction in the parallel state action to adjudicate the claims filed in the federal suit[49] or when the state court agrees to stay its proceedings.[50]

---

[42]   *Moses H. Cone Memorial Hosp. v. Mercury Const. Corp.*, 460 U.S. 1, 16 (1983).

[43]   Id. at 818.

[44]   Id.

[45]   Id. at 820.

[46]   Id. at 818.

[47]   *Moses H. Cone*, 460 U.S. at 25–26.

[48]   Id.

[49]   *Arizona v. San Carlos Apache Tribe of Arizona*, 463 U.S. 545, 559–60 (1983).

[50]   Id. at 559.

D. PREVENTION OF "HORIZONTAL APPEALS" UNDER *YOUNGER* ABSTENTION

Abstention doctrine, as we have seen, governs matters in which a federal court may be asked to decide an unsettled matter of state law or when the federal court would engage in parallel litigation with a state court proceeding contrary to federal policy. In this final section, we turn to the most important of the abstention doctrine, which the Court delivered in its *Younger v. Harris* decision.[51] In *Younger* the Court ruled that a federal district court, barring a small number of exceptions, cannot proceed in a manner that would interfere with an on-going state criminal prosecution. We address this line of cases first. The Court later expanded *Younger* abstention to bar federal-court interference with certain state-court civil actions as well, a matter addressed in the second subsection of our discussion. As we will see, a consistent theme in *Younger* doctrine is the notion that the federal district courts may not sit in review of state court decisions, as under our constitutional system the state courts are deemed on par with the federal courts.

1.   STATE CRIMINAL PROCEEDINGS

Prosecutions for violations of state criminal law are subject to defenses supplied by federal law. Generally these defenses are constitutional in nature. In the typical case, the criminal defendant will present his federal defense to the state

---

[51]   401 U.S. 37 (1971).

prosecution in state court as part of the overall criminal trial. Relying upon federal law as a defense at a criminal trial may not be ideal in every case, however. Indeed, any time one interacts with the criminal-justice system the stakes are high. Given this reality, parties at times have attempted to employ federal law to bar a potentially unconstitutional state prosecution before they are formally charged with a state crime. *Younger* abstention arises out of this context.

The Supreme Court, in *Dombrowski v. Pfister*,[52] allowed suits to enjoin future state criminal cases when the plaintiff filed under 42 U.S.C. § 1983 and the federal suit was filed before the state criminal case began. In *Dombrowski* itself, the plaintiffs feared prosecution under a state law that they argued was in violation of the First Amendment as overly broad and vague. The Court affirmed the injunction of future prosecutions. Thus the plaintiffs were able to present what ordinarily would have been a federal defense in a state-court criminal case in the context of a federal suit for injunction before the state moved against them. The Court later held that this course of action—filing a § 1983 claim to enjoin future state prosecutions—comported with the dictates of the Anti-Injunction Act, codified at 28 U.S.C. § 2283.[53]

After *Dombrowski*, criminal defendants sought to expand the scope of the rule. In particular, criminal

---

[52]   380 U.S. 479 (1965).

[53]   *Mitchum v. Foster*, 407 U.S. 225 (1972).

defendants who had not sought federal review of a
potential criminal prosecution prior to being charged
by the state now sought to file federal suits to enjoin
state prosecutions *after* the state prosecution had
begun. Here the Court took a firm stance. The
Younger abstention line of cases hold that the federal
courts may not interfere with on-going state criminal
trials.

a. *Younger v. Harris*

In *Younger* itself, the state of California formally
charged Mr. Harris with a violation of the state's
Criminal Syndicalism Act in 1966. "Harris ha[d] been
indicted for having distributed certain leaflets,"[54]
which he argued were little more than pro-
communist pamphlets. At the state criminal trial he
moved to dismiss the indictment as contrary to the
First Amendment and later filed a writ of prohibition
against the prosecution in the state appellate court.
Both motions were denied because the United States
Supreme Court in 1927 had found the California act
constitutional in *Whitney v. California*.[55]

Nevertheless, Mr. Harris believed that the
Supreme Court's jurisprudence had since evolved
and that a federal court would find the California act
unconstitutional. As such, while the state
prosecution against him continued, he filed a suit in
federal court to enjoin further state-court
proceedings. The federal district court, finding that

---

[54]   *Harris v. Younger*, 281 F. Supp. 507, 509 (C.D. Cal. 1968)
rev'd, 401 U.S. 37 (1971).

[55]   274 U.S. 357 (1927).

the act was indeed unconstitutional, enjoined the state prosecution.[56] Harris' case, along with several other companion cases, went the Supreme Court for resolution.

While awaiting disposition, the Supreme Court, in a different opinion, held that acts such as California's were unconstitutional under the First Amendment.[57] As a result, it was now patently clear that Mr. Harris had an absolute defense against the criminal charges he faced. The sole issue for the Court, then, was whether a federal court could enjoin an on-going state prosecution, assuming that the state prosecution did, in fact, violate the Constitution. The Court held that the federal district courts could not issue such injunctions.

The Court reasoned that principles of federalism and equity prohibited this type of lower-federal-court review of an on-going state prosecution. The state courts, under our system of federalism, are deemed to be on a par with the federal courts. As such, "[s]ince the beginning of this country's history Congress has, subject to few exceptions, manifested a desire to permit state courts to try state cases free from interference by federal courts."[58] Following this principle, "the National Government, anxious though it may be to vindicate and protect federal rights and federal interests, always endeavors to do so in ways

---

[56]   *Harris v. Younger*, 281 F. Supp. 507, 517 (C.D. Cal. 1968) rev'd, 401 U.S. 37 (1971).

[57]   *Brandenburg v. Ohio*, 395 U.S. 444, 447 (1969) (discussing the California act).

[58]   *Younger*, 401 U.S. at 43.

that will not unduly interfere with the legitimate activities of the States."[59] Moreover, in almost every state criminal case the federal interests at issue are protected because the state courts provide an "adequate remedy at law" for criminal defendants seeking to advance federal defenses such that criminal defendants in state court "will not suffer irreparable injury if denied [federal] equitable relief."[60] Furthermore, for those instances where the state courts fail in this duty, it is the Supreme Court's role on certiorari, not the federal district courts' sitting in equity, to review and reverse state court rulings that are constitutionally erroneous.[61] Therefore, the Court barred the issuance of federal injunctive relief to Mr. Harris because of "the fundamental policy against federal intervention with state criminal proceedings"[62] and "the absence of the factors necessary under equitable principles to justify federal intervention."[63]

b. Ban on Horizontal Appeals

Younger's holding—that "a federal court should not enjoin a state criminal prosecution begun prior to the institution of the federal suit except in very unusual situations"[64]—may be thought of as a ban upon "horizontal appeals." Bear in mind what

---

[59] Id. at 44.

[60] Id. at 43–44.

[61] Id. at 49–50.

[62] Id. at 46.

[63] Id. at 54.

[64] *Samuels*, 401 U.S. at 69.

happened in *Younger* in terms of the interactions between the state and federal court systems. The state courts, both at the trial and appellate level, held the California act constitutional, while the federal trial court, in what was functionally appellate review of these state decisions, disagreed and found the act unconstitutional. Under our system of judicial federalism,[65] however, appellate review of state-court decisions must be done "vertically" up the state-court system's hierarchical chain of command, which ultimately ends with certiorari review by the U.S. Supreme Court. Our dual system of state and federal courts does not contemplate that parties may seek "horizontal" review of state-court judgments from the federal trial courts, because such a scheme is "fundamentally at odds with the function of the federal courts in our constitutional plan."[66]

Younger abstention, then, may be thought of as an instantiation of this principle. So long as the state courts provide an adequate forum for vindication of federal rights, criminal defendants in state prosecutions must wage their battles within the state system exclusively. When they receive adverse judgments, their remedy is vertical appeal within the state-court hierarchy, not a horizontal move to seek an injunction from a federal district court. Such an approach not only advances the notion that "the National Government will fare best if the States and

---

[65]   Post-conviction review of state convictions is the exception. These proceedings, however, are authorized both by statute and the historic role that habeas corpus plays in the common law tradition. See 28 U.S.C. §§ 2241 & 2254.

[66]   *Younger*, 401 U.S. at 43.

their institutions are left free to perform their separate functions in their separate ways" but it also "prevent[s] erosion of the role of the jury and avoid[s] a duplication of legal proceedings and legal sanctions where a single suit would be adequate to protect the rights asserted."[67]

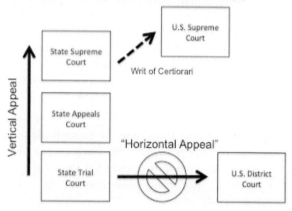

Younger v. Harris
Policy to Prevent "Horizontal Appeals"

c. Expansion of *Younger*

In furtherance of this ban upon horizontal appeals, the Court has been aggressive in the expansion of *Younger* doctrine. Its largest development, perhaps, is in the move from banning federal injunction of state criminal proceedings to the ban upon injunction of certain state civil proceedings. We will reserve that

---

[67]   Id. at 44

topic for now. (See Chapter 10.D.2 below.) In this subsection, we trace the Court's expansion of *Younger* doctrine within the criminal-law setting.

First, *Younger* abstention is not limited to suits for injunction. The *Younger* case itself only barred federal injunctions of on-going state criminal proceedings. But as we have seen in other areas of abstention doctrine, the Court tends to view injunctions and actions for declaratory judgments as equivalents. As such, in *Samuels v. Mackell*, the Court held that federal district courts must dismiss suits seeking a declaratory judgment in regard to an on-going state criminal prosecution.[68] *Younger* abstention also applies to suits at law for monetary damages in regard to an on-going state criminal prosecution.[69] But in these cases, following the general rule regarding abstention in suits at law,[70] the federal court is only empowered to stay the suit rather than to dismiss it.[71]

Second, the Court applies *Younger* abstention not just to federal cases seeking to prohibit an entire state criminal proceeding, but to federal cases seeking to regulate only aspects of a state criminal case. The Court reached such an issue in *Kugler v. Helfant*.[72] There the federal plaintiff sought to enjoin, not the entire state case, but merely the use of

---

[68]   401 U.S. at 73–74.

[69]   *Gilbertson v. Albright*, 381 F.3d 965 (9th Cir. 2004) (en banc).

[70]   See Chapter 10.A above.

[71]   See *Kirschner v. Klemons*, 225 F.3d 227, 238 (2d Cir. 2000).

[72]   421 U.S. 117, 130 (1975).

evidence that had been alleged as unconstitutionally obtained. The Supreme Court held that *Younger* abstention prohibited such a suit in federal court.

Finally, the Court has expanded *Younger* abstention even to those who are not presently criminally charged in state court. *Younger* abstention normally attaches personally to a criminal defendant. What this means is that if two people were involved in conduct that could give rise to a state criminal prosecution, but the state has only charged one person, the person not yet charged may seek a prospective federal injunction against future state prosecution without application of *Younger* abstention.[73] In *Hicks v. Miranda*, however, the Court expanded *Younger* abstention to prevent a person who had not yet been charged in a state criminal case from seeking federal declaratory relief.[74] In *Hicks*, the police seized an allegedly obscene film from a theater. Misdemeanor charges were brought against the two theater employees working at the time of the seizure. The theater owner and his corporation, who were not yet charged in state court, sought declaratory and injunctive relief in federal court. The Supreme Court held that despite the fact that there was no on-going state criminal case against the owner and the corporation when they filed in federal court, "their interests and those of their employees were intertwined [ ] . . . [such that] the federal action . . . [would] interfere with the

---

[73]   *Steffel v. Thompson*, 415 U.S. 452 (1974); see also Chapter 10.D.1.e (discussing viability of Dombrowski).

[74]   422 U.S. 332 (1975).

pending   state   prosecution   [against   the
employees]. . . . [Therefore,] the requirements of
Younger v. Harris could not be avoided on the ground
that no criminal prosecution was pending against
appellees on the date the federal complaint was
filed."[75]

d. Exceptions to *Younger*

While *Younger* abstention's bar against federal
district courts enjoining on-going state criminal
prosecutions is quite broad, it is not absolute.
Importantly, *Younger* did not overrule *Dombrowski*,
it just refused to extend *Dombrowski* to on-going
criminal prosecutions. As such, a plaintiff facing a
concrete and particularized threat of a future
criminal prosecution sufficient to support standing,[76]
can avoid *Younger* abstention if he can meaningfully
proceed in federal court before the state criminal case
begins—and he otherwise does not implicate the
holding in *Hicks*.[77] This timing rule makes sense
when one views *Younger* as a ban upon horizontal
appeals. So long as the federal case substantially
precedes before the state criminal case, the federal
court is not in the position of reviewing state-court
decisions as a quasi-appellate court. Rather, it is
tackling the federal questions of law anew. As such,
if a party substantially proceeds in federal court and,
while the federal case is on-going, a state prosecution

---

[75]   Id. at 348–49.

[76]   Id. at 52–53 (discussing the importance of standing).

[77]   *Steffel v. Thompson*, 415 U.S. 452 (1974). This topic of
filing a federal case before the state case is discussed in greater
detail below at Chapter 10.D.1.e.

begins, then the federal court may enter a preliminary injunction against any pre-trial proceedings in that state criminal case[78] or even a permanent injunction.[79]

Additionally, *Younger* abstention can be overcome in exceptional circumstances where irreparable injury to the criminal defendant cannot be cured by a vertical appeal within the state-court system. For example, the *Younger* opinion itself suggests that state prosecutions brought in bad faith or merely to harass[80] could qualify as exceptions to the rule prohibiting federal injunction. The Supreme Court, however, has never applied these exceptions so as to avoid *Younger* abstention.

Further, federal injunctions to protect interests which are incapable of remedy by way of intra-state-court-system appeal are exempt from *Younger* abstention. In *Gerstein v. Pugh*,[81] for example, a state criminal defendant was held in pre-trial detention without a hearing. The Court held that because this right could be not remedied on appeal within the state system—meaning, an appellate court could not release a defendant from illegal *pre-trial* detention on appellate review *after the trial*—the rationale of *Younger* did not apply. The defendant's injury in this instance was truly irreparable absent immediate injunction from the federal court. Similar reasoning extends this exception to *Younger* to those cases

---

[78]   *Doran v. Salem Inn Inc.*, 422 U.S. 922 (1975).

[79]   *Wooley v. Maynard*, 430 U.S. 705 (1977).

[80]   Id. at 53–54.

[81]   420 U.S. 103 (1975).

where the criminal defendant's double-jeopardy rights are threatened, because a court on appeal after a second trial cannot reinstate a person's right not to have been tried a second time.[82] Such instances of irreparable harm as an exception to *Younger* abstention are otherwise rare. Even speedy-trial claims, which would appear similarly forfeited by the time a case reaches appeal, do not constitute an exception to *Younger* abstention.[83]

Finally, *Younger* abstention does not seem to apply when the United States is a party in the federal case. In rare circumstances, the United States may seek an injunction in federal court of state-court proceedings against non-governmental parties. Because the federalism rationale of *Younger* does not squarely fit in such cases, most courts of appeal hold that *Younger* abstention does not apply in these suits.[84]

e. Determining When a Federal Case Precedes a State Prosecution

Given that the primary exception to *Younger* abstention's broad prohibition upon interference with state criminal prosecutions lies with federal suits that have substantially progressed prior to the initiation of the state criminal proceeding, questions

---

[82]   See, e.g., *Gilliam v. Foster*, 75 F.3d 881, 904 (4th Cir. 1996).

[83]   See, e.g. *Moore v. DeYoung*, 515 F.2d 437 (3d Cir. 1975).

[84]   See, e.g., *United States v. Com. of Pa., Dep't of Envtl. Res.*, 923 F.2d 1071, 1078–79 (3d Cir. 1991); *United States v. Composite State Bd. of Med. Examiners*, 656 F.2d 131, 137 (5th Cir. 1981).

of timing have great import. Put differently, we need to know which court proceeded first in order to effectively deploy *Younger* abstention. We turn now to this topic.

Immediately following *Younger*, it seemed that the Court intended to apply a bright-line rule to these issues. Under this initial approach, a state criminal case was deemed pending when an indictment or information was formally filed.[85] Following this early approach, assuming standing, a plaintiff could file for a federal injunction of a prospective state court prosecution up to the day before the state charges were filed without invoking *Younger* abstention.[86]

The Court in *Hicks*, however, discarded this bright-line approach. As discussed above, the Court in *Hicks* held the owner of a pornographic movie theater subject to *Younger* abstention, even though he was not yet charged in state court when he filed his federal suit, because his interests were intertwined with the state defendants who had previously been charged. The Court offered an additional ground for the application of *Younger* abstention. It noted that the state court had joined the theater owner as a defendant to the state criminal case one day after the owner had filed his federal case. In light of this joinder, the Court ruled that "this Court has [not] held that for *Younger v. Harris* to apply, the state criminal proceedings must

---

[85]   *Younger*, 401 U.S. at 38.

[86]   See *Village of Belle Terre v. Boraas*, 416 U.S. 1, 3 n.1 (1974).

be pending on the day the federal case is filed."[87] The Court then eschewed a bright-line rule for a more malleable standard. "[W]here state criminal proceedings are begun against the federal plaintiffs after the federal complaint is filed but *before any proceedings of substance on the merits have taken place* in the federal court, the principles of *Younger v. Harris* should apply in full force."[88] Despite the fact that the federal district court had rejected an application for a temporary restraining order, the Court held that no substantial on-the-merits proceedings had taken place in the federal court prior to the formal entry of state-court charges against the theater owner.[89] As such, *Younger* abstention applied. Put another way, formally filing in federal court before a state charge is filed is not sufficient to avoid *Younger* abstention. The federal court must proceed with some substantial on-the-merits review prior to the filing of the state criminal case.

The Court revisited this question of timing in *Hawaii Housing Authority v. Midkiff*.[90] In *Midkiff*, the plaintiff filed in federal court and the court issued a preliminary injunction before the state proceedings began. The Supreme Court ruled that a "federal court action in which a preliminary injunction is granted has proceeded well beyond the embryonic stage, and considerations of economy, equity, and federalism

---

[87]   *Hicks*, 422 U.S. at 349.

[88]   Id. (emphasis added). See also *Doran*, 422 U.S. at 929–31.

[89]   Id. at 350.

[90]   467 U.S. 229 (1984).

counsel against *Younger* abstention at that point."[91]
The rule, then, appears to be that merely dismissing
a temporary restraining order is not a substantial
enough federal-court involvement to avoid *Younger*
abstention, while issuing a preliminary injunction is.

One lesson, *but the wrong one*, that could be
gleaned from these cases is that a person facing even
the slightest threat of a state criminal proceeding to
which he has a viable federal defense should run
immediately to federal court before a state case is
filed. Standing doctrine,[92] however, prevents such
federal suits from being filed too early. Cases in the
Younger line uniformly stress the importance of
standing for those seeking a federal injunction prior
to the filing of state criminal charges.[93] Thus, only
truly imminent threats of criminal prosecution will
find standing to support a request for injunction.

Plaintiffs seeking to enjoin a future state criminal
prosecution, then, face a tough task. To have
standing, the threat of criminal prosecution must be
credible and imminent. But to avoid application of
Younger abstention, the federal court must proceed
to substantial on-the-merits rulings, such as the
issuance of a preliminary injunction, before the state
criminal case begins. This leaves but a narrow
window of opportunity.

---

[91]   Id. at 238 (internal quotations and citations omitted).

[92]   See Chapter 8.B.

[93]   See, e.g., *Steffel*, 415 U.S. at 458–60.

When is the federal court first

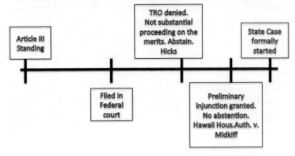

2.   STATE CIVIL PROCEEDINGS

Having reviewed the expansive scope that *Younger* abstention has in relation to state criminal proceedings, we turn in this section to application of the doctrine to prohibit federal-court interference with state civil cases. Recall that *Younger* barred only federal injunction of state criminal proceedings. The Court has since found that *Younger* abstention applies in civil cases where important state interests are at stake.

a. The State as a Party

The Court first began to apply *Younger* abstention to prohibit federal-court interference with state civil proceedings only when: (1) the state itself was a formal party to the underlying state suit and (2) an important state interest was implicated. The Court took this approach first in *Huffman v Pursue, Ltd*.[94] There the state of Ohio began a civil nuisance suit against a pornography theater. The theater owner believed the First Amendment barred the civil suit and sought a federal injunction. The Court applied *Younger* abstention. The Court found *Younger* applicable because the nuisance case was quasi-criminal in nature,[95] the state itself was a party in the state court civil proceedings,[96] and because the strong state interests "which underlie its criminal laws and to obtain compliance with precisely the standards which are embodied in its criminal laws" were implicated.[97] Furthermore, the Court noted the state civil proceeding allowed for intra-state appeal and ultimately certiorari review by the high Court.[98]

The Court applied similar reasoning in *Trainor v. Hernandez*.[99] Here the state of Illinois proceeded civilly against Mr. and Mrs. Hernandez in state court to collect welfare payments that they received fraudulently. At the same time, the state attached the defendants' assets in a bank without due process. Mr. and Mrs. Hernandez sought a federal injunction of the attachment as a violation of federal due process. The Court again ruled that *Younger* abstention applied even though the underlying state case was civil. The Court again noted that the state

---

[94] 420 U.S. 592 (1975).

[95] Id. at 604.

[96] Id.

[97] Id. at 605.

[98] Id. at 605–06.

[99] 431 U.S. 434 (1977).

could have brought a criminal case in this instance, giving the matter, once again, a quasi-criminal character.[100] The Court also noted that *Younger* abstention was grounded by the fact that the state was a party to the underlying civil suit and that it was acting in its sovereign capacity to protect important state financial interests.[101] As such, the Court concluded that "the principles of *Younger* and *Huffman* are broad enough to apply to interference by a federal court with an ongoing civil enforcement action such as this, brought by the State in its sovereign capacity."[102]

In *Moore v. Sims*,[103] the Court once again held that *Younger* applied to prohibit interference with a state civil proceeding. Here the underlying state case was one to remove children from their parents' home. Unlike in *Huffman* or *Trainor*, however, *Moore* lacked a quasi-criminal nature, as removing children from the home lacks a criminal analogue. Nevertheless, the Court held that *Younger* abstention applied because the state was a party to the underlying civil suit and because an important state interest, child welfare, was at stake.[104] Moreover, the Court went on to hold *Younger* abstention "fully applicable to [all] civil proceedings in which important state interests are involved,"[105]

---

[100]   Id. at 444.

[101]   Id.

[102]   Id.

[103]   442 U.S. 415 (1979).

[104]   Id. at 423.

[105]   Id.

even those lacking a link to the enforcement of state
criminal law.

b. The State Not a Party

Having made this step away from quasi-criminal
proceedings and tying *Younger* abstention to
involvement of important state interests, the Court
next came to find that these state interests could
mandate application of *Younger* abstention even
when the state is not a party in the underlying civil
suit. *Juidice v. Vail* is the first case in this line.[106] In
Juidice, a state-court judge found Mr. Vail in
contempt of court for repeated failures to appear and
fined him in the context of a private dispute between
Mr. Vail and a creditor. After the contempt order was
entered, Mr. Vail sought to enjoin enforcement of the
order in federal court. Here, as with *Moore*, the case
was not akin to a criminal proceeding. Moreover,
unlike the prior civil cases in which *Younger* was
applied, the state was not a party to the underlying
civil dispute. Nevertheless, the Court ruled that "[a]
State's interest in the contempt process, through
which it vindicates the regular operation of its
judicial system, so long as that system itself affords
the opportunity to pursue federal claims within it, is
surely an important interest" worthy of respect by
way of *Younger* abstention.[107]

The Court reiterated that important state
interests may garner *Younger* abstention even when
the state is not a party to the underlying suit in

---

[106]   430 U.S. 327 (1977).

[107]   Id. at 334.

Pennzoil v. Texaco.[108] Here, Texaco lost an $11 billion
suit to Pennzoil in a private dispute. Texas law
required the posting of an $11 billion appellate bond
in order to file a notice of appeal within the state
system. Texaco was unable to obtain such a bond.
Texaco sought a federal injunction to bar Pennzoil
from demanding the appellate bond on the theory
that requiring the bond unconstitutionally deprived
it of a right to appeal. The Supreme Court held that
Younger abstention applied because of Texas's strong
state interest in enforcement of its rules of court.[109]

c. State Administrative Action

This broad expansion of *Younger* abstention from
state criminal proceedings, to state civil proceedings
in which the state was a party, to state civil
proceedings lacking a state party, is not the end of
the story. The Supreme Court has also expanded
Younger abstention doctrine to prohibit federal
interference not only with state judicial proceedings
but state administrative proceedings as well. In
*Middlesex County Ethics Committee v. Garden State
Bar Association*,[110] the Court held that the federal
district court must abstain from interfering with
attorney-disciplinary proceedings even when a First
Amendment issue was at the core of the proceeding.
Despite the fact that the proceeding began as an
administrative process, the Court found that state-
high-court review of the administrative hearing

---

[108]   481 U.S. 1 (1987).

[109]   Id. at 11.

[110]   457 U.S. 423 (1982).

rendered the matter sufficiently judicial to fall within the ambit of *Younger*[111] and that there was a no showing that the attorney was prohibited from presenting the First Amendment issue.[112] The Court next found that the state had an "extremely important interest in maintaining and assuring the professional conduct of the attorneys it licenses,"[113] which was worthy of deference under the *Younger* line of cases.

In *Ohio Civil Rights Commission v. Dayton Christian Schools*,[114] the Court took the next step by holding that state administrative procedures were subject to *Younger* abstention even when they had not yet been passed on to a state court for final determination. In this case, private Christian-school administrators refused to retain female teachers who became pregnant on the grounds that their religion mandated that women stay at home with their children. A dismissed teacher filed a grievance with the state civil rights commission, alleging gender discrimination. The school, claiming First Amendment rights, sought to enjoin the administrative proceeding. The Court held that *Younger* abstention applied to bar federal-court interference with administrative proceedings. The Court rested its decision upon the important state interest in preventing discrimination.[115] Moreover,

---

[111] Id. at 433.

[112] Id. at 436.

[113] Id. at 434.

[114] 477 U.S. 619 (1986).

[115] Id. at 628.

the fact that the administrative tribunal lacked authority to hear the school's First Amendment argument did not stop application of *Younger* abstention because the Ohio state courts, upon review, could rule on the issue.[116]

The Court's ever-expanding *Younger* jurisprudence finally came to a stop in *New Orleans Public Service, Inc. v. Council of City of New Orleans*.[117] Here the Court held that a federal district court could enjoin a city council from violating the Constitution. The Court drew a distinction between legislative bodies and judicial bodies for purposes of application of *Younger*, holding *Younger* inapplicable to legislative actions.

* * *

Younger abstention, in summary, plays an important role in preserving the state courts as separate and equal tribunals under our system of government. The doctrine prohibits "horizontal" appeals from the state-court system to the federal, funneling disputes that began in the state system vertically within the state's appellate hierarchy. Thus, a federal court may not enter injunctive or declaratory relief in such a manner that will affect an on-going state criminal proceeding unless the federal right at issue is not amenable to remedy upon appeal. This same principle applies to prohibit federal interference with state civil proceedings in which an important state interest is at stake, even if the state

---

[116]   Id. at 629.
[117]   491 U.S. 350 (1989).

is not a party to the underlying dispute. Finally, *Younger* abstention applies to state administrative, but not legislative, functions.

Taking a further step back, recall that *Younger* abstention is the most important of a family of doctrine that directs federal courts that otherwise are fully vested with constitutional and statutory subject matter jurisdiction to decline to adjudicate the matter before them. The Court finds abstention doctrine an exception to the general rule that a court with jurisdiction must hear the case. These exceptions are justified only when: (1) abstention ensures that unclear issues of state law are referred to the state courts for resolution; or (b) proceeding with the federal suit would lead to an undue interference with state proceedings. While the abstention doctrine falling under the first category are largely now displaced by certification to the state supreme court, that latter grouping of doctrine, especially *Younger* abstention, continue to play an important role in regulating the interactions between the federal and state judiciaries.

INDEX

References are to Pages